INTERNATIONAL PRAISE FOR

Sharing the Work,
Sparing the Planet

IRELAND

"Reducing working time and sharing work better are essential steps towards reducing humankind's impact on the planet. Well-written, fast-moving, Hayden's book makes a compelling case."

Richard Douthwaite, author of The Growth Illusion *and* Short Circuit

UNITED STATES

"In this comprehensive and impressively documented study, Anders Hayden examines the wide range of reduced work-time initiatives that have been implemented in industrialized nations during the last ten years, analysing each policy's outcomes, successes, and flaws.

This book is highly recommended for public officials, policy-makers, caring business people, and labour and environmental activists; indeed, for anyone seeking political and economic policies that are socially and economically just, and also serve both human and ecological needs."

Barbara Brandt, U.S. Shorter Work-Time Group, author of Whole Life Economics: Revaluing Daily Life

GERMANY

"If you are wondering how social and ecological agendas can coincide, get hold of this book! Clearly argued, highly informative, it provides an intellectual cornerstone for a post-growth society."

Wolfgang Sachs, author of Greening the North

CANADA

"For too long we have pitted protection of the environment against the protection of jobs. Here at last is a real vision for the new millennium that integrates a profound understanding of ecology with a practical strategy for job creation and the expansion of leisure time. Hayden unmasks the pitfalls of development strategies based on blind growth, and demonstrates convincingly that unbridled consumption limits rather than enhances our quality of life. This book should be in the hands of every policy-maker concerned about protecting our planet and creating a better and more secure future for our children."

Ronald Colman, Ph.D., Director, GPI Atlantic

"The struggle over time will be one of the most important arenas for social justice activists in the coming years. Anders Hayden gives us an insightful, nuanced, and controversial overview of this issue. It's well worth reading."

Jim Stanford, Economist, Canadian Auto Workers

"Hayden handles well what may prove to be the most important policy and societal change issue of the coming decade."

Professor Robert Paehlke, Trent University

Sharing the Work, Sparing the Planet

WORK TIME, CONSUMPTION, & ECOLOGY

ANDERS HAYDEN

Zed Books Ltd
London & New York

Between the Lines
Toronto

Pluto Press Australia
Sydney

Sharing the Work, Sparing the Planet

First published in Canada in 1999 by
Between the Lines
720 Bathurst Street, Suite #404
Toronto, Ontario
M5S 2R4

Published in Australia and New Zealand by
Pluto Press Australia
6A Nelson Street
Annandale, NSW 2038
Sydney, Australia

Published outside Canada, Australia, and New Zealand by
Zed Books Ltd
7 Cynthia Street
London, England
N1 9JF
and
Room 400, 175 Fifth Avenue
New York, NY 10010
U.S.A.

Distributed in the U.S.A. exclusively by
St Martin's Press Inc.
175 Fifth Avenue, New York, NY 10010

Canadian Cataloguing in Publication Data
Hayden, Anders, 1969-
        Sharing the work, sparing the planet
Includes bibliographical references and index.
ISBN 1-896357-28-8
1. Hours of labour.   2. Sustainable development.   3. Consumption (Economics).
I. Title.
HD5106.H39 1999   331.25'7   C99-930189-6

Zed Press edition (outside Canada, Australia, and NZ)
ISBN 1 85649 817 4 Hb
ISBN 1 85649 818 2 Pb

Pluto Press Australia edition (Australia and NZ)
ISBN 1 86403 111 5

Cover and text design by Jennifer Tiberio / Point of View
Front cover image by Michael Engel

Printed in Canada by University of Toronto Press

Between the Lines gratefully acknowledges assistance for its publishing activities from the Canada Council for the Arts, the Ontario Arts Council, and the Government of Canada through the Book Publishing Industry Development Program.

for Thomas

Contents

Preface

The most fascinating thing for me about work-time reduction (WTR) is how it brings together so many varied issues: job creation for the unemployed and underemployed, improved quality of life for the employed, balancing the demands of work and family, the division of labour between women and men in the market and household, and changing notions of the meaning of leisure, among others. Questions about work time can range from the details of shift scheduling to fundamental questions about how we define progress, the good life, and our individual sense of meaning and purpose. In this book I touch on these and other issues to varying degrees, but focus mainly on the contribution that WTR can potentially make to the achievement of an ecologically sustainable model of development in the wealthy nations of the North.

It was through the work of André Gorz that I first took an intellectual interest in the idea of WTR as a possible utopia that could combine ecological concerns with humanist aspirations for more satisfying ways of living. Juliet Schor, Alain Lipietz, and Bruce O'Hara, who have pointed to WTR as a central element of a more ecologically sound economy, have also been fundamentally important influences. I have drawn on the work of a number of thinkers in the emerging field of ecological economics—people such as Herman Daly, Paul Ekins, and Bill Rees. Critiques of the consumer society and its vision of the "good life" are another important influence, as are the alternative visions outlined by many green thinkers who aim for a less materialistic society oriented towards quality of life rather than quantity of consumption. Benjamin Hunnicutt's work on the history of work-time issues in 20th-century North America has been an important reminder that not so long ago the growth of leisure was a central objective in the struggle for a better life on this side of the Atlantic. I am especially indebted to Wolfgang Sachs for his intellectual inspiration and for encouraging me to continue exploring the idea of more wealth in time as a way to address the challenge of consumption sufficiency.

This book first emerged as a master's thesis in the Faculty of Environmental Studies at York University in Toronto. I received indispensable help from the members of my thesis committee: Ellie Perkins, Greg Albo, Roger Keil, and particularly Peter Penz, who provided essential insights just when I needed them. Thanks also to Ron Colman, Julie White, Jim Stanford, Chris Roberts, Murray Macadam, Barbara Montgomery, Bob Jeffcott, Silvia Langer, Kathryn Scharf, Sean Fitzpatrick, and Ken O'Hara for the information and expertise they provided at a later stage. Of course, no one mentioned here is to blame for any of the book's shortcomings.

My involvement with 32 HOURS: Action for Full Employment, a Toronto-based organization committed to a reduction and redistribution of work time, has given me additional opportunities to reflect on the issues addressed here. I currently work as 32 HOURS' Research & Policy Coordinator (three days a week, in case you're wondering). Very special thanks to Mark Hudson, Debbie Field, and Valerie Hepburn. Thanks also to Michael Jacek, Ray de Boer, Joe Polito, and the other volunteer members of 32 HOURS for their support. I am grateful to those active in the Shorter Work Time Network elsewhere in Canada, particularly to Bruce O'Hara for his years of determination and Tom Walker for his insights. An important word of warning is also in order: the opinions expressed here are my own and are not necessarily those of 32 HOURS or the Shorter Work Time Network.

It was a considerable challenge to revise this work at a time when I was no longer in an academic setting but instead involved in activism to build support for the idea of WTR. In a university environment, you have more of the luxury of calling things as you see them. Outside, you have to worry much more about how well your ideas will "sell." This book was never intended to be a "sales pitch" for WTR. Indeed, I say some things that will certainly make many supporters or potential supporters of the idea uncomfortable. I hope that it will stimulate discussion and that my "productivist" friends and allies will still talk to me after they read it. Given the widely recognized need to stimulate debate about new economic alternatives and revitalize progressive political thinking, I am confident that they will.

When I started on this work, I couldn't have imagined there would be such an impressive revitalization of the movement for WTR in Europe, which has been happening ever since France announced in October 1997 that it would introduce a 35-hour workweek. I want to thank those who took the time to meet with me while I was researching the recent developments in Europe: Pierre Larrouturou, Aldo Battaglia, Vittorio Milano, Antonio Panzeri, Gerhard Scherhorn, Wolfgang Sachs, Willi Hilger, Reinhard Bispinck, Manfred Muster, Christoph Scherrer, Eckart Hildebrandt, Jan Peter Van den Toren, Diana de Wolff, Stephan Schrover, Bernard Tuyttens, and Michel Rocard. Special thanks to Roos Vervoordeldonk for her friendship and help while I was in the Netherlands and since then.

I would like to acknowledge Barbara Brandt for her thinking on this issue, for helping to keep the flame alive in the United States through the Shorter Work-Time Group, and for her words of encouragement. Thanks to Mike Delacour, Gina Sasso, Roger Wilkins, Marion Syrek, Tom Condit, and others in Berkeley for their hospitality and inspiration in campaigning for a 35-hour week. I'm also indebted to Danny Wong, Malcolm Rogge, and Lee Davis-Creal for their support along the way.

I am grateful for the support of the team at Between the Lines. Thanks to Robert Clarke, Paul Eprile, Ruth Bradley-St-Cyr, and Steve Osgoode for their determined work on this project, and to the others who have played an important role behind the scenes.

The combination of activist work with 32 HOURS and intellectual work on this book has at times led my housemates—Mike Whitla, Lisa Haberman, Becca Whitla, Alan Gasser, and George Hartley—to call me "the guy who works 24-hours a day for a shorter workweek." Partly due to their good-natured teasing, I've been getting better at being less of a walking contradiction.

1

Introduction

Eight hours for work, eight hours for rest, eight hours for what we will.

Labour movement anthem, 1880s

So long as there is one man who seeks employment and cannot find it, the hours of work are too long.

Samuel Gompers, U.S. labour leader (1850-1924)

We are today paying the debt for the material growth that characterized the postwar "Golden Age": disfigured landscapes, polluted air and water, erosion of the ozone layer, the greenhouse effect. Since the Third World also needs significant growth of its material production, only a reorientation of the overdeveloped countries towards a model of development centred on the immaterial growth of free time is capable of guaranteeing our common future.

Alain Lipietz, French Green Party economist, 1996

Ever since the beginning of the industrial revolution, working people and their allies have sought a reduction in the hours of work. They have pushed for this as a way of gaining, for everyone, the right and the opportunity to live dignified and healthy lives, and they have seen a reduction in work hours as a way of creating more jobs through a better distribution of the available work. Today these dual historical motivations—of creating jobs and increasing time away from the job—are every bit as pertinent, but they have now been joined by a powerful new motivation: the increasing recognition of ecological limits.

Environmental concerns have brought into play the notion of "sustainable development"—of how, in the words of the Brundtland Commission, the world can meet "the needs of the present without compromising the ability of future generations to meet their own needs."[1] While a disproportionate amount of the debate regarding sustainable development focuses on the poorer nations of the South and fears about overpopulation, the global environmental crisis is in fact deeply rooted in the overconsumption of resources in the wealthy nations of the North.[2] The apparently insatiable appetite of the planet's wealthiest nations for energy and material resources, and the consequent generation of various forms of pollution, have led to severe environmental degradation around the globe. Not only are Northern levels of consumption unsustainable, but they are also held up to the majority of humanity in the South as the model, and striving for this goal promises an ever more intense assault on the environment.

"Human beings and the natural world are on a collision course. Human activities inflict harsh and often irreversible damage on the environment and on critical resources. If not checked, many of our current practices put at serious risk the future we wish for human society." So begins the "World Scientists' Warning to Humanity," signed in November 1992 by more than half of all living Nobel Prize-winning scientists. One of the many manifestations of this crisis is, in the words of ecologist David Suzuki, an "eco-holocaust" as more than 50,000 species vanish annually.[3] Perhaps even more serious—and certainly not unrelated—is global climate change, a phenomenon that threatens to critically disrupt weather patterns, ecosystems, and human activities across the planet. In 1999 two islands in the Kiribati Archipelago in the South Pacific were the first to be submerged by rising sea levels due to global warming, and others in the area were in danger.[4] The potentially devastating economic costs to those of us in the North are also becoming apparent. In the 1990s insurance companies, for example, paid close to four times the weather-related claims in the entire decade of the 1980s.[5] Driving the rising temperatures are the emissions of carbon dioxide and other greenhouse gases, resulting primarily from the rapacious consumption of energy by our frenetic economies, which race to churn out vast quantities of material goods to feed the affluent North's pumped-up consumption demands and the inexorable drive for profit.

There are two main responses to the problem of overconsumption: the paths of "sufficiency" and "efficiency." The idea of sufficiency has been favoured by much of the green movement. Many of its members argue that given prevailing global ecological constraints we have to respond effectively to the question of "how much is enough." The idea of sufficiency calls attention to the first and most neglected of the environmental "three Rs": reduce. Embracing sufficiency may start by questioning consumer choices, cutting out purchases that we can do without, and rejecting the advertisers' notion that non-material needs—for belonging, self-esteem, and status, for instance—must be satisfied with material goods. But the idea inevitably takes us even further, leading to a wholesale critique of Western civilization's concept of progress. From the sufficiency perspective, sustainability is not just a question of technology and economics, but of ethics and aesthetics, of a "fresh inquiry into the meaning of the good life" and a new emphasis on lifestyles of "moderation and mindfulness."[6] Many greens have called for a fundamental transformation of values in Northern societies, a radical overhaul of industrial society, and a significant reduction in levels of material consumption. They emphasize that life can be better in a less materialistic society and that a lower quantity of consumption does not necessarily mean a lower quality of life. The sufficiency approach is based on a hard-headed, scientifically informed assessment of the unsustainability of present economic and social practices,[7] but it has suffered from both the lack of a practical strategy for implementing it and an inability so far to gain widespread popular support.

The efficiency school of thought, which has gained momentum in recent years, instead puts the emphasis on streamlining humanity's use of nature[8] in order to reduce environmental impacts without material sacrifice and without necessarily abandoning the pursuit of unlimited economic growth. Infinite growth on a finite planet is clearly impossible. However, efficiency advocates, among others, point out that it is not the growth of Gross Domestic Product (GDP) itself that creates environmental problems and faces limits, but the growth of "throughput"—that is, resource and energy input and pollution output. For instance, more energy-efficient automobiles or refrigerators could, at least in theory, reduce the total amount of energy consumed and pollution generated through their use even as the output and value of these products continue to grow. Most of the discussion around sustainable development places an overriding faith in the ability of improved technology and better social organization to achieve an "eco-efficiency revolution" that would allow economic growth without throughput growth or, in other words, the progressive "dematerialization" of economic output.

GROWING, GROWING, GONE?

Although the ecological crisis does clearly call for a more efficient use of non-human nature, this response has serious limitations. Growth in GNP without throughput growth is little more than a theoretical possibility at present, and in any case zero throughput growth is not enough. Significant reductions in throughput in the North are necessary. At the 1997 Kyoto conference on climate change, Canada committed itself to achieving, by 2010, a 6 per cent reduction from 1990 levels in carbon dioxide emissions. Yet a 1999 report showed that the chances of meeting this ultra-minimal target were next to zero. Emissions actually rose in 1990-97, a period during which GDP grew by 13.4 per cent and 8 per cent more vehicles were on the road.[9]

Some people look to Europe as a better example, and in some respects it is. In 1999 the European Environment Agency (EEA) reported that carbon dioxide emissions fell about 1 per cent from 1990 to 1996 in Europe—a positive sign that perhaps the link between GDP growth and throughput growth could in practice be broken.[10] Unfortunately, this example provides little cause for celebration; with a cumulative problem like the buildup of greenhouse gases, which remain active in the atmosphere for many decades, it only means that Europeans are adding to the problem at a slightly slower pace than before. The statistics also leave Europe with a very long way to go to reach a more ecologically rigorous 35 per cent reduction in carbon dioxide emissions by 2010, which would be a first step towards a 90 per cent reduction by 2050, the goal thought necessary to limit global warming in an internationally equitable way.[11] While the EEA report pointed to a few positive signs, such as the expansion of wind energy, increased use of bicycles in cities, and growing preference for organic food, on the whole its conclusions cast serious doubt on the potential for decoupling economic growth from throughput growth. It noted that the quality of Europe's environment has shown no significant improvement and has been degraded in a number of areas, despite 25 years of environmental policies. The EEA says that economic growth of 45 per cent is expected over the period 1990-2010. Despite improvements in eco-efficiency per unit of output in key areas such as energy efficiency, due to growth (that is, more units of output) there will still be an increase in total energy consumption, as well as more atmospheric emissions, more transport, more environmentally damaging forms of tourism, and more garbage. It foresees increased mortality and respiratory problems from growing air pollution, growing risks from pesticide and nitrate pollution, and increased production of dangerous chemical products and toxic wastes.[12]

The age of growth without significant new environmental impacts has certainly not yet arrived. Low GDP growth, or even no growth, is almost certainly far more compatible with ecological sustainability than a rapid growth strategy. That does not mean, however, that we should necessarily target zero-growth of GDP, or any other rate of economic growth whether positive or negative, as a goal in itself. This would not be an adequate target from an ecological perspective, because the real challenge is not to change an abstract economic indicator like GDP, but to significantly reduce the consumption of resources and emission of pollutants—on the order of roughly 90 per cent in the nations of the North by the year 2050, according to Germany's Wuppertal Institute for Climate, Environment and Energy.[13] At the same time the scope exists to expand a wide range of ecologically benign and socially valuable activities such as public transit, energy conservation retrofits, reforestation, growing natural alternative materials such as hemp, development of non-polluting products and processes, and higher quality health care and education—which could show up as increases in GDP. But just as sustainable forestry involves a more selective form of harvesting, sustainable economics requires that we be much more ecologically selective about how we create economic value, rejecting the "clearcut" economics of the conventional growth paradigm.

Rather than aiming for any particular rate of economic growth, we should make ecological sustainability the first economic priority. Doing so will require dramatically scaling back the throughput flows between the environment and the economy, which, in turn, will in all likelihood restrict economic growth over the long run. To instead make rapid GDP growth the priority and then hope that even more rapid improvements in eco-efficiency will follow to reduce our environmental impacts would be utterly reckless. It would be like setting out to barrel down a steep and winding mountain road, with a deep precipice below, without knowing for sure that the brakes are in working order. Productivism—the belief in economic growth as a supreme value in itself—will always threaten to undermine ecological goals because it forces us into a never-ending race to constantly improve eco-efficiency simply to keep environmental impacts from growing, let alone reduce them from their currently unsustainable heights. In addition to seeking improvements in eco-efficiency,

Figure 1.1

we have to confront the more challenging issue of sufficiency if we are to have a realistic hope of keeping our demands on nature within sustainable limits.

While environmental sustainability represents the greatest long-term challenge for humanity, in the short term public debate continues to focus on more traditional economic issues. Mass unemployment and underemployment are now the norm throughout much of the North—at levels that were considered politically intolerable only a few decades ago. In 1998 more than 35 million people in the "developed" countries of the Organization for Economic Co-operation and Development (OECD) were unemployed.[14] In Canada in May 1999, despite more than half a decade of "economic recovery," official unemployment stood at 8.1 per cent, somewhat lower than a few years earlier but still staggeringly high compared to previous decades. (See Figure 1.1.) At the same time, many of the employed are working longer hours, resulting in high levels of stress, poorer health, and a lack of time for the things that make life worth living. Many young people are losing hope of ever finding decent jobs. The costs of unemployment—such as unemployment benefits, social assistance, and health-related expenses—drain the public treasury. Economic insecurity provides fodder for a politics of intolerance, in which immigrants, minorities, and the poor become scapegoats for

Figure 1.2

Figure 1.2

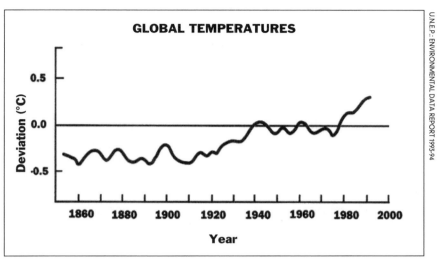

U.N.E.P.: ENVIRONMENTAL DATA REPORT 1993-94

society's failures. Technological advance, which once promised to bring on an "Age of Leisure," instead seems to be depositing a downsized and devastated scrap heap of humanity in its wake.

People across most of the political spectrum see economic growth as both the means of solving such problems and an end in itself. But pursuit of the infinite growth of GDP not only threatens to bring more environmental degradation; at a time when the majority of people in the North have already achieved a high level of material abundance, ever-higher levels of output are very unlikely to bring any improvement in well-being. In the words of Ronald Colman, who is working on a Genuine Progress Index for Nova Scotia, "There is no more pervasive and dangerous illusion in our society than the equation of economic growth with well-being and prosperity."[15] Statistical indicators that are more comprehensive than GDP have shown declining levels of well-being in Northern countries since the early 1970s, despite significant economic growth. A 1995 Merck Family poll in the United States found that three-quarters of Americans had more possessions than their parents, but less than half said they were "happier."[16] Keynesian economics—based on governments pumping money into the economy to counter an economic slowdown—is now not in fashion, yet many of us remain committed in our personal lives to an ineffective form of "Keynesian psychology"—heading to the mall when we feel down and trying to spend our way out of depression. Essentially, most people in the North already have enough stuff—though a substantial minority do not have their fair share. More advantageous, surely, than seeking to continually increase output would be to work at solving unemployment problems, improve the quality of life for everyone, and create opportunities for building a better society and stronger communities by focusing on the expansion of non-material forms of wealth.

Work-time reduction (WTR), most commonly thought of as a shorter workweek but covering a much wider range of possibilities—from parental and education leaves to phased-in retirement—is potentially one way of addressing issues of overconsumption while creating greater time affluence.[17] WTR can serve a progressive[18] environmental vision that recognizes the need for a pragmatic starting point for a "sufficiency revolution" in a number of ways: as one essential element in an environmentally sound response to unemployment, a focal point for an alternative vision of progress based on growth in free time rather than growth in production, a source of the time needed for people to think and act as participants in building an ecologically sustainable and socially just society, and a way to create new opportunities for "simple living" and the subversion of consumerism. Along with efficiency-oriented measures, such as an ecological tax reform, WTR could if widely adopted help to bring about the urgently needed reduction in the North's demands on the environment.

Certainly, working to achieve WTR will be a distinct and complex challenge. But even greater is the challenge of ensuring that its implementation serves ecological ends. There is no guarantee that WTR will in practice challenge the productivist vision of unbounded economic growth—it could find itself co-opted into that broad sweep. We need, then, to consider how we might strengthen the ecological merits of WTR, avoid the pitfalls of productivism, and overcome the other political, economic, and cultural obstacles that stand in the way of achieving a green vision of working less, consuming less, and living more. This vision recognizes that, as long as certain basic material needs are satisfied, we can live better, more balanced, and more fulfilling lives by focusing on the non-material wellsprings of well-being and on activities that exist—or certainly can exist—outside the "work-and-spend" cycle, such as learning, caring for people, taking the time to prepare a good healthy meal and to celebrate it fully with others, playing sports, conversation, spending time with our kids, getting involved in our communities, discovering the natural world around us, making music, making love (which, apparently, many couples are too busy to do very often these days), political participation, taking on personal projects—including what some people will consider to be satisfying forms of work—under our own direction rather than under the control of a boss, and occasionally allowing ourselves the indulgence of just lazing around.

Another part of the challenge is to determine the shape of work-time policy and practice. In Canada recent decades have seen little progress on work-time issues, although Canada's record compares favourably to the United States, which is surpassing Japan to gain the dubious distinction of being the North's long-hours champion. At the same time, working people in the South are routinely subjected to hours of work reminiscent of the worst abuses of the early industrial revolution. In contrast, the European experience, including the revitalization of a political movement for WTR following France's decision to legislate a 35-hour week, illustrates an impressive variety of shorter work-time options in practice and shows that a WTR "tool box" contains a range of possible measures, from legislation to expanding individual choice. A number of related policy and strategy questions arise. Should we focus on a shorter workweek or on a broader range of options for reducing work time over the human life cycle? What is the appropriate balance between individual and collective decisions to reduce hours, and the closely related issue of voluntary versus legislative action? Should WTR come with or without a loss in pay? Can

RICARDO LEVINS MORALES, NORTHLAND POSTER COLLECTIVE

the full promise of WTR be achieved within capitalism, particularly its current globalized form, or is the real struggle one of a higher order to change broader economic structures?

TOWARDS A GREEN LEFT

This is a book about one possible green economic and social vision. One important issue within green politics is the relationship with the left. Green parties have often referred to themselves as "neither left, nor right, but out in front." It's a good slogan, but not one I adhere to. I try to emphasize the importance not only of ecological sustainability, but also of full employment (based on everyone working, but working less), an equitable distribution of wealth, and a high quality of life for all people. I also recognize that the dynamics of a capitalist economic system tend to run counter to these goals, and therefore these objectives will not be achieved without considerable struggle. As such the vision I put forward here falls clearly on the left of the political spectrum, and I hope it will make a contribution to the development of a green-left or, if you prefer, a left-green political movement in Canada and perhaps elsewhere.

This work, then, is addressed not only to those who think of themselves as greens, environmentalists, or ecologists, whether or not they have any affiliation with Green parties, but also to all those who seek alternatives to the socially and environmentally destructive neo-liberalism that has spread, like a virus, into so many nations and so many minds. I especially hope that the book will stimulate debate and discussion among those on the political left and in the labour movement, whose values, traditions, and energies are fundamentally important to ensuring that wealth and opportunities for leading a good life are distributed equitably.

The problem, however, is the definition of a good life: much of the left has become too attached in practice to creating more equitable opportunities for consumerist excess, and far too committed to crudely maximizing economic growth, without making a distinction between those activities that ought to grow and those that should be curtailed, as the foundation of a progressive economic alternative. For instance, a friend recently sent me an article, whose title—"Workers Toil Longer to Buy New Vehicles"—reflects the dual social and ecological crisis we are facing. The article showed that in 1997 it took several more months of labour for the average Canadian worker to purchase an automobile than it did in 1973.[19] My friend's intention was to point out that the system is squeezing working people, who are in many cases working longer and harder for less. Indeed, that is an inequity that should be challenged; however, the problems of making do without a new car would not appear to be one of the great justice issues of our time. Rather than basing our critique of the system on the difficulties of purchasing a new vehicle, progressives in this age of ecological crisis ought to question the notion of private car ownership and propose alternatives to make it possible to live well without it, from more compact design of cities to car-sharing cooperatives.

Of course the problem in this case—and let's be clear on this point—is the automobile and not the auto worker. If scaling back environmentally damaging forms of production means less labour is required in some sectors, we need to create opportunities for workers to shift into socially useful alternative activities, such as manufacturing public transit vehicles, not to mention spending more time with their families or in self-directed projects by virtue of shorter hours of work. Meanwhile, automobile workers themselves have some very good ideas about ecologically sound forms of production that merit expansion.[20] Questioning the wastefulness and destructiveness of technologies like the automobile is perhaps not a popular thing to do in a society in which so many people drive to work and work to drive—and in which so many "good jobs" currently depend on the excessive output of the auto industry—but it ought to be a natural point of convergence between left and green. As eco-socialist theorist David Pepper has argued, neither socialists nor greens want a further mushrooming of a "hedonistic consumer society with a high throughput of goods and a low output of human fulfillment."[21]

Just as there are many types of "socialists," ranging from the tepid Third Way centrism of Tony Blair and his followers (if we can still call them socialists) to militant armed revolutionaries, so too there is a broad range of positions on the green political spectrum. Political theorist Andrew Dobson provides a useful distinction between two main camps: "ecologists" (also known as radical greens or dark-greens); and "environmentalists" (light-greens). According to Dobson, "environmentalism" takes a "managerial approach" to environmental problems, "secure in the belief that they can be solved without fundamental changes in present values or patterns of production and consumption." In contrast, "Ecologism holds that a sustainable and fulfilling existence pre-supposes radical changes in our relationship with the non-human natural world, and in our mode of social and political life. The Queen of England does not suddenly become a political ecologist by having her fleet of limousines converted to lead-free petrol."[22] (Among ecologists themselves further distinctions exist: eco-feminists, eco-socialists, social ecologists, socialist ecologists, deep ecologists, spiritual ecologists—to name a few.)[23] A strong overlap is clearly evident between "ecologism" and a "sufficiency" perspective, while "environmentalism" is content to rely on "efficiency" alone.

As for myself, I like to think I qualify as an ecologist, as a radical green prepared to go the roots of environmental problems and not simply treat the symptoms. Yet at the same time I am looking for pragmatic options that allow us to begin the herculean challenge of turning things around. I certainly don't share the views of some greens at the extreme end of the spectrum who believe the only options are "total change or total annihilation," nor would I go as far as some in calling for the de-industrialization of society. In looking for pragmatic steps forward, there is always the danger that one doesn't think or act ambitiously enough and that one's ideas become co-opted by the existing system. Some radical greens will undoubtedly think that the ideas in this book do not go far enough in promoting a fundamental break with the " 'evil' inertia of the megamachine."[24] But achieving an ecologically sustainable and socially equitable model of development in the wealthy nations of the North— one that the South can realistically hope to attain as well—requires ideas that are both visionary enough to lead to significant change and pragmatic enough to be realizable; and work-time reduction, I strongly believe, is one such idea.

2 | Overconsumption, Efficiency, and Sufficiency

> *We are sufficiently aware of "political reality" to appreciate that many of the proposals we shall make . . . will be considered impractical. However, we believe that if a strategy for survival is to have any chance of success, the solutions must be formulated in the light of the problems and not from a timorous and superficial understanding of what may or may not be immediately feasible. If we plan remedial action with our eyes on political rather than ecological reality, then very reasonably, very practicably, and very surely we shall muddle our way to extinction.*

The Editors of *The Ecologist*, 1972

> *Earth Politics will have to be very pragmatic. It must take a realistic account of the present and its power structure, and not demand the impossible of either the people or the decision-makers. It must recognize the contemporary bias towards economics and offer, so far as possible, economically viable strategies.*

Ernst von Weizsäcker, 1994

Most of us are familiar—perhaps all too familiar—with the statistics regarding the gross inequalities in consumption between North and South. Anyone who has followed debates around global environmental issues is most likely numb from the constant barrage of facts: that the developed countries, for instance, consume 12 times more commercial energy per capita than the developing countries, 11 times more steel, and 15 times more paper.[1] Unquestionably, on average an additional person in

WHAT'S FOR DESSERT?

the North consumes far more and places far greater pressure on natural resources than an additional person in the South. Consumption levels in the North have led to global problems such as the build-up of greenhouse gases, depletion of the ozone layer, exhaustion of fisheries, unprecedented species extinction, the loss of forests, and more. Quite evidently, as Ernst von Weizsäcker puts it, "It is just not possible for the amount of energy, land, water, air and other natural resources consumed by 10% of the world's population—directly or indirectly—to be matched by the remaining 90% without total ecological collapse."[2] Matthias Wackernagel and William Rees calculate that if everybody on Earth walked through life with the same size of "ecological footprint" as North Americans—that is, enjoyed the same ecological standard of living—using prevailing technology we would require three Earths to satisfy aggregate material demand.[3]

Clearly, instead of getting sidetracked by questions of which is the greater problem, overconsumption or overpopulation, the affluent in the North need to begin taking responsibility for finding ways of reducing our resource consumption. Perhaps the most obvious response to this issue is to say that people in the North must simply reduce their material standard of living. This perspective generally brings with it demands for radical transformations of both values and social structures and a fundamental overhaul of industrial society, and often involves advocating a shift towards decentralized, self-reliant communities. Greens have made many calls for just such a transformation.

The authors of *Blueprint for Survival* wrote in 1972, for example, that the solution to the environmental predicament "requires urgent and radical measures, many of which run counter to values that in our industrial society we have been taught to regard as fundamental." They add, "The developed nations consume such disproportionate amounts of protein, raw materials and fuels that unless they considerably reduce their consumption there is no hope of the undeveloped nations markedly improving their standards of living."[4] British ecological activist Jonathon Porritt states, "If you want one simple contrast between green and conventional politics, it is our belief that quantitative demand must be *reduced*, not expanded."[5] Ted Trainer writes in *Abandon Affluence!*: "The most obvious requirement is that the alternative society must be one in which per capita rates of consumption of non-renewable resources are far lower than they are now in developed countries. The fundamental realization must be that a safe and just society cannot be an affluent society."[6] Bill McKibben argues that there are places that "produce decent human lives with less money, less energy, less . . . stuff" and thereby provide lessons "for climbing down from the untenable heights on which we find ourselves."[7]

Greens often point to apocalyptic scenarios if the world does not heed such advice, while at the same time holding out the promise of a better quality of life in a less materialistic society if we do change course. Greens generally maintain that human needs are not best satisfied by continued economic growth as we know it, and some say, "A society of decentralized, self-sufficient communities should be a much happier place."[8] Despite the plausibility of these arguments given the widespread social ills and sense of malaise in "developed" nations—where mood disorders are rising and sperm counts falling[9]—they clearly have not yet been widely embraced. At the Earth Summit in Rio, U.S. President George Bush stated emphatically that the American way of life was not up for negotiation—symbolizing the rejection of such fundamental change.

SUSTAINABLE GROWTH TO THE RESCUE?

Radical environmentalism has been fighting since the 1960s to save the living world from destruction by our technology, population, and appetites by seeking controls on all three, thus posing a fundamental challenge to many elements of modern Western civilization.[10] But the call for a fundamental overhaul of industrial society has not been accepted, for several reasons, including a lack of consensus over the essence and extent of the ecological crisis, a resistance to and fear of difficult change, the perceived lack of a coherent and feasible green economic strategy, and resistance to change by those who profit most from the status quo. A further obstacle is that less radical measures have not yet been pushed to their limits. Ernst von Weizsäcker and Jochen Jesinghaus argue, for instance, that the path of drastic reductions in material living standards in the North is politically hopeless when more desirable options, such as seeking major increases in resource efficiency, have yet to be tried.[11]

Regardless of the reasons, the call for swift and radical change does not appear likely to be taken up any time soon unless some form of acute crisis compels a dramatic change in consciousness. In the meantime, many people have sought a less intimidating path—which accounts for the appeal of "sustainable development" across much of the political spectrum. The watered-down mainstream interpretation of sustainable development suggests that environmental considerations can be integrated into economic decision-making without any fundamental change in social values and structures, and without questioning the vision of endless growth. Proponents of this perspective often speak of "sustainable growth" or, even more ominously, "sustained growth." In other words, "We can eat our development cake and have the environment too."[12]

Much shallow thinking has resulted from this search for an easier way. The Brundtland Report's advocacy of a "new era of economic growth" and acceptance of a "five- to tenfold increase in world industrial output" is, to put it mildly, ecologically reckless.[13] There is, in addition, a completely uncritical acceptance of the idea of "development" in the mainstream sustainable development discourse, and a failure to recognize its role in generating not only ecological degradation but also, in many cases, poverty itself. Perhaps most important is the resultant narrowing of the debate. According to Wolfgang Sachs, the unwillingness "to reconsider the logic of competitive productivism which is at the root of the planet's ecological plight" reduces to a technical problem "what in fact amounts to no less than a civilizational impasse—namely that the level of productive performance already achieved turns out to be not viable in the North, let alone for the rest of the globe." The result is the disappearance of the fundamental debate over "how society should live, or what, how much, and in what way it should produce and consume." Instead, the concept of sustainability has become "infected by the time-honoured certainties of the ruling economic world-view."[14]

Robert Goodland, a critic of the vision of endless growth, praises the Brundtland Report for being excellent on three of the four necessary conditions for achieving sustainability: producing more with less, reducing the population explosion, and redistribution from overconsumers to the poor. He also states: "Brundtland was probably being politically astute in leaving fuzzy the fourth necessary condition to make all four sufficient to reach sustainability. This is the transition from input growth and growth in the scale of the economy to qualitative development, holding the scale of the economy consistent with the regenerative and assimilative capacities of global life-support systems."[15]

This refusal to challenge the perceived imperative of economic growth in the North may very well be politically astute. The idea of sustainable growth clearly draws support because it is more in line with today's economic and political constraints than with a radical green vision. The question remains as to whether this interpretation of the idea of sustainable development can respond adequately to the ecological imperative of a significant reduction in the North's consumption of energy and resources.

THE ECO-EFFICIENCY "REVOLUTION" AND AN ECOLOGICAL TAX REFORM

The mainstream approach to sustainable development ultimately depends on increasing the efficiency of humanity's use of energy, materials, and "environmental services." (Environmental services include nature's "work" to assimilate human-generated wastes, such as water purification and the atmosphere's absorption of the carbon dioxide produced by our industrial economic activities, as well as its "work" to moderate the climate, maintain soil fertility, and perform other functions essential for human life on this planet to continue.) We have seen dramatic reductions this century in the amount of labour input required for each dollar of economic output.[16] Similarly, the goal of "eco-efficiency" is to reduce the requirements from nature for each unit of economic output, allowing a reduction of environmental impacts even as growth continues. In other words, the objective is to "decouple" growth from resource use and pollution, or to increasingly "dematerialize" economic activity.

Some researchers believe that the material intensity of consumption in industrial countries can be reduced by a factor of up to ten to accommodate the need for growth. A slightly less ambitious target is "factor-four" efficiency improvements. According to von Weizsäcker and co-authors Amory B. Lovins and L. Hunter Lovins, "The amount of wealth extracted from one unit of natural resources can quadruple. Thus we can live twice as well—yet use half as much." They provide an impressive array of factor-four examples: houses in Northern climates heated mainly through passive solar design, super-efficient windows, energy conservation retrofits, renting and reuse of hazardous chemicals rather than their outright sale by producers, and low-cost quadrupling of the capacity of railways, among other innovations.[17]

To achieve such efficiency gains, emphasis has to shift from increasing the productivity—output per unit of input—of labour to increasing the productivity of energy and resources. The designs of products, processes, and urban environments must also change to reduce the need for material throughput. Major gains could come through rethinking the *raison d'être* of many businesses—restructuring them to provide "services" rather than physical products. For example, Xerox in Europe stopped selling photocopiers and instead began selling "photocopying services," providing duplication of documents at a fixed price per copy to clients who rent or lease its machines. Since it continues to own and be responsible for the copiers, Xerox now designs them for easy repair, upgrading, and the reuse of parts—resulting in dramatic reductions in the need for raw materials and waste disposal. Energy supply companies can—with the right legislative and regulatory framework—also be transformed into energy service companies, profiting not only by delivering megawatts to customers, but also by seeking out "nega-watts"—reducing the very need for energy by helping customers use it more efficiently, all the while ensuring that customers continue to get the warm room in the winter and cold beer in the summer that they actually want.[18]

Better environmental policies are also essential to trigger an eco-efficiency revolution, and a comprehensive ecological tax reform (ETR) is arguably the single most important policy measure. An ETR would include new green taxes and charges in a range of possible areas (for example, energy/carbon, primary materials, water, polluting emissions, pesticides, landfill disposal, road use, disposable products, non-returnable containers). But it would go much further, amounting to a wholesale tax reform. An ETR could include the elimination of ecologically destructive subsidies—such as the billions in tax dollars spent on unsustainable fossil fuel extraction at Hibernia off Newfoundland or the tax breaks for employers who encourage driving by giving free parking to workers—and, perhaps most important, the reduction of existing taxes on income, profits, or employment. The idea is that instead of taxing "goods"—that is, things we want—we should be taxing "bads," such as waste and pollution.

An ETR package could also include marketable depletion quotas, tradeable emissions permits,[19] a reduction of sales taxes on "green products" such as insulation and recycled goods, and new investments in public transport, energy efficiency, or reforestation. These reforms could provide strong and enduring incentives for investing in new technologies geared to reducing the energy and raw material inputs per unit of output. The potential "double-dividend" includes not only environmental improvements but also new jobs due to the expansion of ecologically beneficial activities and lower taxes on the employment of labour.[20]

One proponent of ETR, William Rees, argues, "There is no getting around the fact that material consumption is at the heart of the sustainability crisis." He adds that we can respond to the overconsumption issue in two ways: an imposed absolute reduction in average material standards of living; or a massive increase in material and energy efficiency. According to Rees, consumerist values make reducing living standards politically unfeasible in the North. Therefore, to achieve the required gains in efficiency we need to begin to make the consumption of energy and materials increasingly expensive. (Rees does recognize the possibility of a third way—a shift in the prevailing cultural values away from consumerism towards sufficiency. He argues that this is conceivable and may be necessary in the long run; however, it remains the choice of a tiny minority so far.)[21]

A wide range of voices, from left to right and running from Greenpeace in Germany to the international Business Council on Sustainable Development, have called for an ETR. *The Economist* magazine, the standard-bearer of neo-liberal economics, has stated its support for the idea in principle, largely as a means of achieving environmental goals with less "burdensome regulation" and of making markets work more efficiently by having prices more accurately reflect true costs. Jacques Delors, socialist and ex-president of the European Commission, endorsed the idea in the 1993 European Union White Paper on growth, competitiveness, and employment. He stated, "If the double challenge of unemployment and pollution is to be addressed, a swap can be envisaged between reducing labour costs through increased pollution charges."[22] Interestingly, while von Weizsäcker, who stresses "pragmatism," is among the main boosters of this idea, the radical *Blueprint for Survival* also features it as a key element.[23] This suggests that it has potential appeal to both the radicals and pragmatists among us, and within each of us.

The favoured approach of ETR proponents such as Rees and von Weizsäcker is to introduce tax changes gradually over several decades to maintain a constant, predictable, and manageable pressure on private enterprise for innovation. While today industry and business generally find it more profitable to consume resources than to employ people, over time an ETR that included reductions in taxes on employment would reverse that tendency. It should gradually, according to Rees, become "more profitable to lay off unproductive kilowatt hours and barrels of oil than to lay off people." Making labour cheaper for employers, without reducing wages for employees, would also encourage job creation in labour-intensive processes such as reuse, repair, reconditioning, and recycling.[24]

A note of caution is in order here for North Americans about the potential to create jobs by reducing labour costs through an ETR. The debate and practice on this issue are most advanced in Europe, where linking new green taxes to lower payroll taxes has been a central item of discussion. However, payroll taxes are considerably lower in the United States than in Europe, and even lower still in Canada—although you would never have guessed as much from the anguished cries of the Canadian business lobby—leaving less scope on this side of the Atlantic for their reduction.[25] A more appropriate approach might be to use green tax revenues directly to employ people in ecological initiatives like energy retrofits or reforestation, or in ecologically benign public services like health care and education, along with targeted income tax cuts to benefit low-income and middle-income earners.

An ETR, then, could help significantly to reduce environmental damage, and it is clearly within the realm of the possible in the not-so-long term. It could allow for win-win-win situations that benefit employers, employees, and the environment at no cost to government budgets. While workers often see environmental measures as a threat to jobs, an ETR carried out on a large scale and managed properly could lead to increases in employment. German studies have shown that a 7 per cent annual increase in the price of energy over 15 years, with the revenues returned to households, would not undermine the economy's general competitiveness, but it would reduce energy consumption by 21 per cent, create more than 500,000 jobs, and favour the poor over the rich.[26] In Britain, economic simulations of an escalating road-fuel duty and a carbon tax, with the revenues used to lower employer payroll taxes (National Insurance Contributions), showed substantial environmental benefits and economic gains, with up to a million jobs created.[27] A measure addressing environmental objectives while reducing some of the most unpopular existing taxes has a readily apparent political attractiveness. Higher energy

Box 2.1   Examples of Ecological Taxation in Europe

- Finland, in 1990, became the first country to introduce a carbon tax, start-ing with coal and later expanding the tax to other forms of energy.[1]

- Sweden pioneered the linking of new green taxes with cuts to other taxes. In 1991 the Swedish government made income tax reductions possible by adding new ecotaxes on carbon dioxide, sulphur, and nitrogen oxides. The effects of the carbon tax were limited because it was scaled down due to opposition from industry based on arguments of competitiveness. The sulphur tax, however, triggered a 40 per cent decrease in the sulphur con-tent of fuel oil in two years—a positive environmental result, although one that led to lower revenues than expected. Since the mid-1970s, to encour-age the development of cleaner alternatives Sweden has introduced a range of ecotaxes, including taxes on fertilizers and pesticides, batteries, domestic aviation fuel, and differential fuel taxes. According to govern-ment evaluations, most of these taxes have had significant positive effects on behaviour and technological development.[2]

- In 1994 Denmark increased taxes on energy, transport fuels, water, and waste. In return the government cut income taxes from an average level of 52 per cent to 44 per cent.[3] At first it applied most of the new taxes only to households, but in June 1995 it increased the carbon dioxide tax on energy use in manufacturing and removed some energy tax exemptions. This step was met with strong resistance by some industries, particularly cement and steel. Energy-intensive production processes could still be exempted from the carbon dioxide tax if the firm agreed to undertake the best available technology savings.[4]

- In 1996 the Netherlands introduced new taxes on gas and electricity, which affect all households and 95 per cent of commercial activities. The 2.1 billion guilders (about C$1.5 billion) in revenue were to be recycled through cuts to income tax and employer-paid social security premiums. Basic energy needs in poorer households were exempted.[5]

- Under the slogan "Taxing Waste not Jobs," Britain announced a landfill tax in 1995, with the intention of using the revenues to make cuts in employers' National Insurance Contributions. Also introduced was a road-fuel "escalator" tax scheduled to increase 5 per cent annually over an undetermined number of years, providing a gradual, long-term price sig-nal. More controversial was the introduction of a value-added tax on domestic fuel, which threatened to hit low-incomes households with poor insulation particularly hard.[6]

- France, Netherlands, Germany, and Denmark operate a system of water charges and rebates in which revenues from pollution taxes are used to subsidize cleaner production methods and waste treatment.[7]

- In 1998 Italy's government promised the introduction of a carbon tax to finance employment-creation measures. This followed a 1994 report proposing a comprehensive tax reform, including a shift of taxes "from people to things."[8]

- France's Green Party has pushed for new ecological taxes on carbon, diesel, water consumption, and chemical fertilizers. The government was reluctant to act boldly without European coordination, but it announced some initial steps in 1998, such as a progressive increase in diesel taxes. New taxes on polluting sectors—chemicals, metals, and energy—were announced in May 1999, with the revenues used to support firms that create jobs through introduction of a 35-hour workweek.[9]

Notes

1. Kai Schlegelmilch and Susan Callan, "Green Taxes Come to Europe," *Yes! A Journal of Positive Futures*, Winter 1997, p.47.
2. Jean-Phillipe Barde, "Environmental Taxation: Experience in OECD Countries," in *Ecotaxation*, ed. Timothy O'Riordan (London: Earthscan, 1997), pp.233, 236; David Gee, "Economic Tax Reform in Europe: Opportunities and Obstacles," in *Ecotaxation*, ed. O'Riordan, p.102.
3. Gee, "Making Pollution Pay," *New Statesman and Society*, April 14, 1995, p.30.
4. Gee, "Economic Tax Reform in Europe," p.101.
5. Hans Vos, "Environmental Taxation in the Netherlands," in *Ecotaxation*, ed. O'Riordan, p.254; Ernst von Weizsäcker, Amory B. Lovins, and L. Hunter Lovins, *Factor Four: Doubling Wealth—Halving Resource Use* (London: Earthscan, 1997), p.209.
6. Gee, "Economic Tax Reform in Europe," pp.81, 95; von Weizsäcker, Lovins, and Lovins, *Factor Four*, pp.205, 209.
7. Gee, "Economic Tax Reform in Europe," p.94.
8. "Maternità, assegno di 200 mila lire e aumento per le pensioni sociali," *La Repubblica* (Rome), Nov. 10, 1998; Gee, "Economic Tax Reform in Europe," p.86.
9. Hélène Crié, "Taxes Vertes: Les Projets Murissent, Jospin Hesite," *Libération* (Paris), May 14, 1998; Isabelle Mandraud, "Un gros cadeau fiscal aux PME, des petits aux ménages," *Libération*, July 23, 1998; Nathalie Raulin, "Jospin règle le Meccano de la deuxième loi," *Libération*, May 19, 1999.

taxes could also encourage the local self-reliance favoured by most greens by making the long-distance transport of goods more costly relative to finding local sources.[28]

Still, the implementation of an ETR faces large obstacles. Both business enterprises and individual citizens may resist the notion of paying for items, such as water, that they have long accepted as being free.[29] More importantly, certain sectoral and regional interests—including both business and labour in those areas that will bear the greatest costs—will put up strong resistance, partly but not exclusively due to concerns about international competitiveness. The defeat of Bill Clinton's proposal for an energy tax (BTU tax) in the early days of his first administration suggests that the path is not easy. Likewise, in Canada, the petroleum industry's efforts managed to end, at least temporarily, talk of a carbon tax. Green taxes, like sales taxes, can hit lower-income people hardest as a percentage of their incomes, raising questions of equity. Additional hurdles are rigid neo-liberal orthodoxy, which rejects government intervention even when the goal is to make the market function more efficiently, and the shift of environmental concern to the back burner in the 1990s.

These obstacles are real, but not insurmountable. Sectors not heavily dependent on energy and resources would actually benefit if other taxes were simultaneously reduced. An essential challenge in the politics of an ETR is enlisting these winning sectors to counter the vested interests that will oppose it. Although not an ideal solution, temporary tax exemptions and concessions can also be granted to those sectors that are hit hardest.[30] Since an ETR could help reduce budget deficits and encourage the development of efficiency-oriented technologies that will increasingly be in demand worldwide, providing new export opportunities, a carefully structured ETR could improve international competitiveness and lead to macroeconomic gains.[31] Meanwhile, governments can use some of the vast revenues generated from the new taxes in a variety of ways to compensate low-income earners for the increased burden and thus make the whole package progressive.[32] Equity concerns can also be addressed by providing tax-free thresholds for consumption of basic necessities such as energy and water.

Despite the great political challenge, there is no inherent reason why ETR cannot be set in place. Indeed, it would be surprising if it were not eventually implemented. Ultimately, if capitalism is to mount any serious response to the environmental destruction generated by its expansionary dynamics, it has few, if any, other options to turn to that can lead to the same level of improvement with as little disruption. A number of

European countries have already introduced significant elements of an ETR package. (See Box 2.1.) The first countries to act were social-democratic Nordic nations. By the late 1990s, with Green parties participating in left-of-centre governments in the European Union's largest nations—France, Italy, and Germany—the potential had grown for the idea of ecological taxation to spread. International harmonization would increase the effectiveness of ETR and avoid problems related to sectoral competitiveness.[33] The European Union could serve as a space for achieving continental harmonization and act as an example for the rest of the world.

THE LIMITS TO EFFICIENCY

As one commentator stated about the possibilities of an ETR, "It could be one of the Big Ideas that we all are waiting for."[34] Nevertheless, there are serious limits to the gains from efficiency alone.

More energy-efficient cars are now being designed and built, but with more cars on the road and more miles driven there is more—not less—energy consumption in transport. More efficient water use may simply feed further urban sprawl into desert areas. E-mail, hailed for reducing the energy consumed per message[35] and for creating opportunities for paperless communication, may very well be leading to increased paper use as the quantity and flow of information increase and people inevitably print out a good deal of it. Meanwhile, in Germany better heating and insulation technology has coincided with increased household energy consumption due to the spread of detached housing and an increase in the housing space per person from 15 square metres in 1950 to more than 37 square metres in the 1990s.[36]

Part of the problem is the type of growth. A separate problem is the rate of growth. Environmental impacts will continue to increase if efficiency gains do not keep pace with economic growth. For example, one team of techno-optimists highlights the great success of Japan and Sweden in achieving energy productivity improvements of more than 2 per cent annually before the fall in oil prices in the mid-1980s.[37] At the same time they advocate economic growth rates of 3 per cent per year. Even if other countries could match the vaunted energy-efficiency achievements of the Japanese and Swedes, the moderate rates of economic growth called for would still lead to absolute increases in energy use. Other defenders of "sustainable growth" refer to forecasts showing that end-use demand for energy in Canada will grow only about one-third as fast as GDP between 1995 and 2020 (27 per cent versus 70 per cent).[38] Given that the Earth is not forecast to grow at the same pace, a 27 per cent increase in energy use means the problem will only get worse, not better. Such statistics are especially worrying given that Canada is already heavily dependent on unsustainable fossil fuel and nuclear energy. Some techno-optimists, forced to take such realities into account, admit that while material intensity *per unit* of economic activity has declined, *total wastes* have increased as economic and population growth has multiplied the volume of products and objects.[39]

What if massive increases in efficiency well beyond the rate of economic growth could be achieved, in the 80-90 per cent range, as suggested by some ETR proponents? Even if this were possible, the end results would still be minimal if we keep increasing our demands and remain committed to an economy based on exponential growth. Some advocates of the factor-four economy, aware of this problem, point out that with a growth rate of 5 per cent per year all the gains from a factor-four efficiency revolution would be devoured in less than 30 years.[40] At a more moderate 3 per cent rate of economic growth, the efficiency revolution would be entirely undone in a mere 47 years. At that time we would find ourselves with the original amount of resource consumption and pollution but with a much greater difficulty in reducing it any further, because the easiest and cheapest technological solutions would already have been exhausted.[41]

Eventually we will reach the limits of increased efficiency. Even if drastic efficiency improvements that outpace growth rates can be achieved over a few years, the exponential growth in efficiency required could not continue indefinitely. At some point there would be diminishing returns to new technologies. For example, we might be able to double the fuel efficiency of our current vehicles without excessive technical difficulty, but would we be able to double that efficiency again and again and again to keep up with the growth in automobile use at home and around the world? Eventually we run directly into the laws of physics, which state that even with perfect efficiency a certain irreducible minimum amount of energy is needed to move people from point A to point B. Other critics point out that we will never be able to produce goods and services without using materials and energy. Recycling can limit this problem but not overcome it, because recycling too can never be perfectly efficient—some percentage of the materials is inevitably lost and new energy inputs are required for recycling itself to take place.[42] The exaggerated faith of some

believers in efficiency and the dematerialized economy prompted ecological economist Herman Daly to quip that perhaps McDonald's will introduce an "infoburger," consisting of "a thick patty of information between
two slices of silicon, thin as communion wafers so as to emphasize the
symbolic and spiritual nature of consumption."[43]

Progress in technological efficiency can also lead to an increased net
consumption of resources. This phenomenon was first observed in the
19th century by economist William Jevons, who noticed that the increasing efficiency of coal use was accompanied by a tenfold increase in total
consumption. As Rees points out, one of the explanations for this
phenomenon is known as the "rebound effect." Greater efficiency allows
firms to raise wages, increase dividends, and lower prices, which in turn
allows increased consumption by workers, shareholders, and consumers.
If, for instance, you decide for environmental reasons to switch from taking the bus to riding a bicycle, you could save both energy and money at a
rate calculated to be 51,000 BTU per dollar. But if you also spend those
savings on consumer items with an energy intensity greater than 51,000
BTU per dollar, the shift to the bicycle is in vain from an ecological perspective. This explains, at least in part, why energy intensity *per unit* of
GNP in OECD countries fell by 23 per cent from 1973-87, but *total* energy
consumption rose by 15 per cent from 1975-89.[44] (The overall energy
consumption record over that period was actually even worse—there was
a relocation of some energy-intensive production from North to South,
so some of the apparent reduction in energy intensity was simply
displacement to another part of the world.)[45]

These considerations call into question the argument of some proponents of ETR who see it as a way to boost economic growth. The World
Resources Institute, for example, estimated in the early 1990s that if an
ETR allowed income taxes in the United States to be lowered so that after-
tax hourly earnings were 10 per cent higher, people might be willing to
work 2.5 per cent longer; and savings might be 4 per cent higher if taxes
on capital were 10 per cent lower. As well, if $100 billion of taxes could be
replaced with "non-distorting" forms of green taxes, U.S. real income
could be $40-60 billion higher.[46] Reducing demands on the environment
through greater efficiency so that the demands can then be increased by
further revving up the growth machine hardly provides an answer to
problems of overconsumption.

Many efficiency boosters seem to forget that it is not enough to simply avoid further increases in environmental impacts; the North must
reduce its demands on the environment. Jesse Ausubel states, for example,

that the United States could "maintain its current levels of cleanliness" even with a twelvefold increase in output by 2100.[47] Even if this prediction were correct, the main problem would still exist, namely that the United States consumes well beyond a globally equitable and ecologically sustainable share of resources and environmental services such as carbon dioxide absorption.[48]

In contrast, Paul Ekins estimated in the early 1990s that a 50 per cent reduction in environmental impact was needed to attain sustainability. He makes use of the equation $I = PCT$, which indicates that environmental impact (I) is driven by three factors: population (P); consumption per capita (C); and the environmental intensity of consumption, reflecting the level of technology (T). Ekins points out that population (P) is expected to double to 10 billion by 2050, while moderate economic growth of just under 3 per cent results in consumption (C) expanding by four times over 50 years. For a 50 per cent reduction in environmental impact (I) to be achieved, technological improvement would have to reduce the environmental impact of each unit of consumption by 93 per cent over the next 50 years ($T_2 = 1/16 \ T_1$). One need not be a technological pessimist to doubt the feasibility of such a tall order.[49] Ekins adds that if we allow consumption per capita to quadruple only in the South, while rich countries experience no further consumption growth, technology must then decrease the environmental impacts of each unit of consumption by 78 per cent. He argues that although this, too, would be an enormous task, it could be achievable with all the support of green consumerism, environmental taxation, and regulation that Northern societies are able to muster. He adds, "It is simply unrealistic for Northern societies to expect GNP growth as well."[50] Some people might quibble with the figures Ekins uses in the equation, but the exact numbers are not the issue here. The essential point is the need to seek environmental solutions on all three fronts—population, consumption, technology—due to the enormity of the challenge. Allowing "C" to grow indefinitely threatens to undo any achievements with respect to "P" or "T."

Similarly, researchers at the Wuppertal Institute for Climate, Environment and Energy have outlined a number of short-term (2010) and long-term (2050) environmental targets in areas including primary energy consumption, materials consumption, and pollution emissions. They estimate that Germany needs reductions of 80 to 90 per cent by 2050 to reach globally equitable and ecologically sustainable levels. While hailing the potential for efficiency improvements, they emphasize,

"Continuing economic growth makes it impossible to achieve the long-term environmental targets."[51]

As with any "technical fix," we also need to consider the possible ecological dangers of new, more "efficient" technologies. The devastating effects of CFCs were not foreseen at the time of their introduction. We have to wonder what damaging new technologies will be encouraged because of an excessive faith in technical innovation. The potential horrors of biotechnology, often touted as a saviour for pushing back environmental limits but already raising genuine concerns about "Frankenstein foods," come quickly to mind.

Just as technologies can have perverse effects, so too can a single-minded reliance on market incentives, such as eco-taxes. John Dryzek has raised troubling questions about a reliance on market incentives to achieve environmental ends. Such policies, he argues, help to constitute a world "in which no moral judgements are made about the intrinsic moral rightness or wrongness of pollution." In his view, a world that promotes rational egoism and profit maximization, displacing *homo civicus* with *homo economicus*, means more problems of the "tragedy of the commons" variety and a decrease in the provision of public goods, such as environmental quality.[52] Given the magnitude of the environmental challenge, neither better technologies nor market incentives can be entirely dismissed as solutions. Still, these concerns highlight the importance of going beyond those solutions in both debate and practice.

TOWARDS A SUFFICIENCY REVOLUTION

In considering the issues of overconsumption and environmental degradation, we need to recognize that an approach relying solely on more efficient resource use is limited to revising means (how to achieve further economic growth?) and avoids questioning ends (how much do we really need anyway?). Solutions to the environmental crisis require a more balanced approach.

As Wolfgang Sachs puts it, "Ecological reform must walk on two legs: scrutinizing means as well as moderating goals." He adds, "An increase in resource efficiency leads to nothing unless it goes hand in hand with an intelligent restraint of growth."[53] An efficiency revolution could be very useful, allowing us to meet our needs and desires with less damage to the environment. It could also allow us to "buy time" to lay the

PARTICIPATE BY NOT PARTICIPATING!

groundwork required for more fundamental changes to Northern societies. However, even the efficiency-boosting authors of *Factor Four* recognize, "We cannot ultimately escape the need for establishing civilisational limits to growth."[54]

Resolving the problem of over-consumption in the North may not necessarily involve an embrace of some radical greens' vision of a *major* reduction in material living standards. The more that improved efficiency allows us to meet our needs and desires with less environmental impact, the higher the material standard compatible with ecological sustainability. However, if we are to sustain the ecological gains from efficiency improvements, the affluent majority in the North will at a minimum have to *restrain* its material ambitions. According to economist Juliet Schor, "Difficult as it may be to tame northern appetites for consumer goods, there may be no other choice if the planet is to escape environmental crisis and at the same time experience significant growth in consumption per head in the South."[55]

While embracing the benefits of greater efficiency, we must begin to ask ourselves how much is enough and set about creating institutions consistent with a society based on sufficiency. Taking this route requires a redefinition of "quality of life" in a way that rejects the ideology of limitless growth and endless acquisition of commodities—the foundation of the existing consumer society. Such a change in our vision of "progress" and "the good life" could even make us better off. Just as the idea of an ecological tax reform has both visionary and pragmatic sides, we have to be both visionary and pragmatic in thinking about how to put this idea of sufficiency into practice.

3 | Working Less, Consuming Less, and Living More: The Ecological Promise of Work-Time Reduction

Sharing the work can create full employment—and it won't cost the Earth.

Bruce O'Hara, 1996

The road to happiness lies in an organised diminution of work.

Bertrand Russell, 1932

Work-time reduction could be the most practical way to begin a "sufficiency revolution" to complement the equally necessary "efficiency revolution." Unlike radical green calls for major reductions in material living standards or a fundamental overhaul of industrial society, WTR has a realistic possibility of gaining widespread popular support in the North. The promise of a 35-hour week was central to the June 1997 victory in France of a left-of-centre government (including the Green Party), an event that helped set in motion a revitalized movement for WTR in much of Europe. In Canada, after years of largely unfulfilled promises about "jobs, jobs, jobs," a small but growing number of voices are calling for shorter work hours as a way of lowering unemployment. Despite persistent mass unemployment, many people with jobs are working more hours than ever and suffering from a serious "time crunch" in their lives. In response to this irrational paradox, reducing and redistributing work time have the potential for improving the lives of both the unemployed and overworked.

But how exactly will WTR benefit the environment? Although French Green Party economist Alain Lipietz argues that WTR is "at the core" of

31

ecological macroeconomics,[1] the links between work time and an environmental agenda are not all that obvious to many people. In general terms WTR can be a key component in enabling people to "live more lightly on the earth" by working less, consuming less, and living more. More specifically, WTR connects to an ecological vision in four principal ways. First, it is a central element in an ecologically sound response to unemployment. Second, shorter work hours can form the core of a new, non-material vision of progress by providing a green way to benefit from economic and technological advances. Third, WTR can provide people with the time necessary to participate in the creation of an ecologically sustainable and more equitable society. Finally, an enhanced ability to choose shorter work hours would open up new opportunities for a more "simple" or "frugal" way of living, based on a lower quantity of consumption and a higher quality of life—and such choice could contribute over time to the subversion of consumer society.

AN ECOLOGICALLY SOUND RESPONSE TO THE EMPLOYMENT CRISIS

Northern countries continue to face a serious employment crisis, despite experiencing an "economic recovery" following the recessions of the early 1990s. More than 35 million people in the "developed" nations of the OECD were unemployed in 1998. In early 1999 the official unemployment rate in Canada remained above 8 per cent, with youth unemployment nearly double that level and the real rates, including those who had given up hope of finding work, much higher still. Although greens would generally reject the idea that jobs are the be-all and end-all of the good life, continuing high unemployment rates clearly have to be recognized as intolerable. For the time being at least, the statement "full employment is still the centrepiece of a decent society" carries plenty of truth.[2]

Over a decade ago green economist James Robertson foresaw this problem, predicting, "The impact of labour-saving technology, the competitive pressures of international trade, and the reluctance of taxpayers to finance more public service jobs, clearly suggest that, if substantial economic growth ever does come back as we still understand it, much of it is likely to be jobless growth." Others, including Jeremy Rifkin, have gone as far as predicting that over the next quarter-century we will see the virtual elimination of blue-collar, mass-assembly-line workers from the production process and that similar job loss is likely in the service sector as it too begins to automate. Even if we don't completely accept that the "end of work" is at hand, we still need to recognize that an astonishingly large number of human beings are in danger of becoming economically superfluous.[3]

The effects of the jobs crisis are apparent in increasing levels of poverty, eroded self-esteem, family breakdown, and crime. There is a growing social polarization between an increasingly poor, "redundant" underclass and a small, rich, technical-professional elite.[4] The marginalized and the excluded, with an increasing sense of desperation, are beginning to sense that they are considered expendable. The employment crisis, coupled with rising inequalities and the erosion of the social safety net, is generating high levels of insecurity that provide nourishment for far-right politics based on scapegoating, paranoia, and hate.

Run Ever Faster, or Slow Down?

The steady increase in labour productivity (output per hour of labour) threatens to displace many workers from their jobs, leading to some critical issues for Northern countries. As productivity advances, we are faced with three main options for maintaining employment levels: increase production; reduce work time; or take a neo-Luddite approach of trying to stop new technologies from being introduced in the first place. The Luddite option is not necessarily as outmoded as most people think. For example, the use of capital-intensive, highly "productive" fishing trawlers—which have utterly devastated many fishing grounds—makes much less sense than smaller-scale efforts that spread work and wealth more evenly, given the limited availability of the resource. But that is a far cry from saying that it would be best, let alone possible, to stop the introduction of new technologies across the board. The real question is the choice between output expansion and work-time reduction.

Throughout the history of capitalism societies have compensated for the labour-displacing effects of productivity advances largely by increasing the output of the product in question or by expanding other industries and new key sectors, leading in either case to increased demands on nature. This is the logic of the treadmill—the need for never-ending economic expansion simply to maintain employment levels. New advances in automation, information, and communication technologies raise serious doubts about whether employment can now be created as quickly as technology destroys it.[5] The term "jobless growth" has become commonplace, and there is at least some evidence that the number of jobs

JOSEPH HENZ

created for a given increment of GDP has declined.[6]

Even if growth could generate new jobs quickly enough, in a world with evident ecological limits to economic expansion "success" of this sort would be a mixed blessing at best. Capitalism's ability to create "work without end" is arguably more troubling than "the end of work." The proliferation of expressways and automobiles, bigger houses, urban sprawl at the expense of prime agricultural land, clearcuts, fossil fuel and hydro dam megaprojects, foreign trade missions to peddle arms or nuclear reactors, and the incessant promotion through advertising of artificial needs to generate demand for ever more stuff—to name a few of the tried and true components of our expansionary economic strategies—no longer provide viable answers to our job problems. As Stanley Aronowitz and William DiFazio argue, "in the light of mounting evidence of ecological crisis," economic policy must stop relying on growth as the solution to problems of technologically induced unemployment and as the means to raise living standards. "Yet in a remarkable example of failure of political imagination and will, uncontrolled growth remains the basis of world and national efforts to resolve long-term economic woes in nearly every major country."[7]

Neither the right nor the traditional left has fully integrated ecological realities into employment strategies. Both continue to take for granted the need to maximize growth. The right proposes to achieve growth by staying the neo-liberal course of free trade, deregulation, privatization, anti-inflationary policies, and deficit-cutting. The left rightly criticizes the inequalities generated by those policies. It also perceptively recognizes that when applied on a global scale such "competitive austerity" is a recipe for the erosion of social standards and an economic crisis of overproduction, with inadequate demand for the goods being produced because workers lack the purchasing power to buy them.

Conventional left solutions, such as domestic expansionary policies and more ambitious schemes to create a pro-growth regime for the global economy,[8] may be more socially desirable than those of the right, but they are for the most part just as environmentally suspect. Although some left proponents of expansionary measures do recognize ecological concerns related to growth, they often do so only as an afterthought and without full consideration of what types of activities are socially and ecologically desirable enough to merit expansion and, equally importantly, which others ought to be scaled back. If growth is necessary to solve problems of poverty in the world, as many on the left will argue, then growth should focus on the poor South, not the rich North. Like generals who have learned all the lessons of a previous war, many on the left call for full employment through a renewed commitment to unselective growth, failing to recognize that no lasting solution to today's economic difficulties is possible at the expense of nature. It is for this reason that greens like Lipietz argue that WTR—and not increased purchasing power and government intervention to stimulate rapid growth, which proved to be the solution to the crisis of the 1930s—has to be the main solution for unemployment in the North today.[9]

Green Employment Options

WTR that leads to a more equitable distribution of existing employment is one essential option for creating jobs without environmental damage. There was much hoopla in France surrounding Toyota's autumn 1997 announcement that it would create 1,500 jobs by building a new auto plant. As the French Green Party pointed out, "Creating jobs by pushing automobile production is not without consequences for the degradation of the environment." Green Party critics added that the same job-creation effect would be experienced if two large firms, each with 12,500 employees, brought in a 35-hour week or, alternatively, if 2,500 small firms with ten employees did the same.[10] In 1996 auto workers in Canada provided a positive example when they bargained for an extra ten paid days off over their three-year contract. Due to this small provision and a similar one three years earlier, the Big Three automakers hired an extra 2,000 people in Canada. In West Germany, 43 per cent of all full-time jobs created from 1983-92 were due to WTR.[11] In the Netherlands, a key factor in reducing unemployment from 12 per cent in 1983 to 3.4 per cent by spring 1999 was a significant reduction of work hours, reaching, by the best estimates, the lowest average annual level in the industrial world.[12]

Some critics maintained that the Dutch success was illusory because it was based largely on WTR rather than on conventional growth-maximization strategies. One right-wing critic argued that the Netherlands was "underproducing in relation to a supposedly low unemployment rate."[13] This line of reasoning would suggest that we are vastly underproducing today compared to the days when 70-hour to 80-hour workweeks were the norm. Apparently with such criticisms in mind, former Prime Minister Ruud Lubbers noted:

> It is true that the Dutch are not aiming to maximize gross national product per capita. Rather, we are seeking to attain a high quality of life, a just, participatory and sustainable society that is cohesive. . . . While the Dutch economy is very efficient per working hour, the number of working hours per citizen is rather limited. . . . We like it that way. Needless to say, there is more room for all those important aspects of our lives that are not part of our jobs, for which we are not paid and for which there is never enough time.[14]

Emphasizing WTR does not rule out seeking environmentally sound ways to generate employment by selectively expanding some types of desirable economic activity. In addition to WTR, a green employment strategy should explore other avenues, including: new jobs in "green industries"; ecologically selective public investment in areas such as energy conservation and building retrofits, public transport, and affordable housing—particularly within urban core areas rather than sprawling suburban zones; expanded employment in public services, such as child and elder care, health, and education; local, non-market production and exchange alternatives like the Local Employment Trading Systems (LETS); and employment in non-profit social organizations—the so-called "third sector."[15] A model for third-sector employment could be France's popular youth jobs program, announced in 1997, in which public institutions, local communities, and the voluntary sector were to be funded to hire 350,000 young people in jobs that meet social needs left unattended by either the state or the market.[16] An ecological tax reform that shifted taxation from labour to resources would also encourage the employment of people rather than the exploitation of nature. The potential of linking WTR, ETR, and ecologically selective economic expansion was confirmed in 1998 by the Dutch Central Planning Bureau, which found, as *The Economist* reluctantly reported, that "the proposals of the Green Left party would lead to the biggest drop in unemployment, mainly by shortening the work week and using taxes on pollution and profits to finance more public-sector jobs."[17]

The service sector is often touted as the most likely source of new environmentally sound jobs. No practical ecological limit exists to the number of people who could be employed cutting hair, giving massages, or offering spiritual guidance. But much service-sector employment remains subject to the same ecological limits faced by manufacturing. Stephen Cohen and John Zysman point out that even in a service-oriented economy, manufacturing is the anchor for services, especially for the high-value-added service jobs that are most in demand. "Lose manufacturing," they argue, "and you will lose—not develop—those high wage services."[18] Likewise, an increase in high-wage service employment in many cases depends on an increase in the manufacturing that it complements. The Economic Council of Canada (before being killed off by the Mulroney Conservatives) issued a similar message: "Service industries need the demand originating in the goods sector." The Council added, therefore, that it was a grave distortion to suggest that the economy could ever be "service-based."[19] Although we should indeed pursue the creation of new, ecologically sound service employment that meets human needs, we must also recognize that much new service employment cannot be isolated from manufacturing's resource consumption and pollution.

Another factor is that some service-sector jobs could more accurately be labelled as a return of the "servant sector,"[20] in which one overworked and overpaid member of the economic elite hires an otherwise unemployed person for some economically marginal activity such as organizing dinners or dog-walking. Wouldn't it be more sensible to have a redistribution of work time so that both parties would have access to good jobs and quality time with their own dogs?

And if you think that the high-tech information economy has allowed us to transcend physical limits and enjoy clean, dematerialized, unbounded job growth, think again. In the United States the region with the densest concentration of Superfund hazardous waste sites is none other than California's Silicon Valley. On average it takes 8,610 litres of water, 6 cubic metres of gases, and 9 kilograms of liquid chemicals to make a single 15-centimetre silicon wafer, the building block of a few dozen chips. Not until the early 1970s, when local computer chip manufacturing was booming, did this once-blooming agricultural zone have to start importing water. The elite information workers of the Valley have used the incomes generated by "clean" info-technologies to pave over some of the world's prime agricultural land—which in the 1940s produced 50 per cent of the entire planet's prunes, apricots, and cherries—in a wasteful form of auto-dependent suburban sprawl, for which they are now paying by choking on a serious smog problem. Chip manufacturers have come up with innovative techniques to reduce the amount of toxic waste emitted per unit produced, but because production is still increasing, so too are overall pollution levels. The sewage emissions of the virtual economy, laced with heavy metals such as cadmium, nickel, and lead, have helped to devastate San Francisco Bay. Shoreline communities once harvested about 15 million pounds of oysters annually from the Bay, but since 1970 the entire oyster population has been too contaminated to eat. Not only has the region's environment been devastated by the reliance on toxic chemicals, but production workers have also paid the price with their health. If the environment critique isn't enough, Silicon Valley employees also have among the longest work hours in workaholic America, due in no small part to high-tech products like beepers, E-mail, and cell phones that make it ever more difficult to escape from work.[21]

Although there is still a lot of work to do and many human needs remain unmet, and policies to create employment in those areas are needed, a lot of work is being done that would be better left undone. In the words of Paul Wachtel, "There are literally millions of people . . . whose daily work detracts from rather than adds to the common good."[22] In Japan, for instance, a wave of resistance emerged in the late 1990s to growth-stimulating, "make-work" infrastructure projects like dams, airports, roads, and bridges that were, in many cases, akin to state-sponsored vandalism of the environment and local communities.[23] In the United States a significant share of recent economic growth is due to the expansion of the "prison-industrial complex." Imprisonment grew at a rate of 6.2 per cent per year throughout the 1990s, a most impressive rate of expansion that has resulted in one in every 150 Americans (and a higher percentage still of Americans of colour) being behind bars,[24] due not only to deteriorating social conditions but also to lobbying by for-profit prisons and other fear-mongers for ever-harsher sentencing. There is no particular ecological problem with the incarceration economy, but certainly U.S. society would be better off without this form of socially cancerous growth.

An ecological approach demands both that we refuse to create jobs artificially at the expense of nature and society, and that we begin the phase-out of unnecessary and destructive forms of production, from land mines to lawn chemicals. An ecological restructuring of the economy will inevitably lead to some disruption of existing jobs. The net employment effect can still be positive.[25] But in any case, rather than furiously scrambling to make new work that is often meaningless and of low or no social utility, we should seek to share equitably the work that needs to be done, the leisure dividend from the work we choose to no longer do, and the wealth generated.

Box 3.1   Genius Calls for Shorter Work Time

The following are excerpts from Albert Einstein's "Thoughts on the World Economic Crisis," written during the Depression of the 1930s.

As I see it, this crisis differs in character from past crises in that it is based on an entirely new set of conditions, due to rapid progress in methods of production. Only a fraction of the available human labour in the world is needed for the production of the total amount of consumption goods necessary to life. Under a completely free economic system this fact is bound to lead to unemployment. . . .

Of one thing I feel certain: this same technical progress, which in itself, might relieve mankind of a great part of the labour necessary to its subsistence, is the main cause of our present troubles. Hence there are those who would in all seriousness forbid the introduction of technical improvements. This is obviously absurd. But how can we find a more rational way out of our dilemma?

If we could somehow manage to prevent the purchasing-power of the masses, measured in terms of goods, from sinking below a certain minimum, stoppages in the industrial cycle such as we are experiencing to-day would be rendered impossible. . . .

In each branch of industry the number of working hours per week ought so to be reduced by law so that unemployment is systematically abolished. At the same time minimum wages must be fixed in such a way that the purchasing power of workers keeps pace with production.

Source: Albert Einstein, *The World as I See It* (Secaucus, N.J.: Citadel Press, 1979), pp.70, 72.

Jobs, Solidarity, and New Political Alliances

WTR as a response to the crisis of unemployment is clearly related to a host of larger considerations. If opportunities for paid employment are increasingly limited, is there any justice in a society that inflicts serious financial and psychological penalties on those who cannot find jobs? Do we need to shift our attention away from paid employment as the main source of our incomes, by moving towards some form of guaranteed annual income? (If so, how can this be financed in an age of globalized capital? Are controls on capital movements needed, or perhaps more fundamental changes to socialize the ownership of the wealth-creating but job-displacing machinery?) Must we find alternatives to the "job culture" in which employment is the principal source of our identities, status, and possibilities for self-realization? Should we seek to create as many paid jobs as possible in ecologically sound activities that meet fundamental human needs, or begin shifting the focus to meeting these needs outside of the context of paid employment, through a revitalization of the household and community economy? What, ultimately, is the point of the frenzied work obsession of modern societies? What, in this age of ecological constraints, is the nature of the good life?

WTR responds to some of these issues in important ways. Although it can only serve the goals of social justice if it is linked to an equitable distribution of income, WTR reflects a recognition that a better distribution of income alone is not enough. The non-material benefits of access to good jobs remain extremely important, and a failure to recognize this point could lead to a concentration of opportunities for rewarding employment in the hands of a shrinking elite, while a growing number of people are driven into marginal low-wage jobs or kept alive, and politically contained, by some form of meagre guaranteed income.[26] In contrast, reducing and equitably distributing work time open up the possibilities for participating in employment and benefiting from opportunities for activity outside of paid work. Rather than forcing some to come to terms with an abrupt decline of their work hours to zero, WTR can facilitate a more gradual society-wide shift away from the current obsession with work and towards other priorities.

The promotion of WTR as a response to the jobs crisis is driven, in the first instance, by a concern for social justice and a desire to avoid the consolidation of a two-tier society of haves and have-nots. According to Lipietz, a Green Party proponent of France's move to a 35-hour workweek followed by a progressive reduction to 30 hours, the push to share work is above all an expression of *solidarity*. He argues, "Putting back together a society which has been torn apart is today's prime imperative, too long hidden by expectation of a mythical economic recovery."[27]

Although resolving employment problems and, more generally, creating greater economic security are clearly valuable in themselves, they also carry indirect ecological benefits. If it is to achieve widespread appeal, a green vision must recognize and respond to the variety of material and psychological needs now being met through paid work. Employment insecurity, and the perceived jobs-versus-environment trade-off, are among the central obstacles faced by a green vision. As Aronowitz argues, the environmental movement has to recognize that it cannot win battles by saying, "We don't care about your jobs." Instead it needs to build links with the labour movement.[28] By providing an ecologically sound response to employment concerns, WTR could be a bridge for establishing such links. It could also help reduce pressure for environmentally unsustainable rates of growth, overcome the perception that environmental measures are a threat to jobs, and promote a climate in which short-term economic considerations are less dominant. According to Bruce O'Hara, "When we're no longer blackmailed by the either/or choice of jobs or the environment, we can take the needed steps to establish a friendly and sustainable relationship with the natural beauty of [the] environment."[29] By responding to a concern as pressing as unemployment, WTR could also serve as a wedge for bringing fundamental questions about societal priorities onto the agenda.

AN ALTERNATIVE VISION OF PROGRESS

We've got enough stuff. We need more time.

William Stumpf, U.S. industrial designer[30]

WTR can be more than a defensive response to the disappearance of jobs. It can be linked, and has been so historically, with a different vision of progress. "Progress" is by now largely associated with the expansion of GDP and increases in material living standards. At the root of such progress is the continued increase in labour productivity, that is, hourly labour output. While technological advances, more effective forms of work organization, and improvements to worker skill levels will most likely bring continued improvements in *productivity*, there is no inherent reason why they must also lead to increased *production*. WTR can instead channel productivity gains towards the non-material benefits of more free time. This argument is perhaps the most significant way in which WTR fits into an ecological vision, standing as it does at the crossroads of a utopian vision and a pragmatic recognition of what is achievable in the not-so-distant future.

This vision combines a sense of both necessity and possibility. According to Lipietz, "Creating a society which gauges progress by the growth of free time more than by the accumulation of wealth is an imperative stemming from responsibility"—that is, the responsibility of sparing the planet from the effects of an indefinite growth of mass consumption.[31] In return for fulfilling this responsibility, the people of the North stand to benefit. If labour productivity continued to rise at a normal rate, and the resulting gains went exclusively towards increased free time rather than increased incomes, it would take only a few short decades to cut the work hours of the "consumer class" of the North in half. Breaking out of the "work and spend" cycle would create abundant time for a wide variety of self-directed activities.[32] According to Lipietz, in the past people might say to each other, "Ten years ago, I could not afford this make of car or a Club Méditerranée holiday; ten years ago I did not have a stereo." Under an alternative vision people might instead say, "Five years ago, I could not have spent the whole of April [hiking]. I got home an hour too late in the evening, so I could not have learnt to play the piano, or play with my children, or chat with my friends in the late afternoon. And in two years' time, I intend to take my year off and publish a book of photographs of my home town."[33]

WTR could help free many people from the "time squeeze" they face. Time pressures are such that one-third of Canadians say they are constantly under stress, trying to do more than they can handle. It often seems as if people have "a choice between having a job and having a life."[34] The effects of the time crunch, and the benefits of WTR, are particularly evident in family life. There is a widespread feeling that people do not have enough time for their partners, their children, or the care of relatives of all ages. The average working couple in North America reportedly spends only 20 minutes a day together, while the average father talks to his child for only 10 minutes a week. This is not only a question of individuals lacking time for the truly important things in life. The "sinister social implications" of an "80-hour workweek," in which both parents are employed full-time, are cause for concern, even at the neo-liberal *Economist*.[35]

The answer to the negative effects of the time squeeze on family life and social cohesion is not, as some would have it, to push women back into the home. The reduction of time devoted to paid labour potentially has much to offer those who seek an equitable distribution of both market and household labour between men and women. It creates an opportunity to help further the changing roles of women and men by reducing the burdens of the "double day of labour" for women and by challenging the dominance of the male career model, in which success requires long hours of paid employment and a wife to take care of the "details at home."[36] Combined with efforts to get men to take on a greater share of household labour, WTR provides an opportunity to consolidate past achievements in gender equity and allow for further positive changes.

Improved health is another significant benefit, given the negative effects of overwork for stress, workplace accidents, and general deterioration of physical and mental health. In Japan, for instance, *karoshi* (death from overwork) is a recognized medical syndrome linked to the deaths of as many as 10,000 people a year.[37] Carmen Sirianni makes a link between the effects of time scarcity and the pressured pace of life on the health of both humans and nature: "The ecological crisis is reflected in a pace of production, consumption, and disposal that exceeds nature's ability to recycle wastes and renew basic resources, as well as in the mental and physical shocks of various forms of 'hurry sickness' that have become endemic to contemporary life."[38] In response, WTR could help remove a good deal of the stress felt by humans and the natural world alike.

Shifting priorities from growth in production to growth in free time implies a gradual shift from employment to leisure as the focus of our societies and individual lives. This opens up the potential for the emergence of a new autonomous sphere of life governed not by corporations or the state but by individuals and voluntary associations. There is the potential of going beyond "trivial leisure" based on passive entertainment and escapism to a "serious leisure" of active participation in political life, cultural expression, study and thought, community affairs, amateur sports, personal relationships, and any number of self-directed projects. Reducing work time could do more than simply create time free from work; it could free time for what is really worth doing.[39]

A positive vision of "working less and living more," a vision that aims to create "an advanced lifestyle appropriate for a post-industrial era,"[40] is extremely important for green politics, which has suffered from the general impression that it involves an embrace of Malthusian austerity and dour asceticism. A vision of progress centred on reducing work time gives substance to the green claim that life can be better in a less materialistic society. According to Juliet Schor, "The centrality of growth in our political and economic culture means that moral or pragmatic environmentally-motivated appeals may not be successful. But, with widespread perceptions of cultural and economic decline, the promise of a higher 'quality of life' may be."[41]

A Future with a History

It is worth recalling that the vision of working less and living more has strong historical roots. Among the first fruits of the industrial revolution were work hours of a length unprecedented in human history. Early capitalism generated workdays of 14 hours and longer, followed closely by the struggle of working people to shorten those days.[42] Workers had an overwhelming desire to gain the time necessary to live dignified human lives—time outside of necessity, domination, and control.

Demonstrations for the eight-hour day were held in the major industrial cities of the United States on May 1, 1886. A labour protest on May 4 in Chicago's Haymarket Square turned violent after police intervened, and seven police and four workers were killed by a bomb. Four labour movement leaders, widely believed to be innocent, were executed. On May 1, 1890, the first international May Day demonstrations were held to commemorate the action of the Chicago workers and demand eight-hour legislation.[43] International Women's Day dates back even further, to 1857, when female garment workers in New York protested abysmal working conditions, including 12-hour days.[44]

The struggles of the labour movement and its allies eventually paid off. With hindsight, it now seems remarkable that some of the original reforms were seen as such significant achievements in their day. For instance, the Factory Act of 1833 in England limited the workday to 12 hours for children between ages 13 and 18 and to 8 hours for those between 9 and 13. The employment of children under age 9 in manufacturing was, with some exceptions, forbidden, as was night work from 8:30 p.m. to 5:30 a.m. for those between ages 9 and 18.[45] Women and later men gained similar protections, through measures such as England's Ten Hours Law. A major movement for the nine-hour day began in Canada in 1872, with some successes, such as the strike by printers in Toronto against employers led by *Globe* newspaper publisher George Brown.[46] The eight-hour day became law in 1917 in Bolshevik Russia, starting a wave of similar legislation in 1918-19 throughout Europe. The standard of eight hours grew increasingly common in North America as well; in 1914 Henry Ford became one of the first business leaders to accept this labour demand. Ford was also a pioneer in introducing a two-day weekend, which he did in 1926.[47] In contrast, Saturday remained a normal workday in some European countries until well into the late 1960s

Workers demonstrate for a nine-hour day, Hamilton, 1872. From An Illustrated History of Canadian Labour, 1800-1974.

and early 1970s. In Canada the average manufacturing workweek declined from 64 hours in 1870 to 60 by 1900, 43 by 1950, and under 41 in 1960.[48]

As these struggles evolved, so too did the intellectual critique of long hours of work and the excessive compulsion to produce, along with a vision of an alternative based on expanding leisure. Businessman and utopian socialist Robert Owen, with a letter to the London press in 1817, became the first of his contemporaries to voice the demand for the eight-hour day. He had previously been the first to limit the workday to 10 hours, taking that step at his factory at New Lanark in 1810.[49]

Karl Marx denounced the Dantesque horrors of the inhumane hours of work in British industry. In volume 1 of *Capital*, he cites the case of the 20-year-old Mary Anne Walkley, who worked shifts averaging 16 and a half hours and sometimes up to 30 hours without a break. One day, after working 26 and a half hours straight making dresses for women of the nobility, Walkley fell ill and, to the astonishment of her employer Madame Elise, died before completing the work at hand.[50] In a proposal to the Geneva Congress of the First International in 1886, Marx wrote that limiting the workday was "a preliminary condition, without which all further attempts at improvement and emancipation must prove abortive." He proposed an eight-hour legal limit "to restore the health and physical energies of the working class . . . as well as to secure them the possibility of intellectual development, sociable intercourse, social and political action."[51]

Marx saw the contradictory nature of capitalism at play with respect to work time. On the one hand, the drive for profit creates pressures for ever longer work hours: "In its blind unrestrainable passion, its were-wolf hunger for surplus-labour, capital oversteps not only the moral, but even the merely physical maximum bounds of the working-day."[52] On the other hand, "despite itself," capitalism plays a progressive role by building up the productive forces: capital is "instrumental in creating the means of social disposable time, and so in reducing working time for the whole society to a minimum and thus making everyone's time free for their own development."[53] Of course, Marx believed that capitalism would have to be overthrown before people could fully realize their emancipation from the life of toil that the system made possible.

John Stuart Mill was one of the first thinkers to link a critique of the industrial status quo, ecological concerns, a new vision of progress, and WTR. He wrote:

> I confess I am not charmed with the ideal of life held out by those who think that the normal state of human beings is that of struggling to get on; that the trampling, crushing, elbowing, and treading on each other's heels which form the existing type of social life, are the most desirable lot of human kind, or anything but the disagreeable symptoms of one of the phases of industrial progress. . . .
>
> Those who do not accept the present very early stage of human improvement as its ultimate type, may be excused for being comparatively indifferent to the kind of economical progress which excites the congratulations of ordinary politicians; the mere increase of production and accumulation. . . . I know not why it should be a matter of congratulation that persons who are already richer than anyone needs to be, should have doubled their means of consuming things which give little or no pleasure except as representative of wealth.[54]

In contrast, Mill called for a better distribution of wealth and for more access by more people to "sufficient leisure . . . to cultivate freely the graces of life." These would be important features of a stationary-state economy, in which population and the amount of capital would cease to grow, allowing "natural beauty and grandeur" and the "spontaneous activity of nature" to be preserved. Mill added: "If the earth must lose that great portion of its pleasantness which it owes to things that the unlimited increase of wealth and population would extirpate from it . . . I sincerely hope, for the sake of posterity, that they will be content to be stationary, long before necessity compels them to it." In contrast to his contemporaries who looked at an end to growth with "unaffected aversion," Mill pointed out:

> It is scarcely necessary to remark that a stationary condition of capital and population implies no stationary state of human improvement. There would be as much scope as ever for all kinds of mental culture, and moral and social progress; as much room for improving the Art of Living and much more likelihood of its being improved, when minds cease to be engrossed by the art of getting on. Even the industrial arts might be as earnestly and as successfully cultivated, with this sole difference, that instead of serving no purpose but the increase of wealth, industrial improvements would produce their legitimate effect, that of abridging labour.[55]

The 20th-century economist John Maynard Keynes, often misinterpreted as a believer in perpetual growth due to his advocacy of demand expansion to combat unemployment, also wanted to see a shift away from production towards higher pursuits. He looked forward to three-hour shifts and fifteen-hour weeks. He perceived the emergence of technological unemployment as a sign that humanity was beginning to solve its central economic problem, the struggle for subsistence. He cautioned that the 15-hour week and the age of general affluence would take time to achieve—roughly a hundred years, he estimated in 1930. Among the advantages of this new age would be the ability to "rid ourselves of many of the pseudo-moral principles which have hag-ridden us for two hundred years." Keynes foresaw a humane future in which "the love of money as a possession—as distinguished from the love of money as a means to the enjoyments and realities of life—will be recognized for what it is, a somewhat disgusting morbidity, one of those semi-criminal, semi-pathological propensities which one hands over with a shudder to the specialists in mental disease." A further benefit of resolving the economic problem would be the downgrading of economists in people's eyes to nothing more than "humble, competent people, on a level with dentists."[56]

Philosopher Bertrand Russell was even more audacious than Keynes, arguing in his 1932 essay *In Praise of Idleness* that a four-hour day had already been proved possible by the First World War. In his view:

The war showed conclusively that, by the scientific organisation of production, it is possible to keep modern populations in fair comfort on a small part of the working capacity of the modern world. If, at the end of the war, the scientific organisation, which had been created in order to liberate men for fighting and munition work, had been preserved, and the hours of work had been cut down to four, all would have been well. Instead of that the old chaos was restored, those whose work was demanded were made to work long hours, and the rest were left to starve as unemployed.[57]

Russell went on to illustrate the absurdity of long hours of work in the modern age:

Suppose that, at a given moment, a certain number of people are engaged in the manufacture of pins. They make as many pins as the world needs, working (say) eight hours a day. Someone makes an invention by which the same number of men can make twice as many pins as before. But the world does not need twice as many pins: pins are already so cheap that hardly any more will be bought at a lower price. In a sensible world, everybody concerned in the manufacture of pins would take to working four hours instead of eight, and everything would go on as before. But in the actual world this would be thought demoralising. The men still work eight hours, there are too many pins, some employers go bankrupt, and half the men previously concerned in making pins are thrown out of work. There is, in the end, just as much leisure as on the other plan, but half the men are totally idle while half are still overworked. In this way, it is insured that the unavoidable leisure shall cause misery all round instead of being a universal source of happiness. Can anything more insane be imagined?[58]

Even some capitalists shared the belief that economic progress should allow workers to experience the benefits of leisure. One of them, W.K. Kellogg, introduced a six-hour day at his Battle Creek, Michigan, facility in 1930, at the beginning of the Depression. His action not only created desperately needed jobs but also proved a highly profitable way to produce breakfast cereal. The shorter day reduced fatigue, improved morale, and boosted hourly productivity. According to leisure historian Benjamin Hunnicutt, several business and financial publications also saw Kellogg's scheme as offering a permanent solution to technological unemployment, based on "elimination of the work, not the worker." Hunnicutt notes that these observers saw revealed the true miracle of welfare capitalism: leisure. They believed:

> Under the direction of enlightened industrialists such as W.K. Kellogg, the exchange of goods, services, and labor in the free market need not result in mindless consumerism or eternal exploitation of people and resources by government-supported capitalism. Rather, capitalism's destiny was revealed as a new freedom from work for more and more people, achieved through the marketplace. Workers would be liberated by higher wages and shorter hours for the final freedom promised by the Declaration of Independence—the pursuit of happiness.[59]

Ditching Shorter Hours for Work without End

Matters have not turned out as the proponents of a non-material vision of progress hoped, at least not yet. One key reason for the abrupt halt in the trend towards shorter hours in North America was the rise of consumerism. A "new economic gospel of consumption" was successfully promoted, and the idea that people can ever have enough was largely dismissed.[60] The promotion of pseudo-needs through advertising and emulation played a part in this, but the drift to consumerism was more than a "capitalist plot." As Gary Cross documents, mass consumption was quite willingly embraced by the masses.[61]

Associated with the emphasis on increased consumption was the focus on solving unemployment through growth, supplemented by government job-creation measures and expansionary intervention into the economy. Hunnicutt recounts how the Roosevelt administration explicitly promoted New Deal public works measures, minimum wages, regulation of industry, and union rights, all at least in part to head off the 30-hour workweek legislation sought by the labour movement and members of Congress.[62] Rather than accepting that the economy had reached a certain maturity and that future progress should be in the form of *freedom from work*, the state introduced a set of measures to promote growth and generate *more work for more people*. This "Fordist" or "social-democratic" compromise set the stage for the postwar Golden Age of capitalism and the explosion of mass consumption.

While the first Constitutional Convention of the United Auto Workers in 1936 declared, "The automobile worker . . . asks that hours of labour be progressively reduced in proportion as the modern machinery increases his productivity," what transpired was the "Fordist era exchange of work for consumption."[63] By 1949 United Auto Workers leader

Walter Reuther was already explaining the abandonment of the fight for a shorter workweek:

> The 30 hour week is a popular demand. . . . But what is our problem when we talk about workers' needs? Is our problem that we have got too many things in terms of clothing and housing, radios, automobiles, educational opportunities? Do we have too much of these things now and the fight is to quit making these things and have more leisure? . . . Our fight is we still don't have enough material goods . . . things that go into making up a high standard of living. . . . When we get to the point that we have got everything we need, we can talk about a shorter work week, but we are a long way from that place as far as my understanding is concerned.[64]

Aronowitz and DiFazio describe this change of labour strategy by arguing: "Since the end of World War II, working people have been encouraged to mortgage everything, including their souls, on the assumption that, economic ups and downs notwithstanding, there was no real barrier to ever higher living standards. The historic demand for shorter hours that accompanied the introduction of labor-replacing technology has been ditched in favor of work without end."[65] This shift had profound environmental consequences, with the unprecedented destruction of the last 50 years being closely linked to the explosion of mass consumption. Environmental considerations today add a powerful reason, and provide a new opportunity, to revive this vision of expanding free time and thereby expand the horizons of our humanity.

Two Reasons to Change Course
The need for an alternative vision of progress is based on two parallel arguments. First, the emphasis on growth and consumption will not give us what we want (the welfare critique). Second, for reasons of ecological sustainability and global equity, the affluent in the North need to redefine what it is we want (the environment critique).[66]

Schor argues that the existing preferences for time over money are not being met due to market failure and a bias against leisure in capitalism. U.S. surveys over the years have repeatedly indicated that people there want increases in free time. Yet despite this, productivity increases have been passed on almost exclusively in the form of higher wages.[67] Also, because much consumption is positional—that is, based on relative comparisons with others—people may gain little if any benefit from increased growth and consumption. In other words, the problem with trying to keep up with the Joneses is that if both the Joneses and the Smiths get higher incomes, neither shows a relative improvement—both keep working their long hours at the grindstone without getting ahead.[68]

A case can also be made that the economies of many Northern countries have grown beyond their "optimal scale," with the costs of growth, including environmental costs and the disruption of communities, outweighing the benefits.[69] Herman Daly points out that in a poor country, growth can satisfy "relatively basic wants" such as food, clothing, shelter, basic education, and security. In a rich country growth more often amounts to the "satisfaction of relatively trivial wants" while "simultaneously creating ever more powerful externalities that destroy ever more important environmental amenities."[70] At a certain point we find ourselves clearcutting forests to produce disposable chopsticks, or destabilizing global climate for the sake of electric toothbrushes, butt busters, or bread machines that end up buried in some cupboard or closet. According to Daly's measure, the Index of Sustainable Economic Welfare, the countries of the North have been getting worse off since the early 1970s, despite significant GNP growth.[71] Picking up on John Stuart Mill's vision, Daly advocates a steady-state economy for the affluent North with a stabilized population level and no growth in the stock of physical wealth. He adds that a policy of "nonmaterial growth, or leisure-only growth" would be a key element of such a steady-state economy.[72]

To the extent that the market does have a bias against our desire for leisure, or that consumption is driven by relative comparison, or that the costs of growth outweigh the benefits, then considerable potential exists for increasing well-being if we can only find ways to break out of the "work and spend" cycle. Many of us in the North could be better off, *even without changing our preferences and values*, if we worked and consumed less. This is not to deny that increasing numbers of marginalized people in Northern societies need higher incomes. We also need to re-create conditions under which working people can receive their fair share of productivity gains. But neither of these points detracts from the importance of shifting societal priorities from growth in production to growth in free time.

The second strand of thought in this vision is the need, for environmental reasons as well as global justice, to put a greater emphasis on nonmaterial sources of well-being. What this amounts to is a quest for a "New American Dream." While the traditional left has focused on the "redistribution of wealth," we also urgently need a "redefinition of wealth."[73] Part of this equation is the continued effort by environmental activists and others to expose the atrocious consequences of consumerism and to persuade people to revise their priorities and follow a less materially intensive path. Increasing numbers of "downshifters" and seekers of "voluntary simplicity" can play an important role in leading by example.

The experience of WTR itself, and the corresponding benefits for quality of life, could help serve as a catalyst for promoting a further shift towards postmaterialist values and encouraging a rethinking of the nature of "progress" and "the good life." Donald Reid argues that leisure not only is a product of change but also can be a transformation mechanism itself.[74] For instance, when Bell Canada asked its technicians initially in 1994 whether they would voluntarily accept a cut of 8 per cent in their workweek—with a proportional cut in pay—only 10 per cent responded favourably. Some four months later, with the measure in place, only 15.4 per cent wanted to return to full-time. This led Robert Lacroix to conclude that those employees who taste the shorter workweek end up liking it.[75] The example carries echoes of the voice of worker Marcelle Evans in a 1932 survey. After tasting a six-hour workday at Kellogg's, Evans said, "I'd never work 8 hours or longer again if I could help it."[76]

Efficiency and Sufficiency: A Two-Front Strategy
This alternative vision that measures progress by non-material factors such as free time goes beyond the defensive, albeit useful, tactic of reducing work time to redistribute available employment. Although not a panacea for overconsumption, a focus on non-material growth is vitally important for an ecological vision. Channelling productivity gains towards more time rather than more production clearly does not in itself lead to *absolute reductions* in the demands that Northern societies make on the environment; but it could be extremely effective in *limiting* or even *halting* increases in consumption and further environmental degradation so that action on other fronts can lead to environmental improvements. Lipietz has argued, for instance, that the nations of Europe could realistically hope to achieve ecologically sustainable and globally equitable quotas of carbon-dioxide emissions through the introduction of eco-efficiency measures stimulated by ecological taxes and other reforms. This would only be possible, though, if efficiency gains were not wiped out by further large-scale increases in production; hence the importance of taking advantage of productivity gains in the form of WTR rather than higher output.[77]

TIME TO THINK, TIME TO ACT

What do you think would happen in this country if, for one year, they experimented and gave everybody a twenty-hour week? How do they know that the guy . . . who is mildly disturbed at pollution doesn't decide to go to General Motors and shit on the guy's desk? You can become a fanatic if you had the time. . . . Time, that's the important thing.

Mike LeFevre, steelworker[78]

Some activists have noted the irony of finding themselves doing ecologically and socially destructive things to make a living, and only having the chance to do constructive things—like paying their respects to corporate polluters—in their scarce spare time. WTR, on its own, would not eliminate the first problem, but it would create more time for engaging in constructive activities, including taking part in the building of an ecologically sustainable and socially just society.

This useful work includes the more labour-intensive but environmentally sound practices that will be part of a sustainable society. Many ecologically beneficial activities—such as growing more of your own food, letting the sun dry your laundry on a clothesline rather than in a nuclear-powered or fossil-fuel-powered electric dryer, mending clothes and repairing goods rather than buying new items, and using alternatives to disposable products—take a little extra time. WTR could also allow a new type of consumption that, in turn, can match a different and less environmentally damaging form of production. Robin Murray points to the case of food. With long work hours, he argues, people have a greater need for highly processed convenience foods, such as Kraft Dinner or McDonald's burgers. At the other end of the spectrum is unprocessed organic food, which takes more time and more skill to prepare at home.[79] (The equitable distribution between men

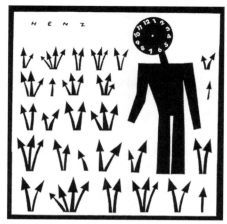

JOSEPH HENZ

and women of these more ecologically sound household activities also has to be addressed.)

By giving people more time outside paid work, shorter work hours can also contribute to the revitalization of household and community economic activity outside the market. Green economic thought has focused to a considerable extent on locally based production and exchange alternatives in opposition to the profit-driven, corporate-dominated, and energy-intensive transfer of commodities across the globe. Alongside the "formal economy," green economists stress the importance of non-market exchanges such as local barter, voluntary community services, and neighbourhood reciprocity, which meet needs unfulfilled by the state or the market. The reduction of the time spent in paid work would increase the opportunity for people to engage in these non-market exchanges and perform what James Robertson has referred to as "Ownwork" (self-organized work). According to Gorz, the shorter workweek would permit people to organize and create neighbourhood services (caring for children, helping old and sick, teaching each other new skills) on a co-operative or mutual aid basis.[80]

The importance of time for these local initiatives can be seen in the example of Local Employment Trading Systems, often lauded by greens as an ecologically sound alternative to the global money system. The expansion of initiatives like LETS is held back by many people's lack of disposable time for contributing something of value back into the system, not to mention the time required to figure out how to benefit from it. Likewise, credit unions, car-sharing and renewable energy co-ops, co-housing projects, community gardens, and other democratically organized economic institutions—which could represent the seeds of a green economy struggling to break through the asphalt of global capitalism—are often heavily dependent on the time of committed volunteers. A symbiotic relationship could clearly develop between WTR and these green economic alternatives. The more time free from employment, the more energy people can devote to these alternatives outside of the global market. The more developed these alternatives, the less dependent people will be on employment in the market to meet their needs.

Time is also clearly necessary for active citizen participation in political activity. This is not only good in itself, as part of an alternative vision of progress, but it is also centrally important to a progressive-green politics that requires the time of informed and committed people working for political change. Overworked, overstressed people are much more likely to spend their evenings gazing semi-consciously at the TV screen than attending committee meetings, educating themselves about the details of key issues, writing letters to the editor, or engaging in acts of protest. It is probably no coincidence that Americans both work more and watch more television than Europeans, while the Japanese until recently beat the Americans on both counts.[81] When people get beyond the TV today, it is often only to move as far as the mall. In the words of Barbara Brandt: "In an economic system in which addictive buying is the basis of corporate profits, working a full 40 hours or more each week for 50 weeks a year gives us just enough time to stumble home and dazedly—almost automatically—shop; but not enough time to think about deeper issues or to work effectively for social change."[82]

Historically, labour's push for shorter hours included a desire for time to read, learn, carry out the responsibilities of citizenship, and take part in social change.[83] Today, WTR would benefit a left-ecological politics as it seeks to resist the onslaught of the right and promote positive alternatives. According to Ernest Mandel, there is no possibility of worker self-management, much less the self-management of society, without ample time for decision-making. Thus the long-term vision of a society based on democratic participation and self-managed institutions, a vision shared by greens and many on the left, requires emancipation from the regime of work without end.[84]

NEW OPPORTUNITIES FOR "SIMPLE LIVING" AND SUBVERTING CONSUMERISM

A man is rich in proportion to the number of things he can afford to let alone.

Henry David Thoreau[85]

None of the previous arguments involves using WTR to bring absolute reductions of consumption levels in the North. Redistributing available employment could serve as an alternative to ecologically destructive forms of growth-oriented job-creation. Receiving future productivity gains in the form of time rather than money could limit or even halt future increases in consumption, but it would depend on action on other fronts, like the promotion of eco-efficiency to reduce demands on the environment. Meanwhile, the idea that the liberation of time from work would allow participation in the building of an ecologically sustainable society is based on the opportunities that WTR would create, though there is no guarantee those opportunities will be seized. But if carried out on a more dramatic scale—beyond the level needed to give the unemployed access to work, or at a rate above the growth in productivity—WTR would lead directly to reductions of production and consumption.

Like the alternative vision of progress, WTR on this scale is based on a less materialistic conception of the good life. But by embracing less consumption, it represents a deeper shade of green and a far more fundamental challenge to existing values and economic structures. It involves an embrace of frugality, which according to James Nash is "a revolt against the Sumptuous Society. For the sake of personal, social, and ecological well-being, it rejects the gluttonous self-indulgence, compulsive acquisitiveness, competitive consumerism, casual wastefulness, and ostentatious materialism promoted by the peddlers of economic 'progress.' "[86]

It is unlikely that in the near future whole Northern societies will be prepared to accept major income reductions in exchange for significant reductions in work hours. Still, some pioneers within these societies are exploring ecologically sound lifestyles based on a lower quantity of consumption and a higher quality of life. These pioneers include so-called "downshifters" who have given up successful and demanding careers, as well as some environmental activists, New Age spiritualists, Christian evangelicals, and others who believe in voluntary simplicity.[87]

Much of this interest in the simple life is apolitical, focusing solely on individual change, and its potential would be greater if its enthusiasts, and others, more fully recognized the enormous difference between a social environment that sustains simple living and one that acts against it.[88] For example, political efforts that ensured the right to choose shorter work hours could help make a lifestyle based on voluntary simplicity more practical. Greater choice over work hours would give people a greater ability to shape their incomes according to their needs. As Sachs puts it, this form of "time sovereignty" would "open up new possibilities for economic underachievers."[89]

According to Gorz, a "policy of free choice of working hours" is a key element of a path that leads "in freedom to a more frugal, ecologically sustainable consumer model based on self-restraint."[90] The free choice of work hours could contribute to the revival of traditional economic norms, where for the worker "the opportunity of earning more was less attractive than that of working less. He did not ask: how much can I earn in a day if I do as much work as possible? but: how much must I work in order to

Box 3.2   500 Years Ahead of His Time?

The Utopians divide night and day into twenty-four hours of equal length and assign only six to work: three before midday, after which they go to lunch; after lunch they have two hours in the afternoon for rest; after that they work for another three hours before dinner. . . . The purpose is not to allow them to waste this free time in wild living or idleness, but to enable them to apply their minds to whatever useful pursuit they wish in their free time. . . .

For as they spend only six hours in work, it might be that you think a shortage of supplies must follow. This is quite the reverse of the truth. In fact, this period of time is enough and more than enough to provide everything needed to support life or make it more comfortable. You will easily understand this if you remember how large a part of the population is idle in other countries. . . .

In Utopia, where everything is in good order and the state well established, it happens only very infrequently that a new site is chosen for building. They quickly repair present faults and also take precautionary measures against those that are likely to arise. So the buildings last for a very long time with only a slight expenditure of labour, and workmen in that field occasionally have practically nothing to do . . .

While elsewhere four or five woolen cloaks of different colours are not enough for one man, and as many silk tunics, and for a more fastidious man not even ten are enough, in Utopia each man is content with one and it generally lasts him two years. For there is no reason why he should want more; if he obtained them, he would not be any better protected against the cold, nor would he seem one jot more attractive in his clothing.

So with everyone practicing useful crafts and fewer men needed for each, as there is great abundance of supplies, occasionally they lead out a huge crowd to repair the public roads if any are worn away. Very often not even such work is required and so they make a public announcement of fewer working hours. For the magistrates do not exercise the citizens against their will in unnecessary work, since the institution of this republic has this one chief aim—that, as far as public necessity allows, all citizens should be given as much time as possible away from bodily service for the freedom and cultivation of the mind. For there, they think, lies happiness in life.

Sir Thomas More, "On the Occupations of the Utopians," chapter 4, *Utopia* (New York: Washington Square Press, [1516] 1965), pp.52-53, 55-56.

CARROLL & SIMPSON

"We could afford it if we both worked three jobs...
But then, we'd never be home anyway."

earn the wage . . . which I earned before and takes care of my traditional needs?"[91]

Policy measures such as "Right to Shorter Work Hours" legislation could ensure that no employee is denied a request for reduced hours unless this step would endanger the firm. A measure like this was expected to become law in 1999 or 2000 in the Netherlands largely through the efforts of the Green Left party.[92] Likewise, employment standards legislation could guarantee the right of all employees to options such as sabbaticals, extended parental and educational leaves, and phased-in retirement—all of them common in Northern Europe. Measures to reduce the disproportionate wage, benefits, and career penalties accompanying the choice of part-time work could also help make it more attractive to work and consume less. These kinds of policy changes could allow more people to pursue ecologically sound, satisfying lifestyles. In turn this could help in attaining a "critical mass," making voluntary simplicity a more socially accepted and hence more appealing option.

But what would happen in a capitalist economy dependent on high consumption levels if large numbers of individuals, or entire Northern societies, opted out of the consumerist way of life? According to Nash:

> Frugality is not a major problem for the Sumptuous Society when it is
> only a personal virtue, even when practiced by a couple of million

earnest individuals or thousands of conclaves of the committed. It is then more of an eccentric nuisance to a vast economy. But if frugality became a widespread social practice . . . it would cause severe economic dysfunctions under the current system. The damning drawback of frugality as a social norm is that it is a formula for market depression in a socioeconomic system that depends on expanding levels of production and consumption to keep the system going and growing.[93]

Nash adds that widespread frugality under the present system not only means less consumption and production, but could also have devastating social and psychological consequences, particularly for the increased numbers of poor and unemployed people. It would make a more equitable distribution of limited resources even more essential, but perhaps more difficult to achieve. Although "imperative for sustained human and biotic welfare," frugality also "could be a source of human agony under existing conditions. It is an essential condition of justice but potentially a temporary cause of injustice." Nash concludes—correctly—that frugality demands a new economic paradigm—more precisely, a new economic system—consistent with the strict need to adapt to biophysical limits.[94]

If introduced on a large scale, WTR, at least in theory, could on its own reduce Northern consumption levels. While having the greatest potential for ecological improvement, reducing work time on a dramatic scale would clearly face far greater obstacles than if the reduction were limited to redistributing employment or absorbing future productivity

"She was always buried in paperwork...
So it was her last request."

gains. Nevertheless, improving the ability of individuals to choose significant reductions in their work hours is entirely feasible, and it could play an important role in the eventual subversion of consumerism.

Linking WTR to a large-scale rejection of consumerism would be the most ambitious and utopian part of the project. But a path of less work and less consumption runs into serious difficulties within capitalist economic structures. Not only does capitalism make a widespread embrace of frugality highly problematic, but it also creates pressures that could undermine the ability of WTR on a more moderate scale to serve ecological ends.

4 | Perverted by Productivism? Work-Time Reduction and an Expansionary Vision

In 1914, Ford reduced the daily hours in his plant from nine to eight; in 1926 he announced that henceforth his factories would also be closed all day Saturday. His rationale was that an increase in leisure time would support an increase in consumer spending, not the least on automobile travel and automobiles. This was a prescient view, for the weekend did eventually become associated with outings and pleasure trips.

Witold Rybczynski, *Waiting for the Weekend*, 1991

Despite the ecological promise of work-time reduction, no guarantee exists that, once in practice, WTR will challenge a productivist vision of endless economic expansion. Indeed, many different visions and versions of WTR representing different interests and ideologies are possible—and these alternative approaches could deflect the project from serving ecological goals.

In France, for instance, by the mid-1990s the debate was no longer even about the desirability of adopting WTR—that much was accepted across most of the political spectrum. Rather, the debate was about how to proceed, with conservatives, socialists, communists, and greens all putting forward their own positions.[1] In Canada, where the debate is not as advanced, similar distinctions have begun to emerge. While the labour movement has long favoured the introduction of WTR with no loss in pay, the business community has shown at least some interest in the issue from its own angle. A 1996 business magazine article called for a legislated 32-hour week in return for "sidelining the social safety net" by eliminating all unemployment insurance and welfare spending apart from disability payments—and ending government-legislated standards for vacation pay, severance pay, and sick leave.[2] Significantly, Nazi Germany and fascist Italy recognized the value of paid vacations and structured leisure as vehicles for fostering political loyalty, which suggests that WTR can be appropriated by just about any political vision imaginable.[3]

A green vision will have to contend above all else with a "productivist" version of WTR based on a belief in the possibility and necessity of infinite economic expansion. In that model WTR would be part of an enlightened social compromise that would restore the high rates of economic growth of the postwar era, to the benefit of both capital and labour. This is a model that has a close affinity to a social-democratic or Fordist approach to creating a "win-win" capitalism, and although it can share some common ground with a green vision, it stands in sharp contrast on a number of key points. Anyone interested in WTR as a contributor to an ecologically sustainable way of life, then, must watch out for the pitfalls of productivism, including the dangers of at least partial co-optation.

WORK-TIME REDUCTION AS A STIMULUS TO ECONOMIC GROWTH?

Rather than seeing it as an alternative to a growth-oriented vision, productivist advocates of WTR argue that it is positively correlated with economic growth. For instance, one of France's most influential proponents of a four-day week, Pierre Larrouturou, argues, "One should not contrast the reduction of work time and growth. Far from being mutually exclusive, they should be mutually reinforcing. It is when there is more growth that the reduction of work time is easier to negotiate. . . . Inversely, the reduction of work time will reinforce growth."[4]

In theory this growth stimulus can result from a number of factors. First of all, WTR can lead to increases in hourly labour productivity in the remaining hours of work, largely because of reduced fatigue and burnout, lower absenteeism and employee turnover, and higher morale and commitment to the job. A general rule of thumb is that 50 per cent of the reduction in work hours is compensated for by increased productivity. This means that a firm that reduced work hours by 20 per cent would, *even without any new hiring*, on average experience only a 10 per cent loss in production.[5] The redistribution of a given quantity of work hours from people working long hours to people who are unemployed or underemployed would thus increase total production. By keeping the labour market tight, shorter hours would reduce employment insecurity and increase consumer confidence, eliminating a main fetter on economic growth. This effect would, in turn, provide more stable markets for producers looking to invest. It would also increase the number of people paying taxes, reduce the number receiving unemployment benefits and social assistance, and cut other costs—like health-care spending—that are being driven skyward both by overwork and unemployment.[6] The result would be lower deficits and/or taxation levels, providing a boost to economic expansion. From a conventional economic perspective, these would all be positive effects.

Growth, though, doesn't always come easily. Fierce global competition and the erosion of national capacities to maintain strong aggregate demand put downward pressure on wages along with labour, environmental, and social standards. This leads, predictably, to an erosion of consumer demand and sluggish economic growth worldwide. Predictions that such pressures could lead to an unravelling of the world economy, rejected as alarmist not long ago, have been taken much more seriously in the wake of the Asian crisis, Russian meltdown, and general economic volatility of 1997-99. In response to these trends, a small but growing number of voices have begun calling for global economic policy coordination to extend Keynesian aggregate demand expansion to the international level and to create a "pro-growth regime for the world."[7]

Similar voices at the national and provincial levels in Canada include the alternative budget proposals put forth by labour and social activist groups. Those proposals rely heavily on economic growth as the solution to Canada's employment, deficit, and inequality problems, though they also attempt to integrate ecological concerns, placing considerable importance on trying to make growth less energy-intensive and materials-intensive. The alternative budgets make a number of sensible recommendations, such as stronger environmental regulation, public investment in environmental infrastructure, and job creation in "non-material" public services such as health, education, and child care. They also highlight WTR, both as a job-creation measure and as an element in a greener economy. Nevertheless, the overall thrust is to rely on faster growth to create jobs and reduce deficits, with an expressed, and ultimately excessive, faith that growth not only is compatible with environmental goals, but also can help achieve them.[8]

"As near as I can make out, it wants a four day week!"

While WTR is not always a part of calls for a new "global Keynesian" or social-democratic compromise, it can be highly compatible with such a vision.[9] WTR can be promoted as a stabilization measure that restores consumer confidence, reduces employment insecurity, and boosts aggregate demand by sharing productivity gains and putting adequate purchasing power in the hands of workers. As part of the deal, labour commits itself to co-operating with capital to achieve a high rate of economic growth and the productivity gains that make it possible, while capital also benefits from lower social expenditures on the costs of unemployment.[10] As such, shorter hours can be part of an attempt to create a more socially enlightened, although environmentally suspect, model to restore rapid growth. The adoption in the late 1990s of major WTR initiatives by some left-of-centre European governments, which were at the same time exploring a coordinated revival of Keynesian growth policies,[11] indicates that this "social-democratic productivist" vision of WTR is much more than just a theoretical possibility.

On the micro level WTR can be co-opted by productivism through the emerging linkage between shorter work hours for individual workers and longer operating hours for capital. The idea is for individuals to work fewer but more flexible hours, a system that makes possible a more intensive use of machinery. The change often includes the reorganization of work through the addition of new shifts or variable work hours that respond to fluctuations in demand. The potential for such a linkage

Box 4.1   Machines Working Longer, Humans Working Less

In response to the threat of 250 lost jobs and the need to be more competitive, Hewlett-Packard's manufacturing facility in Grenoble, France, sought to increase production without adding new investment. Its management has done this by having "machines working longer, humans working less." Under the new arrangement no employee now works more than four days a week, but the plant is kept open 24 hours a day and seven days a week instead of five days as before. The working week varies from 26.8 hours for the night and weekend shift and 33.5 hours for the afternoon shift to 34.5 hours for the morning shift. All 250 employees, including 40 new hirings, are paid on the basis of the old week of 37.5 hours.

In 1988 BMW's Regensburg plant shifted from a five-day, 37.5-hour week to a four-day (4X9), 36-hour workweek, with a six-day (6X9), 54-hour operation of its plant and equipment. The plant increased its workforce from 4,000 to 6,500. By increasing its rate of capital utilization by more than 35 per cent, BMW lowered its overhead costs and its total costs of production, even though it raised its hourly wages to keep its workers' weekly pay unchanged and had to pay social security and unemployment insurance for more workers than before. The plant introduced Saturday shifts—generally taboo at the time in Germany—with each worker coming in every third Saturday, but workers could also end up with five days off in a row.

The same principle of shorter hours for labour and longer hours for capital was behind a 1993 agreement between Chrysler and the Canadian Auto Workers at the Windsor minivan plant. The agreement led to a 7.5-hour day with no loss in pay, a reduction of overtime, the hiring of 800 workers on a third shift, and major cost savings from running machinery around the clock.

Sources: Roger Cohen, "Europeans Considering Shortening Workweek to Relieve Joblessness," *The New York Times*, Nov. 23, 1993, p.A1; Guy Aznar, "La semaine de quatre jours," *Futuribles*, November 1993, p.67; Tibor Scitovsky, "More Workers and Fewer Hours = Higher Productivity," *New Perspectives Quarterly*, Spring 1996, p.39; Edward Dolnick, "Less Is More: Why German Autoworker Brigitte Dunst Loves Her Four-Day Week," *Utne Reader*, May-June 1995, p.65; Advisory Group on Working Time and the Distribution of Work, *Report* (Ottawa: Ministry of Human Resources Development, 1994), p.41.

gained prominence in France with the Taddei Report of 1986, which sought to revise the Socialist government's work-time strategy following failed plans to phase in a 35-hour week in the early 1980s. The report argued that the short weekly operating time of productive equipment in French industrial firms had to be increased to enhance productive capacity and competitiveness by reducing unit costs and increasing the rate of return on capital. The efficiency gains would make possible reduced prices, new hiring, and WTR with little or no loss in pay.[12] This idea has become an important part of work-time practice in Europe.

This strategy of making machines "sweat" to the limits of their capacities is highly compatible with a productivist approach, but an uneasy fit with an ecological vision. Guy Aznar points out that measures like a four-day week combined with the addition of another shift, usually on nights or Sundays, mean increased production—working machines longer produces more. Aznar's concern is: "It is very nice to produce more cars, but you still have to sell them. This solution only applies in sectors where there is unsatisfied demand."[13] More to the point, from an environmental perspective at least, is that it is not so nice to produce more cars.

WTR and work reorganization can be linked to create "more" all around. But the key issue is what kind of "more"? If it is a matter, for example, of extending the hours of public services so people have more access to libraries or health care at lower cost, that is a good thing. But if it is about pushing machinery to churn out more stuff for excess consumption the planet cannot afford, that is a different matter. This problem parallels the eco-efficiency issue. A water-saving technology can be a key tool to help us live sustainably, but it can just as easily encourage more urban sprawl into the desert. The key issue is the kind of progress we hope to achieve through our more efficient use of labour, capital, and nature. Equally importantly, we have to lay down some macro-limits based on what the Earth can sustain, so that greater micro-efficiency does not come back to haunt us (as it did in the case of the "highly efficient" fish trawlers off Canada's east coast). If the institutions of a sustainable or steady-state economy were in place, we could welcome the greater capital efficiency that comes from linking WTR and longer operating hours as a way to reduce the amount of capital investment needed to meet our established level of needs. Since that is not the case, the linkage is cause for concern.

MORE TIME TO CONSUME?

The content of leisure time also distinguishes the green from the productivist visions of shorter hours. The green vision focuses on freeing up time outside of capitalist work so that people can participate fully as citizens in the lives of their communities, build personal relationships, and engage in a wide variety of activities under their own direction. In contrast the productivist vision sees leisure primarily as an outlet for yet more consumption. Gorz argues that the development of capitalism has "left no space in workers' lives for anything but functional paid labour in the service of capital on the one hand, and consumption in the service of capital on the other."[14] While greens seek to create an autonomous sphere of free time not linked to the service of capital accumulation, the productivist vision sees leisure as a new source of profit.

Among the first businessmen to recognize the lucre in leisure was Henry Ford. In addition to understanding that workers needed good incomes to be good customers, Ford realized that a two-day weekend could stimulate the demand for consumer products, most notably his automobiles.[15] WTR has something of the same potential for serving as an opportunity for the expansion of the "leisure industries." (That the term "leisure industries" is not widely recognized as an oxymoron says a great

Box 4.2 Leisure in the Brave New World

The Director and his students stood for a short time watching a game of Centrifugal Bumble-Puppy. Twenty children were grouped in a circle round a chrome-steel tower. A ball thrown up so as to land on the platform at the top of the tower rolled down to the interior, fell on a rapidly revolving disk, was hurled through one or other of the numerous apertures pierced in the cylindrical casing, and had to be caught.

'Strange,' mused the Director, as they turned away, 'strange to think that even in Our Ford's day most games were played without more apparatus than a ball or two and a few sticks and perhaps a bit of netting. Imagine the folly of allowing people to play elaborate games which do nothing to increase consumption. It's madness. Nowadays the Controllers won't approve of any new game unless it can be shown that it requires at least as much apparatus as the most complicated of existing games.'

Aldous Huxley, *Brave New World* (New York: Harper Flamingo, 1994), p.26.

deal about the extent to which leisure has been colonized by capitalist consumerism.) One of the problems for capitalism today is the lack of time available for consumption of the goods being produced.[16] The use of gadgets—home computers, compact disc players, camcorders, and the like—requires time. The purchase of those goods and complementary products—software, CDs, videotapes—is held back by the lack of time available for their use. Time liberated from work could also be a boon to the travel industry, which is already among the largest sectors in the global economy and one of the greatest consumers of energy—particularly due to air travel. Meanwhile, much of capitalism's dynamism is devoted to creating new forms of distractions and escapism that, to be profitable, will require disposable time. This raises the question: "Will leisure simply mean going to theme parks and gazing into the 500-channel universe?"[17]

Leisure is now one of the main sectors of economic expansion. Until the 1960s it was largely self-organized and public, but now leisure is increasingly based on industrialized consumption within the global market. A shift has occurred from time-intensive to goods-intensive leisure, amounting to a "commodification of free time."[18] The consumption of leisure goods—entertainment systems, recreational vehicles, backyard pools, second homes, exotic vacations—has come to be a way for individuals to distinguish themselves from other members of the community.[19] In Japan a recent *reja bumu* (leisure boom) combined with a "rising concern for nature" to increase sales of fuel-guzzling four-wheel-drive Range Rovers from England and cabins made of imported U.S. logs.[20] The "logic" of capitalist consumerism has clearly infiltrated leisure, with major ramifications for the environment. In Germany the leisure sector is responsible for 13 per cent of material withdrawals and 17 per cent of primary energy consumption, making it the third-largest sectoral category. According to researchers at Germany's Wuppertal Institute, the sector's environmental impact "reflects the long-observed trend towards material satisfaction of non-material needs." They add that the transition to a leisure society, given present trends, by no means guarantees resource-saving, sustainable consumption.[21]

Whereas the green vision promotes leisure as an *alternative* to higher incomes and consumption, the productivist vision sees higher incomes as a *requirement* for the enjoyment of leisure. Where productivism prevails, shorter hours create new demands for leisure consumption, which in turn reinforce the desire for more income to pay for goods-intensive leisure. In the green vision productivity gains are to be devoted almost exclusively to more free time rather than more income, while in the productivist vision much of the advance in productivity goes to higher incomes to pay for, among other things, new forms of leisure consumption. By seeing time and money as complements, rather than alternatives, the productivist vision is disposed to a more gradual reduction of work time and the continued pursuit of significant pay increases. In West Germany in the mid-1950s, for example, the achievement of additional leisure increased demand for goods that served entertainment and the demonstration of status. This in turn led to stronger income preferences among workers, with the result that unions had to postpone their original plans to complete the introduction of the 40-hour week.[22] To the extent that the productivist perspective on time and money remains dominant, WTR will be less likely to serve environmental ends.

In addition to being an outlet for consumption, WTR can serve a productivist vision by providing time to equip people with the skills required for economic expansion. Donald Reid fears that rather than a "postmaterialist" future, we may move into a "New Dark Age" in which people will be obligated to use their free time to gain new skills that will ostensibly make them more employable.[23] That age may already be upon us, if all the rhetoric about retraining and "lifelong learning" is any indication. These forms of education are generally not motivated by the value of learning for its own sake, or to create better citizens or expand human capacities, but to produce workers with the narrow skills required to serve capital accumulation. (Attentive viewers of the film *Antz* will have noticed that one of the many propaganda banners prodding the neurotic Woody Allen ant and his fellow workers, as they toil in the service of the totalitarian colony, reads: "Free Time Is for Training.")

GREEN SUSPICION OF SHORTER WORK HOURS

Given these concerns, some greens are less than enamoured with the idea of WTR. According to Dobson, "greens look at the burgeoning leisure industry and see its consumer-oriented, environmentally damaging, industrialized and disciplined nature" as a threat to their self-reliant vision of the "green Good Life."[24] They are also sometimes suspicious of the link between the growth of industrial productivity and the expansion of free time. Many greens see work as a good thing—a noble occupation that uplifts the spirit, helps create and reproduce community ties, and helps people to create themselves. As Jonathan Porritt notes: "The statement of Thomas Aquinas, 'There can be no joy of life without the joy of work', just about sums it up for me." Rather than supporting a vision of "Athens without slaves," in which robots and information machines make an affluent leisure society possible, many greens would agree with Bob Black, who writes: "I don't want robot slaves to do everything. I want to do things myself."[25]

The concerns of these greens cannot simply be dismissed. WTR could, in fact, serve productivist rather than green ends. But the ecological promise of WTR as a pragmatic and potentially attractive way to begin addressing the issue of sufficiency must be kept in mind. The creation of more time outside paid market labour would also bring new opportunities for the type of self-directed work and activities that these greens promote. WTR can indeed be a central element in a green vision—but more thought is needed about how it can be pushed in a green rather than productivist direction.

IT ISN'T EASY BEING GREEN

In practice, within the confines of a capitalist economy it is difficult to call for WTR without making productivist arguments. To be heard, you have to make the case that shorter hours will improve labour productivity, restore consumer confidence, cut costs, lower deficits, and increase or at least maintain competitiveness—all of which tend to be effective arguments in this day and age because they suggest WTR is good for growth. It is next to impossible to avoid compromises on these issues, and perhaps it is not entirely necessary to do so. The difficult challenge for greens is to cautiously and reluctantly accept some productivist arguments, if necessary, as a wedge for advancing WTR as part of a broader ecological critique and alternative vision.

Lipietz, for example, cites the warnings of the Club of Rome and others about limits to the growth of consumer society and argues that our ingenuity should allow us to devote more time to "celebration or meditation" than to "destructive production." Yet he makes clear that his advocacy of a 35-hour week to reduce unemployment is not a call for zero growth. He argues that as long as workers receive at least partial payment for the hours no longer worked, the result will be higher total consumption and expanding markets, *allowing production to increase*. His response to ecological concerns over this expansion is that we can prevent our demands on the environment from growing if our consumption model itself changes, and he calls for individuals and governments to direct their spending power towards the protection and restoration of the environment, aided by eco-tax and subsidy incentives.[26] It is worth emphasizing that Lipietz's argument is about sharing existing work as a way to bring down high rates of unemployment, which differs, as we will see, ecologically and economically from WTR as permanent orientation irrespective of the rate of joblessness.

Another issue—and one that distinguishes "lighter greens" from "darker greens"—is whether labour productivity gains should be actively promoted to hasten the reduction of work time. This is to be distinguished from the position that, for better or worse, labour productivity is continually increasing, and there is a need to find an ecologically sound outlet for it. Gorz has argued that to minimize socially necessary labour and maximize autonomous activity the sphere of basic goods production needs to take the utmost advantage of automation, specialization, and economies of scale.[27] Lipietz argues that to compete in global markets, industrialized nations seeking a socially and ecologically desirable development model, including WTR with little or no loss in pay, must attain high rates of labour productivity growth. This is one of the reasons he promotes new forms of work organization that enlist active worker participation in the struggle for productivity increases.[28] Although Lipietz's view may be a realistic and pragmatic assessment of what is required both economically and politically to achieve shorter work hours, given the current powerful constraints of competition and prevailing social values, it gives rise to a sense of unease about the potential contradictions. Seeking to boost industrial *productivity* on the one hand while limiting *production* increases on the other by channelling these gains to shorter work time is, from an ecological perspective, like stepping on the gas with one foot and slamming on the brake with the other. Critics of this vision argue that increasing industrial productivity is the problem, not the solution. Elmar Altvater, for example, agrees that WTR is essential in the short term as a response to unemployment, but has stated that in the long term the visions of Gorz and Lipietz are not ecologically tolerable. Instead, he argues that we need to stop productivity increases and shift away from machines fuelled by fossil energy to human labour.[29] Similarly, Robertson sees a leisure-oriented vision based on maximizing industrial productivity as being part of a "hyper-expansionist (HE)" future that conflicts with a "sane, humane and ecological (SHE)" path.[30]

As for myself, I must confess to having made productivist arguments in attempts to have the issue of shorter hours placed on the public agenda. I have found myself in the uncomfortable position of arguing, for instance, that firms can gain longer operating hours for capital in return for shorter work time for employees—knowing not only that in today's world this amounts to an argument in favour of more production of industrial commodities, but also that such arguments are important in overcoming dismissal of WTR as "utopian" or "uncompetitive."

The pressure to make arguments about how WTR can serve the cause of capital accumulation also comes into play with respect to leisure issues. Echoes of the productivist "leisure as market opportunity" view were heard when Wayne Roberts and Susan Brandum, two WTR proponents with green leanings, argued that the tourism business had an interest in getting behind the shorter hours movement—although to their credit they urge short-distance tourism rather than, say, the "sun-and-sand" holiday resort packages that drain dollars out of the local economy, consume extravagant amounts of energy through air travel, and are designed for the workaholic looking for a quick hit of relaxation in an "exotic" locale.[31] Likewise, given the competitive pressures and hegemonic discourse of the moment it is difficult to avoid the "free time is for training" argument that more leisure for workers can create new opportunities for a better trained workforce.

AVOIDING THE PITFALLS OF PRODUCTIVISM

The pressure to make concessions to the realities of the day is not unique to the promotion of a green vision of shorter hours; it is a pressure felt by all proponents of reform who also seek more fundamental change in the long term. While accepting that it is extremely difficult to avoid compromises with the discourse and practice of productivism in a capitalist economy, if we make such concessions we have to ask ourselves whether we are no longer challenging the vision of endless economic growth and instead being co-opted into that vision.

In trying to navigate these issues and avoid falling into a productivist trap, we need to ask ourselves a number of questions. Is the objective of WTR to promote growth in production or to create an alternative to such growth? Is it little more than a temporary, second-best measure to reduce unemployment, or a permanent reorientation of priorities? Is it a way to stimulate consumption, or an alternative to higher consumption? Is leisure desirable primarily because it creates new market opportunities, or because it creates autonomous space outside of the market? Is the goal to make the machine of capitalist consumerism work more equitably and more smoothly, or to start subverting that machine?

There is, as we've seen, a distinction to be made between the effects of WTR as a strategy to combat existing unemployment and as a way of benefiting from future productivity gains regardless of the rate of joblessness. Putting more people to work by redistributing available hours would most likely stimulate an increase in production, which would—unless there were corresponding increases in eco-efficiency—in turn create additional negative ecological impacts. However, the increase in production and related environmental damage required to achieve the socially essential goal of lower unemployment would be far less than under a conventional growth strategy with unchanged hours of work. Lower unemployment and greater economic security would also have indirect ecological benefits by reducing the pressure to accept environmentally destructive forms of growth in order to create jobs. Furthermore, the ability to respond to employment concerns through WTR can be an opportunity for greens to pose more fundamental questions about the type of society we want and our criteria for progress. Of particular importance is the potential to build alliances with the labour movement and at the same time encourage labour to rethink its attachment to a vision of ever-expanding consumerism. Creating the precedent of shorter hours, and gaining practical experience in its implementation, can also lead to a more permanent orientation towards reducing work time.[32] That orientation is essential as an ecologically sound outlet for future productivity gains. For these reasons, although it may not lead directly to reductions in the ecological impacts of Northern societies, and although without corresponding measures to boost eco-efficiency it may increase environmental damage in the short term, WTR with the objective of putting the unemployed to work can still serve green ends.

If workers with jobs were prepared to accept shorter hours with lower incomes to allow new hiring, there would be less pressure for concessions to productivism. However, the labour movement, understandably in many cases, tends to resist any suggestion of lower pay, even if it is limited to high-income earners and means more jobs for the unemployed. The insistence on maintaining income levels generates added pressure to find a productivity pay-off to finance shorter hours with no loss in pay as well as new hiring.

One way of finding that pay-off is the trade-off of WTR for longer operating hours, which is about using capital more efficiently to increase production and lower costs. Although in most cases it might seem a concession to productivism, the approach is arguably still potentially useful for advancing an alternative non-material vision of progress. Longer operating hours were central to a 1993 deal at the Chrysler minivan plant in Windsor: 800 new workers were hired on a third shift while the regular daily hours were reduced from eight to seven and a half with no loss in pay. Like the Bell Canada technicians who at first reluctantly, then happily, accepted a reduction of their workweek and pay in 1994, some Chrysler workers were less than enthusiastic about the agreement at first, especially because it meant losing overtime opportunities. A federal government task force reported, though, that it saw signs that "the loss of overtime is less resented as time passes and as people begin to live their lives in a new way."[33] It appears that the very experience of shorter hours, even if it requires a concession to productivism, can make a contribution to the transformation of values and priorities. Such experiences also show that reducing work time is possible in Canada, helping to make the approach a legitimate item of public debate. They provide the precedent and practice needed to establish a more permanent orientation towards reducing work time. For these reasons, even productivist trade-offs in the short term can serve as a useful way of gaining acceptance for the idea of WTR and illustrating the benefits of a new conception of the good life focused more on quality of life than quantity of consumption. Nevertheless, this remains a complicated issue, and advocates of the green position would do well to hesitate before making such concessions.

From a green perspective the issue of how to benefit from future productivity gains is more straightforward, although not without its complications. Income rather than time is the ultimate limiting factor for the quantity of consumption: a lack of money places clear limits on consumption, while a shortage of time can be overcome by more consumption-intensive activities. As a way to benefit from future productivity gains, then, WTR will generate fewer demands on nature than will increases in income. Still, to limit the co-optation of free time as an outlet for more consumption, greens have to push for most or even all future productivity gains to go to shorter hours—in opposition to the productivist vision of a bit more leisure, which reinforces demands for more income to pay for commodified leisure, followed by a bit more leisure, and so on. Inevitably a "battle" over leisure time will also follow, with leisure industries promoting new forms of consumption, greens hoping to encourage non-consumptive lifestyles, and other groups, including religious and political movements, seeking a prominent share of people's "liberated time."

STRENGTHENING THE ECOLOGICAL MERITS OF WORK-TIME REDUCTION

Although green politics should avoid relying too heavily on the hope for "revolutions" in either environmental values or eco-efficiency, both a continued promotion of changes in values and the creation of incentives to use nature more efficiently are key complements to WTR. Continued efforts to promote green values, instil critical environmental awareness, and encourage less materialistic lifestyles will aid in resisting the colonization of leisure by ecologically damaging consumption. It would make a significant difference if most people began wanting to spend their free time walking in nearby natural areas, getting involved in their communities, preparing a meal for friends with food from their own gardens, or playing soccer on a local team (a game that is so internationally popular largely because it requires little in the way of material inputs apart from the ball), rather than helicopter skiing in the Alps, golfing on the former rice paddies of Southeast Asia, or enjoying a game of Aldous Huxley's Centrifugal Bumble-Puppy. We need a vision of "spending time with the Joneses" rather than of keeping up with them,[34] and a new emphasis on local festivals and celebrations rather than long-distance tourist escapism. But a change in values is a slow and complex process, and we can't count on instant revolutions in social values, sudden moral awakenings, or imminent paradigm shifts.[35] We also need to come up with measures that do not depend on value transformations.

Policy measures that promote a more efficient use of nature, such as ecological tax reform, can reorient the direction of the economy and significantly influence the content of consumption. Although such reforms won't replace the need to limit consumption levels, they are still of great importance. An ETR could help provide valuable disincentives for ecologically damaging forms of leisure consumption. Higher fuel prices, for example, could be a significant deterrent to the growth of energy-intensive long-distance travel, particularly air travel. Meanwhile, increased prices for resource, energy, and pollution-intensive goods and services, coupled with increased individual choice over work hours and thus income levels, could lead increasing numbers of people to decide that the consumption payoff from working long hours is not worth the cost of the time and life energy lost. Furthermore, to the extent that sharing work as a job-creation strategy provides a short-term boost to economic growth, measures to promote eco-efficiency become increasingly important as a means of limiting, and possibly negating, the ecological consequences of that growth. Similarly, efforts to create ecologically sound employment in "green industries," expansion of employment in public services such as health care and education, and community-oriented jobs in the non-profit "third sector" are important ways of ensuring that any new growth is ecologically benign. Such efforts would also be aided by an ETR that shifted the burden of taxation from human employment to resource consumption and pollution.

FINDING COMMON GROUND

Green advocates of WTR face a political problem due to limited numbers. WTR, behind which the idea of sufficiency can be promoted, can only go forward if large numbers of people rally around it. However, many potential supporters in the labour movement and on the traditional left do not share the critique of productivism and consumerism. In the short term, political alliances among progressives from a variety of perspectives are needed to oppose neo-liberal policies and propose positive alternatives. In Canada the designing of alternative budgets has created an important space for this kind of discussion. Within such forums, "left" and "green" can find considerable common ground on the need for policies such as WTR, ecological taxation, a more equitable distribution of wealth, and new job-creating investments in ecologically strategic areas such as public transit and energy conservation.[36] Yet the centrality of more rapid growth in the alternative budget proposals has generated debate and division between "left" and "green."[37] With time some of these differences might be worked out and a left-green synthesis emerge—perhaps, for instance, by abandoning growth in GDP as a goal in itself and focusing instead on a selective expansion of ecologically sustainable and socially desirable activities guided by more comprehensive quality-of-life indicators.[38] Still, fundamental differences on the question of growth, and the related question of how to define wealth, may prove difficult to reconcile.

It is certainly not easy for WTR to be put into place in a purely green fashion without concessions being made to the rhetoric and practice of productivism. But some cautious concessions are arguably justifiable to help win acceptance for, and gain experience with, WTR and thus advance a wider ecological vision based on sufficiency. Ultimately the difficulties in reconciling the practice of WTR with an ecological vision can be traced back to the inevitable pressures towards productivism in capitalism. The relentless and insatiable pursuit of profit, the promotion of materialist values and pseudo-needs, the generation of inequalities and envious striving to catch up, and the filling of leisure with passive spectacle and consumption all run counter to a green vision of working less, consuming less, and living more.

5 | Why It's So Hard to Work Less

I owe, I owe, it's off to work I go.

Bumper sticker

When growth ceases to be the central goal or means to effect the goal, the standard objections to the shorter work week evaporate.

Herman Daly and John Cobb, *For the Common Good*, 1989

The road to WTR, whether in its green or productivist form, is blocked by numerous obstacles that advocates will have to both recognize and carefully negotiate their way around. Some of these obstacles are economic, some political, and some cultural.

The business sector has—with some notable exceptions—historically opposed shorter work time, and continues to do so. Support from the most likely champion of WTR and the historical leader on this issue, the labour movement, cannot be taken for granted. Government intervention would help, yet under the hegemony of neo-liberal ideas many governments are moving towards the deregulation, not regulation, of labour-market practices, including work hours. The idea of living better by working fewer hours and consuming less also faces cultural barriers, including a continued societal obsession with growth and consumption, the pervasiveness of an exaggerated work ethic, the difficulties—real or imagined—faced by some people in having to structure and self-manage their own time, and the commodification and trivialization of leisure.

BUSINESS AND THE BOTTOM LINE

Box 5.1   An Argument in Favour of the 12-Hour Day

PARIS, 1923—[The *Herald* says in an Editorial:] However desirable it may be to abolish the twelve-hour day, no progress can be made toward its abolition with the present shortage of labor if the steel mills are to be kept going. The continuous nature of steel-making bars any compromise between a twelve-hour day and an eight-hour day. There must be two shifts or three. And this third shift at present would necessitate the employment in the steel industry of 60,000 more men. Where are these men to come from?

International Herald Tribune, June 29, 1923; reprinted "In Our Pages: 100, 75 and 50 Years Ago," *International Herald Tribune*, June 29, 1998.

The business sector's resistance to shorter hours has been due primarily to concerns about unit labour costs—that is, the cost of labour, including wages and benefits, for each unit of economic output. Business will generally resist the concept of shorter hours, all other things being equal, if it comes with no corresponding reduction in worker compensation. Increases in labour productivity can, however, make it possible to reduce hours without a proportionate reduction in pay and with no loss of profitability. One source of increased productivity is WTR itself, which generally gives a boost to output in the remaining hours of work,[1] allowing a corresponding increase in hourly pay without any harm to the bottom line. A share of productivity gains generated in other ways, such as improved work organization and labour-saving machinery, can also be passed onto workers either through higher wages or shorter hours at the same pay.[2] From a business perspective, WTR with no loss in pay thus seems at first to be much the same as a wage increase with an unchanged number of hours.

A number of reasons exist, however, as to why business may object more strongly to WTR than to wage increases. Schor argues that capitalism has a structural bias against WTR, which she says leads to a failure of the "market in hours." Benefit costs, for instance, are usually a fixed amount per worker, which creates an incentive for employers to have their employees work longer hours, including overtime (even at premium pay) rather than hiring new people and assuming additional benefit burdens. These "hours-invariant costs" have risen significantly in North America, increasing employers' fondness for longer working weeks on the part of their employees. Schor maintains that hours-invariant costs are probably the main reason why the U.S. economic recovery of the 1990s saw so little job growth in its early stages, and why levels of factory overtime rose to record levels. Meanwhile, with salaried work additional working hours are "free" to the employer, creating pressures that result in the "elastic hours of the salaried worker." Employers, moreover, often see a willingness to work long hours as a useful signalling device identifying loyal or hard-working employees. Management in capital-intensive firms that do not have the flexibility of shift work or have a limited supply of labour with the appropriate skills may also oppose reductions in hours to maintain high capital utilization (and avoid the costs of training new workers).[3]

The move to shorter hours can also bring on other costs. Unlike wage increases, work-hour reductions require adaptive shifts in work organization that can be troublesome and costly. Reorganizing production often raises complex issues of scheduling and, if it involves a change in the existing division of labour or pace of work, runs the risk of provoking industrial disputes.[4] Some jobs can be less easily divided into separate tasks than others, making it harder for lost production due to the shorter hours of some workers to be made up by others. (For example, if 100 assembly-line workers go from a 40-hour week to 32 hours, it is relatively simple to hire 25 more workers to take their place on the line. It is more complicated if you have one accountant in the office—simply hiring someone for eight hours per week to take her place on her day off might not be practical, so a more complex process of redefining job descriptions and workloads—and possibly even contracting out some work—becomes necessary.) The costs of recruiting new workers, and the future burdens of redundancy and dismissal payments, add to the mix.[5]

Many people argue that small firms are particularly likely to face difficulties in introducing shorter hours, because they have a narrower range of options for dividing up tasks and reorganizing production. The French experience in reducing the workweek from 40 to 39 hours under the Mitterand government in the early 1980s found significant bottlenecks in small firms. Likewise, during a national effort to reduce hours in the Netherlands, also in the early 1980s, small firms were less likely to put WTR into practice.[6] In Canada the Canadian Federation of Independent

Business, a lobby group for small business, has been particularly vocal in opposing legislated reduction of work time. Still, recent French experience indicates considerable success on this front: many small businesses have been able to profitably take advantage of government incentives to reduce work time, reorganize production, and hire more workers.[7]

The difficulties of organizational change connected to reduced hours will differ depending on a firm's degree of experience in making the changes. Michael Huberman and Robert Lacroix argue that the more often a firm uses a technological or organizational innovation, the more likely it is that the firm can successfully exploit or improve on that innovation. This point applies to the reduction of work hours, which, they say, is not a static experience. The costs to firms of adjusting to shorter hours can fall over time as learning occurs with the accumulation of experience. For example, firms may introduce flexible work teams, organizations, and technologies that facilitate the further adjustment of work schedules. With learning and positive feedback mechanisms, therefore, WTR need not raise costs. Compared to the greater experience of German firms, such as Volkswagen, which have often used the tool of shorter hours during periods of economic slowdown, the relative lack of experience with WTR in North America left Bell Canada facing far greater costs during its 1994 experiment with shorter hours.[8] The lack of recent experience is an additional obstacle to reducing work time in North America, but if the initial steps can be taken the task should become easier with the buildup of experience.

Management can more easily meet the challenge of reorganizing work if it has access to the expertise and information it needs. Recognizing this, the French government has organized a program of technical support for its shorter hours initiatives, as well as a national information campaign to share experiences on work time. This sharing of expertise and previous learning experience can help turn the challenge of WTR into "an asset for the enterprise that knows how to link it to a new organization of work."[9]

The pressures of increasing global competition create additional constraints, including the desire of employers for longer and more "flexible" work-time arrangements. The combination of heightened international competition and growing capital intensity means business is increasingly concerned with both controlling labour costs and making a more efficient use of capital. Firms seek to operate capital equipment as long as possible and want labour available on a "just-in-time" basis—to flow on and off at the flick of a switch or the turn of a tap, like electricity or water, according to fluctuations in demand and the dictates of "productive efficiency."[10] As a result the "rigidities" of the standard workweek have come under attack in many jurisdictions, with business calling for the deregulation of work time.[11]

This point about competitiveness and globalization can be, and often is, overstated. Although it is certainly more than a right-wing fantasy, the cry of "global competition" is often simply a rhetorical tool to stop progressive ideas dead in their tracks. If workers had heeded those who warned in 1898 that "foreign competition will drive out the native product," they would never have achieved an eight-hour day.[12] Moreover, in the first two years after France introduced its 35-hour legislation there were no signs of a flight of investment (if anything, strong job growth illustrated the exact opposite), and a number of large foreign-owned firms agreed to a 35-hour week.[13] It is also far from clear that the U.S. model of longer hours, massive income disparities, and social decay is more competitive (witness the stubborn U.S. trade deficit), let alone more socially desirable, than the pattern in the Netherlands, Germany, and France, with their moves to work-hour reductions. Indeed, a number of reasons exist for why "enlightened" employers could find WTR to be attractive.

Selling Shorter Work Hours to Business

The potential benefits of shorter hours to business can be divided into those that could contribute to profitability and competitiveness even within the existing global order and those that would derive from WTR as part of a more enlightened social compromise.

Shorter hours are not only generally associated with increased productivity in the remaining hours of work—due to reduced fatigue and burnout, lower absenteeism and employee turnover, and higher morale and loyalty. They can also play a role in recruiting and retaining valued employees who reject the stress and lack of work-family balance caused by long hours. The current culture of long hours and "busyness" also has costs for the quality of work, taking us, in the words of one manager, into "the era of the half-assed job."[14] Unlike downsizing, which has on the whole had strikingly poor results for profitability,[15] shorter hours allow firms to hold on to the expertise of their employees and the training invested in them, providing continued access to a broad pool of talent. Such factors have combined to make it possible for some U.S. firms to go as far as implementing a 30-hour week with 40 hours pay, and do it profitably.[16] (See Box 5.2.) Measures such as job-sharing, that is, the splitting of one full-time job among two people, provide opportunities for the

Box 5.2   Profiting from a 30-Hour Week for 40 Hours' Pay

Like many radical labour activists, Ron Healey believes in a 30-hour week with 40 hours' pay. But Healey is a business consultant from middle America.

Metro Plastics Technologies in Columbus, Indiana, was struggling to find skilled employees when it approached Healey. He devised a 30-40 plan that was set in place in July 1996. The firm was flooded with applications from highly skilled people. Productivity gains were impressive and worker morale improved. The quality of work also improved greatly, illustrated by a 72 per cent drop in customer returns. By 1997 Healey had worked with 11 different manufacturing firms to implement 30-40, and he later took the model into health-care service firms.

Healey's approach is an unusual mix of enlightened human resources policies with hard-nosed business tactics. "It's not the number of hours people spend at work that counts," says Healey, "it's what they do while they're there that matters most." His model is based on gaining employee commitment by "giving people their life back" and the belief that "people should spend overtime in life, not work." With six kids of his own, Healey understands the value of a shorter workday for family life. But he also thinks business has to be prepared to say goodbye to employees who do not perform, according to the motto of "hire the best, let go the rest."

The potential combination of improved profitability for business and opportunities for a better quality of life for workers has its attractions, but 30-40 is not without complications. For one thing, 30-40 is based on straight six-hour shifts. Healey maintains that the number of accidents and workers' compensation claims has fallen at 30-40 firms, but some critics wonder about the long-term health and safety effects of eliminating all breaks except trips to the bathroom. It also includes a controversial bonus system, so that if workers are late for any reason they miss out on the 10-hour bonus and only get paid for the 30 hours worked. Critics also ask whether the system simply amounts to a conventional speed-up of industrial work. Finally, it is not a model for redistributing work to create jobs, nor does it represent a break with a productivist growth vision. The point is for the same number of workers to produce as much in 30 hours as they did in 40. Flawed as it may be, more examples of 30-40 in practice might help get the idea of "working to live" rather than "living to work" back on the agenda in North America.

Sources: Marilyn Gardner, "Wanted: Employees to Work 30-Hour Weeks for 40 Hours' Pay," *Christian Science Monitor*, March 20, 1997; Wayne Roberts, "Shorter Hours for Same Pay Adds up to Profits," *NOW* (Toronto), Sept. 18, 1997, pp.29, 31; "30/40 Founder Visits Toronto, Local Firm Weighs 30-Hour Week for 40-Hours Pay," *Better Times: The Newsletter of 32 HOURS: Action for Full Employment*, November 1997, p.4.

training of younger employees and can help in phasing older workers into retirement while maintaining access to their skills.[17] WTR can also be combined with increased work-time flexibility and a reorganization of production to allow longer operating hours, providing capital-intensive businesses with major efficiency gains and reductions of overhead costs.

Whether such benefits are enough to overcome, or at least somewhat mollify, business opposition depends on other factors, such as the degree, if any, to which worker compensation declines with shorter hours and whether changes in government policy provide carrots and/or sticks to encourage the shift in approach. Another factor is the evident instability of the emerging global order and the national capital-labour compromises that are possible within it, raising the question of whether the business elite will eventually come to accept the need for a new New Deal. Global competition is intensifying pressures on firms to reduce wages and employment levels, and the continued introduction of labour-saving machinery adds to displacement. When shown the wonders of the early days of automation in the 1950s, the United Auto Workers' Walter Reuther kept repeating the question, "Yes, but who will buy the automobiles?"[18] In the 1950s a rapidly expanding economy meant that displaced workers could find equally good jobs in other sectors, and automobile sales continued to rise. Today globalization is eroding the ability of national governments to maintain buoyant demand to counter the negative effects of job displacement. The result is persistently high unemployment and underemployment even during a period of "economic recovery," high levels of economic insecurity, and stagnant domestic markets. These conditions, in turn, drive corporate attempts to export into similarly stagnant markets and to engage in further cost-cutting as a principal means of gaining higher profits.

The potential for a downward spiral has led some critics to warn of serious economic and social chaos, and it has generated calls for a new collective framework for economic expansion.[19] Although measures are needed in the near future to create a global economic regime that eliminates destructive forms of low-standards competition, allows the achievement of full employment, and ensures a fair sharing of productivity gains, the answer from an ecological perspective cannot be geared towards maximizing economic growth. While Reuther was right to suggest that serious economic problems would arise if workers could no longer afford the commodities they were producing, today the Earth can no longer afford a form of global expansion that promotes a never-ending increase in the output of material commodities. WTR, which can allow workers to

BACK BENCH

GRAHAM HARRAP

experience their fair share of productivity gains in a non-material way, therefore stands out as a central component of any new social compromise that aims to restore economic balance while respecting ecological limits.

There are as yet few signs that business in North America sees the need for an enlightened productivist compromise with labour, let alone a green pact with nature and future generations. For the time being, business seems to "want it all," relishing its enhanced power to discipline labour, repress wages, and turn the clock back on working conditions. This stance is clearly shortsighted as consumer purchasing power lags behind productive capacity—raising fears about a 1930s-style crash— social cohesion erodes, and nature continues to be despoiled. Yet business has rarely distinguished itself by a long-term perspective on the common good. If the tide is to turn in a more socially and environmentally sound direction, a key factor will be collective organization by workers and citizens.

WORKING TO SURVIVE OR WORKING FOR MORE TOYS?

While the business community in North America remains largely unreceptive to calls for WTR, support among workers is not guaranteed. One discouraging study found that the number of Canadian workers who would prefer shorter workweeks, if the shorter weeks brought a proportionate cut in pay, declined from 17.3 per cent in 1987 to only 6 per cent in 1995. The wording of the survey question, though, was biased: it implied that WTR by necessity had to come with a straight pay cut, and it failed to mention any possible link with job creation. A differently worded survey found in 1998 that 64.5 per cent of Québécois would participate in work sharing (18.2 per cent opposed) and 66.5 per cent would give up overtime hours (17.2 per cent opposed) if the program created jobs for young people.[20]

In any case, many employees continue to prefer gaining money over time. Part of the reason is undoubtedly the desire to accumulate more consumer goods: some rank-and-file workers are "hooked on the consumer goodies which overtime will buy them."[21] Proponents of WTR hear responses such as: "I like having my toys and I want to work overtime to have them. Who are you to tell me I can't?"[22] This desire for more material goods is a real factor; however, the problem goes far deeper than the issue of worker greed.

The 1990s in Canada were marked by a deep recession and weak recovery, a sustained wave of corporate downsizing, major cuts to the social safety net, and a growing gap between rich and poor. These factors have generated intense feelings of economic insecurity. The result, arguably, is a pressure for the employed to grab all the overtime and earnings they can now in case they lose their jobs.[23] High levels of unemployment and increased capital mobility have also strengthened the hand of employers in bargaining, contributing to stagnating or declining real wages. A vicious circle is at work: a downward pressure on wages leads employees to work longer hours to compensate, worsening the problem of unemployment, weakening the bargaining power of workers, and creating new pressures for still lower wages. The need to work longer hours to make up for lost income is particularly acute among families with single parents or with one spouse laid off. Moreover, much recent job creation has been in low-paying and insecure part-time and temporary work. Although workers in these "non-standard" jobs could benefit greatly from the opportunities opened up by shorter hours in more secure sectors, they are understandably unreceptive to any suggestion that they themselves work less. With these factors in mind, writer Jamie Swift points out, "It's simple to say that people should cut back on their consumption, work shorter hours, and live more simply. But . . . it's not so easy to do."[24]

One working group on women and work time points out that more than 80 per cent of women in Ontario earn less than $30,000 a year and argues that most women need to earn more money, not less. They add, "Working people didn't create unemployment by working too many hours. . . . Why should we have to create the solution by 'learning to live with a little less?'" Echoing the arguments of conservative critics, they maintain that sharing insufficient available work between more workers is not the answer.[25] As a result of such concerns, left-wing critics have accused proponents of WTR of advocating the "redistribution of poverty" and the "sharing of misery" among the working class.

The critique from the left is based on a scenario in which wages fall with the reduction in hours. There is obviously a greater openness to shorter hours when the deal comes with no loss in pay—a traditional demand of the labour movement—or as part of a package including measures such as "the creation and protection of decent living wages, more paid jobs, social support systems for dependent care, more worker's control over work time and better employment laws for non-standard workers."[26] The importance of framing the issue is apparent in discussions of overtime: talk of banning overtime is guaranteed to make many labour movement members uneasy, while they warmly embrace the idea of the right to refuse overtime.

Worries regarding the cost of living go hand in hand with concerns about income. Among the most significant obstacles to introducing shorter hours are the costs related to high personal debt loads. The consumer binge of the 1980s, coupled with stagnant real incomes since the 1970s, has left many people saddled with significant debt-service costs. The problem is especially real for people who are paying down mortgages, not to mention recent graduates facing escalating student debt. The easing of interest rates in the second half of the 1990s was a positive countertrend that promised at least some small relief to this problem.

The decline of welfare state spending is another source of pressure. The erosion of collective provision and of the safety net means that individuals must earn more through the labour market to take care of themselves and their families. The decline in social expenditures contributes to the desire for overtime to pay for the new costs, such as higher university tuition for their children. Likewise, falling levels of public pensions might push people to stay in the workforce longer, possibly outdoing any gains in reducing work time elsewhere in the economy.[27] Just as the fear of poverty in old age leads people in the South to have large families as a means of self-protection, contributing to population growth, the erosion of the social provision of income security means that citizens in the North need to find more income to meet their personal needs, thus hindering the adoption of ecologically sound and satisfying lifestyles based on "voluntary simplicity."[28]

The privatization of the welfare state has a further perverse effect. Government cutbacks lead unions with sufficient power to protect themselves by bargaining for improved benefits. This adds to the hours-invariant benefit costs that are a main reason employers prefer overtime over hiring new workers.[29] The obstacle of benefit costs is particularly acute in the United States, where workers—at least those with "good jobs"—receive health-care benefits through their employers and not collectively through the state. If Canada continues to move towards the U.S. social model, these obstacles to WTR will only grow.

That people are often bound into ways of living that are not of their own choosing is a fact that some greens forget, which in turn sometimes results in "blaming the victim" when it comes to choices regarding work and consumption. Commenting on the situation in the United States, Marc Breslow argues, "American society *demands* that people spend incessantly."[30] The heroic and even impossible sacrifices required to live without a car in many North American cities, due to sprawling urban development, poor public transit, and the shift of jobs to the suburbs, exemplify the problem. The lack of affordable housing or neighbourhood security in many city centres can drive people to the suburbs and into car-dependency. Support for a vision of people working and consuming less could be stronger if society was organized differently, with greater collective support for a low-cost way of life.[31] The trend, however, looks to be in the opposite direction. Meeting many core needs—such as education, shelter, and transportation—now requires a higher income than it did in the past. With respect to education, for example, it used to be enough for parents to send their kids to a local public school so that they could be put on the "success track." Today many parents believe that the same result requires private school, followed by increasingly costly undergraduate and even graduate education.[32]

Despite the validity of concerns about how the high cost of basic needs encourages long hours and the need for structural changes to address this problem, emphasis on the need for income can be extended beyond the point where it merits sympathy. For instance, one French worker maintains, "The 32-hour week is a utopia and a joke. . . . You reduce working time and wages. But what is the worker going to do with his extra leisure time if he has no money?"[33] This comment echoes Gorz's point about how capitalism has created people with no identity beyond being worker-consumers, and it shows how dependent many of us have become on the market to satisfy all our needs and wants. Although this dependency is clearly related to capitalism's generation of new "needs" and its hindering of the capacity of people to fulfil their needs and wants outside of the market, the problem also reflects a failure of the imagination.[34] Surely we can still find ways to engage in leisure and provide our own amusements, just as people have done throughout history, without first having to generate income from the sale of our labour.

Workers who are not deterred from their desire to work less by the aforementioned obstacles face further hurdles and costs. As Schor points out, the labour market fails to provide most workers with the option of shorter hours if they so choose.[35] Where the choice does exist, it can come at great cost. In North America, part-time workers are often not only paid lower total wages, but also lower hourly wages with few or no fringe benefits. Opting for shorter hours can also result in a loss of seniority and a reduced chance of promotion.[36] Workers who ask for shorter hours fear that management will interpret their requests as a sign of disloyalty or lack of commitment, and that they will be the first to go if layoffs come.[37] Conversely, intensifying competition for good jobs creates pressure on employees to work long hours as a way of competing and signalling their worthiness. Meanwhile, this competition has strengthened the ability of employers to require such a commitment from workers who want to keep their jobs.[38]

The heavy penalties faced by people interested in working less suggest that there is a strong limit on how much individual workers acting alone can achieve in terms of WTR. Collective action, both through labour unions and government, is important in making WTR available on reasonable terms and avoiding destructive long-hours competition between individual employees. Moreover, the reduction of standard work time for all workers requires the active support of the labour movement.

LABOUR UNIONS AS A FORCE FOR CHANGE

Labour unions have played a central role in the struggle for WTR historically in Canada and elsewhere. Their leadership is extremely important if a new era of work-time reduction is to be achieved; but that leadership cannot be taken for granted.

One of the main obstacles facing the labour movement is the apparent divergence between those who would pay for WTR and those who would benefit. New jobs due to WTR benefit the unemployed, who, in most cases, are not members of the union in question. However, the costs of mobilizing and possibly striking in favour of shorter hours, as well as any reductions in pay or sacrifice of wage increases, are shouldered by union members already holding jobs. Many of the already employed,

particularly those with seniority and a high degree of job security, have nothing to gain monetarily from working shorter hours.[39] In times of economic slowdown and uncertainty, workers with security and seniority sometimes prefer to see others laid off over a reduction of their own hours and incomes. For instance, in 1998 a small number of senior Chrysler workers in Windsor voiced their preference for laying off the third shift rather than losing eight hours of overtime for themselves.[40]

A number of factors could override this problem. For the already employed, shorter hours can provide significant benefits in leisure time and quality of life. Even when a preference for time does not clearly predominate over the desire for money, a potential role exists for union leaders, among others, in seeking to shift the balance of preferences. For example, during its successful 35-hour-week campaign IG Metall, the German metalworkers' union, encouraged the workers to recognize the benefits of more leisure and rest periods.[41] The benefits of leisure can also be linked with an alternative, non-material vision of progress, providing opportunities to unite labour and the environmental movement.

Another key factor is the degree of solidarity within the working class. IG Metall's mobilization of support for the 35-hour week emphasized the collective good of the measure and solidarity with the unemployed as well as within the union.[42] The campaign showed that labour is capable of more than simply standing up for the interests of its most powerful members—it is also capable of offering workable solutions for the unemployed and society as a whole. Similarly, workers at one Western Canadian plant have refused to work unnecessary overtime, thereby avoiding avoiding numerous planned layoffs and leading to recalls of laid-off colleagues.[43] Nevertheless, many unions remain content to draft resolutions in favour of WTR but show little evidence of efforts to build a broader movement for shorter hours or to shift their bargaining priorities.

Canada's decentralized collective bargaining structure may also be holding back union leadership on this issue.[44] Compared to Germany, for example, with its nationwide or regional sectoral negotiations, in Canada those who make sacrifices for shorter hours at the level of individual firms will most likely not reap any increased employment security and the related long-term financial benefits. The issue, then, is not simply one of class conflict, but also a matter of achieving solidarity among workers themselves.

Greater "solidarity" with the jobless could eventually emerge given fears of even higher levels of unemployment. Union demands for WTR in Europe in the 1980s, for example, were driven by more than high unemployment rates. The microelectronics revolution had raised fears that existing levels of unemployment were the first signs of catastrophic or endemically high levels of unemployment due to labour displacement. This strong negative motivation for WTR was enough in many European countries to countervail both relative union weakness in collective bargaining and the less than enthusiastic concern of employees to increase their time for leisure.[45]

A further complication for labour is the growing diversity of employee preferences regarding work hours. Nowadays the call for a shorter workweek does not lay "nearest the heart of every labourer," as the eight-hour day once did.[46] In the 19th century workers universally despised the 70-hour-plus workweek, and the demand for the eight-hour day resonated with all workers because of shared threats to health, lack of time for leisure, and a strong sense of working-class identity. Today far less consensus exists on issues related to time. Many workers actively seek shorter hours so they can better balance their paid work and home responsibilities, for instance, while others stuck in involuntary part-time jobs would like more hours. Labour unions, then, face complex questions about adapting to the diversity of preferences and allowing greater individual choice of different work schedules. Some people fear that the individualization of work time could undermine the practice of standardized wages and conditions, the cornerstone of union policies since the emergence of collective bargaining.[47] Another worry is that various flex-time and part-time options could be used to further segment the labour force—and could serve to solidify, rather than reverse, the inferior status of women in the labour market as well as in the home. According to Carmen Sirianni, the union fears reflect the importance of common time standards in labour's capacity to represent collective interests effectively. By removing individual bargaining over work hours, common standards were central in limiting competition among workers.[48] The labour move-ment can and must learn to creatively manage these complex issues if unions are to remain relevant and effective in a world of diverse employee preferences.

The considerable challenge of mobilizing behind WTR is one way to put the labour movement to the test. Gorz points out that trade unions risk degenerating into a force for protecting a small, privileged labour aristocracy. He maintains that to avoid this possibility and to reverse the marginalization of a growing percentage of the population, "an ambitious policy for a continual, programmed reduction in working hours is indis-pensable." Also essential is an openness on the part of unions to the aspi-rations of other social movements. According to Gorz, "The attitude of the trade-union movement towards the other social movements and their objectives will also determine its own evolution. If it divorces itself from them, if it refuses to be part of a wider movement, if it sees its mission as being limited to the defence of waged workers as such, it will inevitably degenerate into a conservative, neo-corporatist force."[49]

The evidence in Canada on this question is mixed. The continued high levels of overtime despite persistent mass unemployment, and the significant pockets of resistance to any suggestion that the long hours of high-paid workers be limited, are grounds for pessimism. The temptation is to conclude that the philosophy of "business unionism," in which unions have no role beyond promoting the narrow, short-term economic interests of their most powerful members, predominates over a "social unionism" with a broader agenda for building a better society.

Yet signs exist that at least some elements of the labour movement recognize the need to forge alliances with other social movements to resist the neo-liberal onslaught and promote common alternatives. The 1995-98 Ontario Days of Action in opposition to the provincial Conservative government are an example of an attempt to build an alliance of resistance. As for a common program for positive change, some people within the Canadian Auto Workers have argued that WTR is an issue that can mobilize workers in solidarity with the unemployed, women's organizations, environmentalists, and the young. The increasing prominence of WTR among economic alternatives promoted by some unions is encouraging, as is its inclusion in the federal alternative budget, which seeks to build consensus among labour and other social movements around economic policies.[50] Also significant are recent small-scale successes in reducing work time to create jobs. Whether these signs of hope and small successes can be expanded so that WTR becomes a top priority on the collective bargaining and public policy agenda—as unions throughout much of Europe have achieved—remains to be seen.

GOVERNMENT LEADERSHIP IN A TIME OF NEO-LIBERALISM

WTR has the potential to bring major public benefits in financial savings on unemployment insurance, social assistance, and other related costs of unemployment, as well as ecological benefits and improvements in quality of life. Whether through legislation, the creation of financial incentives to favour WTR, or taking the lead as a model employer, government intervention in this imperfect market for work hours would be desirable and justifiable. Such intervention, though, runs counter to the neo-liberal worship of unfettered markets.

In many jurisdictions pressures exist for the deregulation of work hours, for returning work time to the market where it can be "recommodified" into a good that people are free to buy, sell, or dispense with as they choose and with little legal restraint.[51] In Ontario the Conservative government under Premier Mike Harris began considering a number of options to weaken legal constraints on work time. One option among others to remove "red tape" would be to allow employers and labour unions to negotiate "flexible standards" for hours of work that are *longer* than the provisions contained in the current act. This proposal emerged following lobbying by major corporations, such as General Motors, which has sought the "flexibility" of 10-hour days and a 56-hour week, a schedule that would sound pretty "rigid" to most folk.[52] In California under Republican governor Pete Wilson, greater flexibility was also the rhetorical justification for eliminating overtime pay for daily hours in excess of eight. In Germany, despite the success of workers in achieving significant hours reductions through collective bargaining, the Christian Democratic government of Helmut Kohl instead sought an increase in labour-market flexibility. The German business lobby called for government to "get rid of regulations like no weekend work" on the grounds that the "machinery is not Catholic or Protestant."[53] This idea of "flexibility"—which in practice generally means flexibility on the employer's terms—quickly became a global buzzword signifying similar neo-liberal changes in various jurisdictions.

But there are indications that the tide could be turning against neo-liberal thinking on work time. France's 35-hour-workweek legislation in 1997 has revitalized demands for shorter hours legislation throughout much of Europe. In Canada Quebec's Parti Québécois government introduced incentives to reduce long hours of work along with a modest reduction of the standard workweek from 44 to 40 hours, while the New Democratic Party (NDP) in British Columbia announced subsidies for shorter hours linked to new hiring in the forestry sector.[54] The Manitoba and Ontario New Democratic parties passed resolutions in favour of WTR in 1997 and 1998 respectively, while the opposition Labor Party in Australia came out in favour of financial incentives to encourage a range of work-time redistribution options: these are signs that social-democratic parties are beginning to see this as a key issue.[55] Even the OECD moderated its neo-liberal hostility to WTR policies by reluctantly recognizing in 1998 that under the right conditions WTR can successfully create jobs and avoid layoffs.[56] The federal Liberal government in Canada, however, was content to trumpet the fact that it commissioned a fine report in 1994 advocating a reduction and redistribution of work time,[57] followed by another fine reflection on the changing workplace, while showing no signs of commitment to real action.

A CULTURE CONSUMED BY GROWTH

One of the main cultural obstacles to a widespread embrace of WTR is the persistent obsession with growth and consumption. Some observers committed to the growth paradigm see calls for shorter work time as representing a "loser attitude." Conservative economist John Crispo, for example, writes, "What bothers me most about those who advocate shorter work weeks as a way to hire some unemployed is their defeatism. Seemingly having given up on more appropriate ways of reducing unemployment, they are really advocating spreading around the misery in the form of general under-employment and smaller paycheques."[58] The political left remains, for the most part, equally wed to a growth-oriented response to problems of unemployment and poverty. Even some proponents of shorter hours are prone to seeing it as a second-best option, with the preferred path being to rev up the growth machine even further. For instance, while endorsing a range of policies to reduce and redistribute work time, the 1994 federal Advisory Group on Working Time and the Distribution of Work argued that expansion of the demand side of the economy was the key lever for resolving the unemployment crisis.[59]

Advocates of reduced hours have been charged with promoting a "Chicken Little" scenario that fails to appreciate the potential for growth. However, a vision of shorter hours is not a matter of "the sky falling in" but of "the sky opening up," creating new opportunities for balanced, fulfilling lives.[60] The truly bleak scenario holds that we must run ever faster in our ever fouler squirrel cages of growth just to maintain current levels of employment. The trends of "downshifting" and voluntary simplicity notwithstanding, the hegemony from left to right of growth-centric thinking remains a major hurdle to a general embrace of working less.

The societal obsession with economic growth parallels the individual obsession with income and material consumption—another complex and multifaceted problem. Consumerism has continued to thrive largely due to the increasing symbolic importance of goods. It is no longer so much a question of what goods do, but what they say. Products no longer primarily serve the struggle for survival, but increasingly the struggle for experience and the expression of personal identity.[61]

One aspect of the symbolic power of goods is their role in the achievement of status relative to others. According to Schor, the phenomenon of positional consumption, or "keeping up with the Joneses," largely drives the "work and spend" cycle. It is, in her view, no longer mainly a matter of keeping up with the neighbours, but of keeping up with co-workers, friends, and others who are part of a peer reference group. For those who watch a lot of television—most people in North America—the reference group also includes the well-coiffed and well-clothed characters on the screen. This problem is not limited to adults—even teenagers get caught in their own "work and spend" cycles, purchasing the CDs, clothes, shoes, and even cars that are wanted not just for their own sake, but to give the buyers an identity, status, and a sense of belonging with their peers. Many parents increasingly experience the pressure of maintaining their children's consumption standards or, in other words, "keeping up for the kids."[62] As Alan Durning points out, "In the consumer society, [the] need to be valued and respected by others is acted out through consumption." Wearing the right clothes, driving the right car, and living in the right quarters are ways of saying, "I'm OK. I'm in the group."[63]

Status consumption can be taken to ridiculous levels. A 1998 report revealed that some *rich* Americans, with salaries in the $100,000 to $200,000 range, were feeling hard done by because they could not keep up with the *super-rich*.[64] This phenomenon is not limited to the North. In post-Pinochet Chile, with mass credit consumerism on the march, a high percentage of drivers ticketed for unlawfully using their cell phones while in motion were found to be using toy replicas; middle-class motorists pretending to have air conditioning were baking with their windows closed; and school-kids were sticking Velcro-backed insignias from elite academies onto their uniforms to hide their downscale backgrounds.[65]

The issue of relative consumption represents a clear case of a collective action problem. If the consumption standards of our reference group are rising we have to consume more, simply to keep pace. Moreover, people who struggle against the tide by choosing to work and consume less risk ever greater social marginalization, and those brave souls who do so are likely to be few in number. These pressures on individuals to keep up with expanding norms of consumption are a significant obstacle to WTR being achieved through individual choice, which again highlights the importance of collective efforts to combat the work-and-spend cycle and establish norms of sufficiency.[66]

The idea of sufficiency was common not so long ago, although it has been severely eroded. One of the more fascinating aspects of Hunnicutt's study of Kellogg's six-hour day is the change in workers' perceptions about their needs. In the 1930s, during the depths of the Depression, six-hour workers often said they were satisfied that their material needs were being met. They welcomed the additional time as a new form of freedom and recognized that an extra two hours would only give them "extra money." By the time of the consumerist boom years of the 1950s, the language used increasingly expressed the idea of absolute need. Phrases like "can't afford six hours" and "have to work full-time to survive" were common. It was as if, in Hunnicutt's words, "the two extra hours became the figurative difference between life and death." One worker recounts his own conversion as "*learning* that six hours were not enough."[67]

THE OVERWORK ETHIC

Work is the refuge of people who have nothing better to do.

Oscar Wilde[68]

Now it's work, work, work for everybody. . . . Nobody has any time anymore to do anything—even to be with the kids.

Leroy Despins, a Kellogg six-hour worker[69]

Beyond the rewards of consumption, work in itself has a powerful psychological hold over people's lives, to the point that talk of WTR may seem somehow "morally suspicious." Many see working less as a sign of laziness, stagnation, and a decline of the work ethic, something especially intolerable at a time when winning the global competitive race supposedly demands that we work longer hours. For instance, the chief economist of Dresden Bank in Germany argues that although "the four-day work week could be useful in crisis management . . . as a medium-term policy, it is great craziness. You do not resolve a problem by working less."[70] Likewise, Chancellor Kohl was disturbed by the disposition of the German working class to reject long hours of toil.[71] Such attitudes are not just held by bankers and conservative politicians, German or otherwise. A wide spectrum of the population in Canada and other industrial nations has been socialized into a work-centred social system. We have been taught since childhood that hard work is a virtue, and that to get ahead all we have to do is work hard. As a result, any move to a "postmaterialist" society will require major psychological and lifestyle adjustments.[72]

Despite the growing scarcity of jobs, work remains the central source of individual identities in our society. The question "What do you do?" is the first thing we ask when we want to know "Who are you?" According to Aronowitz and DiFazio, more than any other factor—such as increasingly meagre social assistance benefits or any intrinsic meaning or satisfaction derived from work—we are driven to take jobs because most of us constitute the "self" through membership in the labour force. While advocating a "less materialistic and more leisure-oriented society" that would reduce pressures on the environment, Reid asks, "If human self-worth and dignity are built around work at present, and if there is to be less human labour in the future, how do humans construct a self-identity and sense of self-worth?"[73] This link between identity and paid work is

particularly strong for men, whose identities, according to feminist Betty Friedan, have been defined through "wage earning dominance." Moreover, society places a particular stigma on men who opt for less than full-time work.[74]

The excesses of a work-obsessed society are reflected in workaholism, today's "respectable" addiction. According to O'Hara, work provides the perfect drug for people seeking an escape from their families, feelings, or other problems. "You can go binge out on work all you want—not only do you not have to feel guilty, but you can actually feel virtuous." In contrast, one of the main problems faced by those who opt for less work is guilt about being able to have balance in their lives, spend time with their children, and not feel stressed. People think, "I must be cheating somehow because I'm actually happy and centered and fulfilled in my life." It's "tragic," says O'Hara, "when people who have balance and joy in their life feel like somehow they must have ripped the system off."[75]

Bertrand Russell once said, "One of the symptoms of approaching nervous breakdown is the belief that one's work is terribly important, and that to take a holiday would bring all kinds of disaster."[76] A 1998 Canadian study showed that only 58 per cent of the people surveyed planned to take a summer holiday that year, down sharply from 76 per cent in 1992. Similar decisions are trickling down onto the next generation. Parents are putting more intense pressure on their kids to use every moment of time "productively," with summer vacations increasingly devoted to rigidly structured programs at the expense of spontaneity and play.[77] Such decisions are due, in part, to growing economic insecurity—the fear of putting your own job or your children's future at risk if a single moment is allowed to pass by "unproductively." At the same time a "civilized" culture would, surely, draw the line against the inevitable pressures to do and produce more.

In many respects perhaps little has changed since 1883 when Paul Lafargue, in his provocative pamphlet *The Right to Be Lazy*, felt compelled to write: "Cannot the labourers understand that by over-working themselves they exhaust their own strength and that of their progeny, that they are used up and long before their time come to be incapable of any work at all, that absorbed and brutalized by this single vice they are no longer men but pieces of men, that they kill within themselves all beautiful faculties, to leave nothing alive and flourishing except the furious madness for work."[78]

FEAR OF FREEDOM?

Some observers argue that people are inhibited from accepting a vision of expanding leisure because of the threat of having to be responsible for structuring and self-managing their time. Reid states that many workers view the possibility of less work in their lives with considerable ambivalence. He points to the work of psychoanalyst and social philosopher Erich Fromm, who argued that humans have a "fear of freedom." Fromm maintained that rather than welcoming the opportunity to be responsible for managing their own lives, people want instead to rely on some external agent. In medieval times it might have been the church, and today the corporation and paid work.[79] Charles Handy argues that the emerging world of work, in which paid employment takes a significantly smaller place in a person's life, has more appeal to the well-educated members of the professional middle classes who, he says, know how to manage their own lives. He quotes Keynes, who wrote, "There is no country and no people, I think, who can look forward to the age of leisure and of abundance without a dread. It is a fearful problem for the ordinary person, with no special talents to occupy himself, especially if he no longer has roots in the soil or in the beloved conventions of a traditional society."[80]

It is reasonable to argue, as Reid does, that the liberation of time so that it becomes useful to the individual and to society alike will be a major undertaking for those used to having time scheduled and organized externally by others.[81] However, these arguments can be taken too far and can degenerate into a class-biased, patronizing dismissal of the talents and abilities of "ordinary" working people. Although Keynes recognized that it would be difficult at first for many people to adapt to the change, he was confident that ultimately they could do it. As for our ingrained need for work, he maintained that doing more work for ourselves in our free time and putting in "three hours a day" would be "quite enough to satisfy that old Adam in most of us!"[82]

THE COMMODIFICATION AND TRIVIALIZATION OF LEISURE

Yet another problem is the trivialization and devaluation of the idea of leisure. Unlike ancient Athens, when leisure (made possible by slavery) was valued as the basis of a reflective life and active citizen participation in the affairs of the polis, leisure today is not perceived as having an important and useful social role.[83] Hunnicutt has traced the trivialization of leisure throughout the 50-year experience with the six-hour day at Kellogg's. He points out that when the plant introduced shorter hours in the 1930s as both a response to the Depression and a reflection of an alternative vision of progress, activities such as reading, gardening, caring for family members, amateur sports, canning, going to parks, thinking, being a neighbour, and taking time "just to play with the kids" flourished among the workers. Many workers used the time to keep up with skills and interests they had developed in high school or college—music, writing, art, and history, for example. Leisure was not just for resting in preparation for more work, or for passive amusement and mindless consumption. It was "the most important part of the day." By the 1950s these activities were being replaced by mass-market culture. People in Battle Creek began to see leisure as an effortless time: "I've done my work. I've done the important things in life. . . . I've served my time, now I can stop trying. I'm off work, I can kick my heels back, entertain me." Leisure was not only trivialized, but also "feminized." It was increasingly seen to be for "silly women" or "sissy men," in contrast to the serious work of "real men." The gender split in attitudes was readily apparent by the time

Kellogg's six-hour day finally ended in 1985, when 75 per cent of the workers still participating were women.[84]

Leisure has also been commodified. According to John Clarke and Charles Critcher, "The success of the market lies not only in its material domination of the production of leisure goods and services but in its cultural domination of ways of thinking about leisure as a set of commodities."[85] Those who want to promote a new vision of progress based on leisure rather than consumption need to revive the idea of a meaningful or "serious" leisure that is not centred on passive consumption of commodities. Furthermore, as Reid points out, if that way of living is ever to become legitimate and useful, society must assign a value to an alternative leisure lifestyle.[86]

"NICE IDEA, BUT IT CAN'T BE DONE"

Recent years have been a time—at least in the Anglo-Saxon world—when alternatives regarding the direction of society have been quickly dismissed, if considered at all. Whereas the 1960s stand out symbolically as a decade in which imaginations were unleashed and a good many people believed society could be, and was even destined to be, changed for the better, the 1980s and 1990s are perhaps best characterized by the Thatcherite mantra of TINA: "There is no alternative." The belief in TINA has created an additional wall of defence around the neo-liberal agenda focusing on competitiveness, deficit-cutting, and scaling back of the welfare state. It has also contributed to a knee-jerk reaction against alternatives to the agenda, including WTR. Even those who accept WTR as a good idea often argue that it can never be carried out in practice. Those beliefs reflect a basic lack of awareness: WTR has indeed been achieved on a large scale historically; and despite all the obstacles, WTR is now being achieved to varying degrees and in various forms in many countries.

A related problem in North America is the belief that "the 40 hour workweek, 8 hours a day, 5 days a week, 50 weeks a year, is a natural rhythm of the universe."[87] This is clearly not the case. Compared to the early days of the industrial revolution, most of us in the North are already half-time workers. In the mid-19th century, 80-hour weeks and 13-hour days were common in most industrial countries.[88] The subsequent movement for shorter hours succeeded in conditions very different from today, but the task was no easier. The 40-hour barrier has been breached recently in many places and many firms, from Ile-de-France to Indiana. Other forms of WTR have also made advances elsewhere: for instance, a norm of five to six weeks' vacation in most European countries, paid parental leave of 18 months for both men and women in Sweden, or the right for workers to take partially paid sabbaticals in Denmark, Finland, and Belgium.

Lest we think that these reductions of work hours are made possible by industrial society, we should also keep in mind that average work time was far lower in the pre-industrial period. A casual labourer in 14th-century Britain worked an estimated 1,440 hours a year, compared to an average of 1,856 hours for a manufacturing worker in Britain in 1988. Some hunter-gatherers could meet their needs and those of their dependants by putting in a 15-hour workweek.[89]

People need, then, to be reminded both of the successful movement for WTR in the past century and a half and the current examples of shorter hours at home and abroad. Awareness of these examples, particularly those from other countries with a different type of capital-labour compromise, should not lead anyone to believe that an "Age of Leisure" is imminent, that achieving WTR will be simple, or that it will always serve green rather than productivist ends. But the awareness is needed to overcome the overly pessimistic view that it simply cannot be done—the first necessary step in building an effective movement for shorter hours.

The four-day workweek as envisaged in the 1970s.

6

Work-Time Policy and Practice, North and South

The paradox of our times is that many Canadians today work long hours while many others have no work at all.

Advisory Group on Working Time and the Distribution of Work, Canada, 1994

I loved the days off! I miss the days off.

Bobbie, Ontario public-sector worker reflecting on unpaid "Rae Days," 1998

I sleep and I work. I can do nothing else.

Woman worker in Mexican maquiladora (sweatshop), 1994

As important as overcoming the obstacles to work-time reduction are the questions about the form that hours reductions should take, and the most appropriate ways of implementing them. WTR options are certainly not limited to a reduction of the workweek—even though that option attracts the bulk of attention. There are also a number of policy tools, ranging from legislation to individual choice, available for implementing WTR. In addition to exploring these policy questions, the following pages will look at work-time practice in Canada and, briefly, in the United States, Japan, and some of the nations of the South—where workers often experience particularly extreme forms of work-time abuse.

FOCUS ON THE WORKWEEK, OR THE WORK LIFE?

Most people see the issue of work-time reduction as a question of shortening the workweek. The campaign for a 32-hour week, for example, provides a powerful symbolic objective that is not matched by, say, Charles Handy's call for the 50,000-hour work life.[1]

The downside of this focus is that it tends to distract attention from other possibilities, such as better provisions for parental or educational leave, time off in lieu of overtime, longer vacations, sabbaticals, partial retirement, and any number of other ways of reducing work hours over the days, months, or years of a human lifetime. These other possibilities provide options that may suit the needs and desires of certain people in a way that can't be satisfied by a single-minded focus on the length of the workweek. (In addition, many involuntary part-time workers could benefit from longer rather than shorter hours—not to mention better pay and benefits.) In this light, the French appear to have found an important answer in their flexible 35-hour-week initiative—creating the common symbol of 35 hours around which people can rally, while at the same time allowing considerable diversity in the form that WTR takes in practice.

Various factors, such as employment generation, the contribution to meeting other social needs, ecological consequences, and the preferences of the public, merit consideration in weighing the different options. Measures such as the introduction of more statutory holidays, for example, might improve the quality of life for people already holding jobs, but they are unlikely to generate as much employment as other options, such as reducing overtime or introducing gradual retirement (which phases out older and phases in younger workers). An option that deserves particular attention is the expansion of leaves for education, family care, and personal sabbaticals. Such policies, which are particularly advanced in Denmark and Sweden, have several attractions: a contribution to societal and family needs by promoting a better work-life balance, their employment-generating effect, and potential for public support.

The ecological merits of the various options are difficult to judge, but they could vary significantly. Gorz argues: "The demand for reduced working hours has always been the one most bitterly resisted by bosses. They have preferred to grant longer paid holidays. For holidays are a perfect example of a programmed *interruption* to active life, a period of pure consumption, unintegrated with everyday existence, doing nothing to enrich normal life with new dimensions, to give it an expanded autonomy or a content distinct from the professional role."[2] A green vision—

concerned with creating an autonomous sphere of activity outside the market and avoiding the colonization of liberated time through intensive consumption and passive profit-driven leisure—should take this argument into account. Gorz's statement provides a rationale for favouring options such as reducing the workweek or (perhaps even better still) the workday over introducing longer vacations. Ultimately, though, his concern is only one of many factors that have to be weighed.

A TOOL BOX FOR REDUCING AND REDISTRIBUTING WORKING TIME

Regardless of the specific objective—whether a shorter workweek or any other option—a number of overlapping tools are available for achieving WTR.

Perhaps the most obvious tool for limiting the hours of work is *legislation*, which can also establish the right to choose various forms of working less and provide employment standards protections for shorter-hours workers. Legislation, though, is never the final word on work hours. The legislated standard workweek in Germany, for instance, is 48 hours, but collective bargaining has substantially reduced those hours. In the United States the federal 40-hour standard is the triggering point for overtime premiums, but regular hours for many workers often exceed that level. Legislation can also prove more effective when combined with other tools. Legislation for a 35-hour week in France, for instance, has been supplemented by financial incentives, with collective bargaining playing a significant role in working out the details.

Financial incentives policies, which create monetary "carrots" for shorter hours and "sticks" for longer hours, can be an important complement to work-time legislation. The basic idea behind these incentives is that when WTR creates jobs it also generates significant benefits for the public ("positive externalities"). The public saves on the massive financial costs of unemployment, such as unemployment benefits, social assistance, and increased health-care costs. The state can then use these savings to encourage employers and employees to choose shorter hours ("internalization of externalities"). At the same time, those who create costs for the public by opting for long hours can be penalized through higher overtime premiums or taxes on overtime hours—taxes being preferable, because premiums actually make overtime more attractive from the perspective of workers.

Policies to create incentives for employers can take a number of forms, including tax credits, subsidies, or payroll tax cuts for firms that reduce hours and hire more workers. These types of policies have been implemented or are being introduced in several European countries and on a modest level in British Columbia and Quebec. Former French Prime Minister Michel Rocard, now a Member of the European Parliament, has proposed one possible model: reduction of payroll taxes on the first 32 hours of work per week, combined with a significant increase in payroll taxes on hours above 32. A company that stayed at 40 hours would see its payroll tax burden remain unchanged, but would have a powerful incentive to reduce hours and hire more workers. This proposal, endorsed by the European Parliament in 1996, has had a significant impact on work-time debates in many countries.[3] A less ambitious, but important, first step in Canada would be to eliminate perverse incentives for long hours as created by the structure of payroll taxes.

Another incentives-based option is to top up the incomes of employees who choose shorter hours. Quebec economist Paul Morin proposes a refundable tax credit to compensate, in whole or in part, for lower incomes due to WTR.[4] OECD official Bernard Hugonnier advocates using funds spent on unemployment costs to encourage the voluntary choice of part-time work. He suggests that in France, for example, incomes could be topped up so that half-time workers could earn 75 per cent of their former salaries.[5] This could allow gradual retirement for older workers while bringing young people into the workforce. The state could also make financing available for firms to support paid educational and parental leaves and personal sabbaticals, linking payments to a requirement to hire unemployed persons as replacements. To make the best use of limited funds, governments could focus these forms of income support more heavily on workers at the bottom of the income scale. A number of variations on this idea are already in practice in Europe.

Collective bargaining is another fundamentally important tool: the length of work hours is a key issue in settlements between employers and labour unions. Germany, for example, has achieved significant WTR in recent years exclusively through collective bargaining efforts. Although progress in WTR can be achieved in this arena even without government intervention, collective bargaining need not stand in isolation. Incentives for shorter work time can give an important push to collective bargaining. Meanwhile legislation can set the overall goal of shorter work time but leave important details on implementation to collective bargaining. France provides an important example of both these options.

Tripartite consensus entails agreement among government, business, and labour on the broad outlines of economic policy. In the Netherlands, often cited as the model for this approach, a negotiated reduction of work time in return for salary moderation was a key element in a tripartite consensus to resolve the economic crisis of the early 1980s. In Germany the Social Democratic government elected in September 1998 promised new efforts to reach a Dutch-style consensus on employment issues, which would probably include WTR. In Canada, Quebec reached agreement on modest WTR measures at a tripartite summit in 1996.[6]

The *individual choice* of employees and employers to reduce hours is another key tool, which can be supplemented by financial incentives to make opting for shorter hours more attractive. Legislation and collective bargaining are also important in establishing the terms that govern individual choices.

INDIVIDUAL OR COLLECTIVE CHOICE? VOLUNTARY OR LEGISLATIVE ACTION?

Decisions and action to reduce work hours can take place on a range of levels. At one pole is reliance on the voluntary choices of individual employees and employers. At the other is legislated reductions for all members of society. Intermediate possibilities are collective bargaining, legislation that guarantees individuals the right to choose shorter hours, and the creation of incentives to encourage such choices.

A principal advantage of individualized reductions is their response to the growing diversity of preferences among workers: when employees want WTR, they don't necessarily all want standard reductions of the workday or week. The greater divergence of aspirations and situations reflects a larger shift in society towards individualist attitudes and a fragmentation of identities. This diversity makes standardized collective reductions a more difficult "sell" than individual choice.[7] Another benefit of individual choice is that it can increase the value of leisure time for the employee involved. A reduction of hours that does not take into account individual needs can impose unwanted leisure on people, but when workers themselves decide on the amount and timing of their leisure, they are more likely to make the best use of that time.[8]

Individual and voluntary options have a political appeal because of the resistance, both among employees and employers, to standard

TABLE 6.1	LEVEL OF DECISION REGARDING WORK-TIME REDUCTION	
TYPE OF ACTION	Individual	Collective
Voluntary	• Agreements between individual employees and employers • Individual choice of a shorter-hours job	• Collective bargaining between labour unions and employers • Tripartite consensus among government, business, and labour
Legislative	• Creation of incentives to influence individual choice • Guarantees of individual rights to reduce work time • Employment standards protections for short-hours workers	• Legislated reductions of standard workweek, limits on overtime, longer vacations, etc.

measures imposed from above. When workers are concerned largely with stagnant or declining wage levels and the threat of future job loss, and business leaders are leery of blanket measures that call for wholesale adaptation, the individual and voluntary approach would face considerably less opposition and fewer difficulties of enforcement.[9]

Still, collective action remains essential. If people are to be guaranteed the choice of shorter work hours, whether four-day weeks, half-time work, sabbaticals, or other options, either legislation or collective agreements will have to establish these choices as rights. Governments also have a role in enforcing the rights, in addition to other employment standards related to work time. Non-unionized workers and those on the margins of the labour market especially need this protection. Many workers now are simply not able to choose shorter hours; or, if they are, they often face severe penalties in the form of hourly wages, benefits, seniority, and career prospects. The terms governing the choice of shorter hours are thus a matter of collective concern. The incentive structure faced by employers and employees is also key. Society, in the political arena, needs to decide, for instance, whether the structure of benefit costs and payroll taxes hinders or favours shorter hours and whether to provide any income supports for those choosing shorter hours.[10]

Another key question is the effectiveness in creating employment. Some observers argue that voluntary reductions of work time are a more effective way of creating jobs. The costs of those reductions, for instance, are usually borne by workers in the form of lower wages, which means in theory that employers have more money available to hire more workers. In contrast, legislated collective reductions often transfer part of the cost burden to employers through higher salary costs, thus creating a disincentive to new hiring. Rejecting such measures, *The Economist* argues, "If governments restrict firms' freedom they will probably kill jobs, not create them. . . . Job sharing will trim dole queues only if employers and workers freely negotiate such deals themselves."[11]

Despite that warning, to create jobs in any significant number we need to do more than minor tinkering through individual and voluntary reductions. Lipietz argues that WTR has to be substantial and general, requiring legislation or at least a multisector collective agreement to be effective. He argues that without a clear, loud signal firms will wait for somebody else to start the ball rolling.[12] Employees themselves require a similar push. Given a decentralized bargaining system, those who make sacrifices for shorter hours will be less likely to reap the financial or employment security benefits, and workplace bargaining without legislation is unlikely to create the widespread reductions in work hours required to substantially reduce unemployment. Besides, most companies have enough slack and potential for productivity improvements that they can accommodate minor reductions without increasing employment. Some economists maintain that the bigger the reduction in hours, the larger the proportion of the hours-reduction that will be translated into increased employment. A cautious approach will thus have minimal impact. Some WTR proponents have therefore argued that if a reduction of the workweek is to have a significant effect as a job creator, Canada will require a substantive reduction to 35 or 32 hours per week. Similarly, some advocates of WTR in France, including Rocard, have argued that the government's 35-hour-week plan does not go far enough to reduce the country's 12 per cent unemployment by any great degree. They call instead for 32 hours.[13] In most countries such large, society-wide jumps will require a legislative stimulus and/or a strong package of incentives and disincentives.

From an ecological perspective, a drawback of leaving WTR to individual choice is the problem of relative consumption and the lack of a collective norm of sufficiency. If we judge our own well-being largely by comparisons to others, it is important to reduce work time collectively and not simply rely on choice at the individual level. Otherwise most people will continue to compare their personal level of consumption to one achievable only with long hours of work. Similarly, although Gorz argues that it is essential to give workers the right to limit their work time voluntarily, he maintains that it is impossible to obtain an ecological restructuring of production and consumption by that measure alone. The problem is that a commonly accepted norm of sufficiency, which could serve as a reference for self-limitation, no longer exists. Such a norm of sufficiency has to be re-created collectively, shifting self-limitation from the level of individual choice to that of a social project.[14]

Likewise, for a way of life that focuses more on leisure than on work and consumption to be attractive, society has to give it value and legitimacy.[15] This is much more likely to occur if society as a whole moves towards shorter hours than if the choice is simply left to a small number of "32-hour types." We still need voluntary WTR options for individuals to provide new opportunities for "downshifters," increase the numbers of people opting for lives of "voluntary simplicity," and start things moving in the right direction. But the numbers of those who opt for shorter hours and less consumption will be far greater if society makes a collective challenge to the dominant pattern of "work and spend."

A narrow focus on individual WTR could also aggravate existing labour-market inequalities, especially those between women and men. WTR could lead in two opposing directions: towards a more even sharing of work, including household tasks, between men and women; or towards a more acute gender-based segmentation between full-time and part-time workers.[16] The possibility of a more even sharing motivated feminist groups in Sweden, beginning in the 1970s, to campaign actively for a six-hour day, 30-hour week for both men and women. At the same time, Swedish feminists were suspicious of "separate solutions," such as part-time work options and parental leave policies, for women.[17]

Studies repeatedly show that women are more favourable than men towards WTR, including part-time work.[18] One reason is the greater pressure on women to balance the demands of household and market labour due to their disproportionate responsibilities at home. Another factor may be that men's identities and sense of self-worth are more dependent on paid employment. On the surface, this would seem to indicate that women have more to gain from a wider availability of individualized choices for shorter hours. The danger is that an emphasis on individualized WTR alone will lead to greater disparities between men and women in hours, incomes, benefits, career prospects, and pensions, for instance. Whereas reduced hours for all workers would create opportunities for men to take on a greater role in the home, individual options taken up mainly by women could reinforce the dominant pattern of women having sole responsibility for unpaid household labour and caregiving. Some people are thus suspicious of the drive to get women to work less in the paid labour force and do more unpaid work at home as a means of solving both the unemployment crisis and the "crisis of the family."[19] The cause of overcoming that suspicion is not advanced when some proponents of WTR argue: "It would be possible to achieve full employment by a voluntary reduction in hours of work if governments creatively supported this goal. One initial step . . . would be to turn around a recent cultural trend. In the not too distant past, it was expected that one parent would stay at home to look after children when they were young."[20]

In the Netherlands, along with its move, since the early 1980s, towards a 36-hour week as the new norm for full-time, there has also been a dramatic increase in part-time work. One controversial aspect of the model is that those working part-time are mainly women. Day-care space is scarce. Women are still expected to devote most of their time to their children, and men rarely stay home with the kids—although there are signs that the role of men is rapidly changing. Dutch women's groups argue that the gender-based division between full-time and part-time work should be challenged and that the solution is for men and women to reduce their work hours equally and share household tasks.[21] Yet the increase in part-time work opportunities has coincided with the recent increase in female labour participation and helped women balance the demands of paid work and home. While 36.5 per cent of Dutch employees were part-time in 1996, a study in the same year found that only 6 per cent of Dutch part-timers said they wanted a full-time job but could not find one.[22] This finding suggests that the spread of part-time work has occurred in a way that responds to the demands of workers—particularly women—for flexibility in their work time. Meanwhile the Green Left party's campaign for a legislated right for individuals to reduce their hours of work has been motivated largely by its strong feminist beliefs. Its members make the case that such a right will not only help women balance work and home, but will also help further the recent trend of men taking a greater share of household responsibilities.[23] This complicated picture suggests that the promotion of individualized WTR options carries both dangers and opportunities for the cause of gender equality. At the very least, with the expansion of individual options men must be actively encouraged to take advantage of the possibilities, and advocates should continue to make the case for gender equity in the distribution of both paid and unpaid labour.

The pros and cons of individualized versus collective reductions of work time suggest a need for a multitrack approach. We need collective action to reduce average hours worked, through legislated measures such as a reduction of the legal workweek, but individuals should get as much choice as possible over how and when they take their leisure time. Even when legislation reduces "weekly" hours, provisions should allow this reduction to also be taken in the form of more days off per year or longer holidays—whatever best suits those involved—as in France. While a large-scale, legislated reduction of the standard workweek to, say, 32 hours is desirable, it could be some time before political support for such a change can be established. In the meantime—in addition to more moderate legislated reductions such as ensuring a 40-hour standard in all provinces—"Right to Shorter Work Hours" legislation should guarantee people's ability to freely choose to go beyond the standard reduction for society as a whole. Choices of part-time work and extended leaves should be available—to both men and women—without penalty. Legislated guarantees should include equal treatment for part-time and shorter hours workers. Part-time options should also be reversible, allowing people to move in and out of full-time status.[24] Governments also need to ensure that the structure of payroll taxes and benefits does not create disincentives to shorter hours and new hiring, and they should go beyond simply "levelling the playing field" in work hours, as one recent Canadian government report advocates.[25] They should actually tilt the playing field towards shorter hours by creating positive financial incentives. Meanwhile, collective bargaining can play an important role—particularly if workers choose to bargain for their share of annual productivity gains in the form of shorter work hours. A guiding principle for such a WTR package would be "as much individual choice as possible, as much collective action as necessary."

CANADIAN POLICY AND PRACTICE

Canadian work hours are among the most polarized in the affluent North. While unemployment even in "good times" has remained above 8 per cent, nearly one-fifth of all employees, about 1.9 million people, worked overtime in the first four months of 1997, with an average of about nine hours each per week. Some 60 per cent of this overtime was unpaid.[26] International data from 1994 showed that Canada ranked near the top end of OECD countries in the percentage of men working 45 hours or more per week: roughly 23 per cent. The country also had the largest percentage of men working less than 20 hours per week, about 12 per cent. In 1976 almost two-thirds (65 per cent) of

"You're going to have to cut down on overtime, Charlie... no more than 80 hours a week."

Canadian workers put in between 35 and 40 hours per week. By 1997 that number had fallen to 54 per cent, with the number of employees working both very short hours and long hours having risen. This increasing inequality in hours of work is a major factor in the growing gap in incomes in Canada.[27] A reduction and redistribution of work time, then, should have much to offer the overworked, the underemployed, and the unemployed in Canada, although so far only a few provincial governments have shown any signs of being prepared to address the issue.

Government Policies

The federal Labour Code establishes a standard 40-hour workweek and 8-hour day (after which overtime premiums must be paid), a maximum 48-hour workweek, and two weeks' paid vacation (three for employees with more than six years of service). These federal standards have limited effect, though, because they cover only certain sectors of the economy representing only about 10 per cent of workers. Most workers fall under the jurisdiction of the provinces, which have varying standards (see Tables 6.2 and 6.3). Canadian vacation standards are particularly meagre relative to European norms (Table 6.4).

One of the more innovative federal policies is the UI Work-Sharing program. Introduced in 1982, it provides unemployment insurance funds to top up the incomes of workers who agree with their employer to share available work to avoid temporary layoffs. For instance, in a firm with 100 employees, instead of laying off 20 workers for six months, all workers could go to a four-day week and receive UI on the fifth day.[28]

Other federal policies, such as the annual income caps on payroll taxes that fund unemployment insurance and the Canada Pension Plan, create obstacles to reducing and redistributing work time. Once an employee's income surpasses the annual maximum (tax $39,000 in 1999), neither the employee nor the employer pay payroll tax on the additional

TABLE 6.2	WORK-HOUR STANDARDS IN CANADA		
Jurisdiction	Standard work hours after which overtime applies	Maximum hours of work	Hours after which right to refuse overtime
Federal	8/day 40/week	48/week	---
B.C.	8/day 40/week	---	---
Alberta	8/day 44/week	12/day	---
Saskatchewan	8/day 40/week	44/week	44/week
Manitoba	8/day 40/week	---	40/week
Ontario	44/week	8 day, 48/week	8 day, 48/week
Quebec	40/week (by Oct. 2000)	---	---
New Brunswick	44/week	---	---
Nova Scotia	48/week	---	---
P.E.I.	48/week	---	---
Newfoundland	40/week	16/day	---
N.W.T.	8/day 40/week	10/day, 60/week	---
Yukon	8/day 40/week	---	---

Overtime pay is 1.5 times regular pay in all jurisdictions except New Brunswick, Newfoundland, and Nova Scotia, where it is 1.5 times the minimum wage. B.C. also requires double time pay after 11 hours per day and 48 per week. Quebec and the Yukon allow overtime hours to be compensated through time off equal to 1.5 times the overtime hours worked. B.C. allows overtime hours to accumulate in "time banks," to be taken as time off, if the employee requests it and the employer agrees.

Most jurisdictions exempt some categories of employees from the regular standards. Some allow the standard and maximum hours to be calculated as an average for a period of longer than one week, under limited circumstances.

Source: Ministry of Human Resources Development Canada.

income. This policy generates an incentive for employers to have existing employees work overtime rather than hire new workers and pay the additional payroll taxes. Changing these policies to create a "level playing field in work hours" would be an obvious first step towards encouraging a more sensible distribution of work time.

A few provinces have explored innovative work-time policies, although the results have been less than spectacular. In 1996 British Columbia introduced measures to promote shorter work hours and new hiring in the forestry sector. If employers and employees collectively negotiate new work arrangements to reduce hours and create jobs, the government would provide up to $3,500 annually per job created. The financial support would offset additional costs for legislated and negoti-ated benefits, such as Canada Pension Plan and Workers' Compensation, that result from hiring more workers. The government aimed to create

TABLE 6.3   PAID VACATIONS IN CANADA

Jurisdiction	Weeks by law after years of service
Saskatchewan	3 after 1, 4 after 10
Manitoba	2 after 1, 3 after 4
Alta., B.C., N.W.T., Quebec	2 after 1, 3 after 5
Federal	2 after 1, 3 after 6
Newfoundland	2 after 1, 3 after 15
Ont., N.B., N.S., P.E.I., Yukon	2 after 1

In Quebec, employees with between one and five years of service have a right to a third week unpaid vacation upon request.

Source: Ministry of Human Resources Development Canada.

TABLE 6.4   ANNUAL PAID VACATIONS IN EUROPEAN COUNTRIES

Country	Number of weeks, 1996 as determined by law (l) and/or collective agreement (a)
Austria	5 (6 after 25 years service)
Belgium	4 (l), 5 (a)
Denmark	5
Finland	5 (l), 5-6 (a)
France	5 (l), 5-6 (a)
Germany, East	5.4 - 6
Germany, West	5.84 (average)
Greece	4.4 (5 after 20 years service)
Ireland	3 (l), 4 (a)
Italy	4-5 (a)
Luxembourg	5 (l), 5- 6.6 (a)
Netherlands	4 (l), 5-6 (a)
Norway	4.2
Portugal	4.4
Spain	6
Sweden	5
Switzerland	4.8
United Kingdom	4-6

Source: Giuseppe Fajertag, ed., *Collective Bargaining in Western Europe 1995-96* (Brussels: European Trade Union Institute, 1996), p.27.

3,000 jobs through the program and committed up to $20 million. Premier Glen Clark, who at times expressed considerable interest in WTR, said that, if successful, this effort to promote shorter work hours could be extended to other industries.[29] However, the initial results of the program were disappointing. Some critics maintained that none of the parties— business, labour, and government—were particularly committed to the plan.[30] Others argued that workers had made serious efforts to bargain for WTR but were stymied by fierce business resistance. A case in point is the nine-month strike of workers at the Fletcher Challenge Canada mill in 1997. The workers placed a high priority on reducing regular hours and having all overtime banked to be taken as time off. The union wanted to create 1,000 new jobs by reducing work time by 10 per cent. "The employer's position," according to union activist and researcher Julie White, "was full flexibility with its attendant loss of jobs." She adds that despite the setback at Fletcher Challenge, WTR remained a high priority for B.C. pulp and paper workers.[31]

British Columbia's financial support for WTR was one element of the controversial Jobs and Timber Accord reached among government, the major forestry firms, and unions. Environmentalists have criticized the Accord, which sought to create a total of 40,000 new jobs, for weakening environmental protections in the industry. It is unfortunate that WTR, which offers a way to create jobs without increasing environmental damage, has been promoted in British Columbia as part of a larger package that appears to run counter to environmental goals. While WTR has considerable potential to unite labour and environmentalists, British Columbia has experienced an increasingly bitter division between the two movements.

The B.C. health-sector restructuring agreement of 1992 provided a more positive example of WTR in practice. It gave employees the right to maintain a job within the system, even though particular jobs were to disappear. One part of the package reduced the workweek from 37.5 to 36 hours with no reduction in pay, which the provincial government saw as a "no cost" pay increase. The 4 per cent reduction in work time was expected to create the need for 2 per cent more workers. This case is an example of how WTR can assist a major restructuring of employment and how employees can see WTR as a reasonable form of compensation increase.[32]

In Ontario the New Democratic Party government under Bob Rae attempted to reduce public-sector wage costs in 1993 through a "social contract" involving unpaid days off for all public employees with incomes above $30,000 per year. (The days became known as "Rae Days," similar to Manitoba's "Filmon Fridays.") The major flaw was the government's decision to take this action through legislation that reopened existing collective agreements—a move that, understandably, was bitterly resisted by public-sector unions. Relations between the NDP and key union supporters were severely strained, contributing to the party's defeat by the Conservatives in 1995. The Canadian Union of Public Employees has rejected these kinds of imposed unpaid days off because of the loss of wages, the lack of hiring of replacement staff, and increased workloads for the remaining employees.[33] Still, once they experienced them, many workers welcomed the additional days off. Del, a social contract worker, remarked, "For me, the impact of the money reduction was nothing compared to the freedom I got with those extra nine days off." Another worker, Arlette, noted that people who lost income through the Rae Days began to find out "that you don't need as much stuff as you think. You know, I'm a great buyer of clothing. But you don't need as much clothing as we think we do. When you've got less money, you'll find other ways to entertain yourself."[34]

The subsequent government, led by Conservative Premier Mike Harris, allowed the social contract to lapse and embarked on a program to lay off thousands of public-sector workers. The Tories also weakened the mechanisms for enforcement of employment standards, including those related to work hours and vacations. They began looking at ways of allowing employers and unions to negotiate "flexible standards" for work hours that are *longer* than legislated standards and of increasing from 48 to 50 the number of weekly hours before employees can refuse overtime. Other proposals would eliminate the need for permits to exceed 48 hours per week and would average out overtime calculations over a four-week period (making long workweeks without overtime pay possible).[35] Not surprisingly, a protest placard seen on the lawn of the Legislative Building at Queen's Park shortly after the election of Mike Harris carried the words: "Hey, Hey, Bob Rae, You don't look so bad today!"

Quebec has introduced a number of modest policy measures to promote WTR. The government, business, and labour participants at an October 1996 Summit on the Economy and Employment reached a consensus to reduce the standard workweek from 44 to 40 hours (beyond which overtime premiums would be paid) by October 2000. Also announced was a tax credit for firms in the amount of $1,200 per job created in a given year. Firms with more than 25 employees must adopt a voluntary WTR program—including the option for employees to choose shorter workweeks, extended vacations, sabbaticals, and partial retirement—if they are to be eligible for the credit.

In April 1997 the Quebec government moderately strengthened vacation standards by giving workers with between one year and five years of service the right to take a third week of vacation, although employers would only be required to pay for the first two weeks. Quebec also improved unpaid parental leave standards, with mothers and fathers having the right to 52 weeks' leave rather than the previous 34. In 1994 the government began providing a subsidy of $4,000 for each job saved through a program to reduce and reorganize work time.[36]

One Canadian public-sector example that explicitly linked work time and the environment is a case of a compressed, rather than reduced, workweek. In 1976 employees at Vancouver City Hall moved to a four-day week, with the same weekly hours, to reduce traffic into the downtown core as part of "The Livable Region Strategy." The step was intended to serve as an example for other employers to follow. Its documented benefits included: improved ability to recruit and retain staff, improved employee morale, better work-family balance for employees, and reduced absenteeism. Since employees worked longer each day, the public benefited from the convenience of 8:30 a.m. to 5:30 p.m. opening hours, five days per week. By 1998, 1,100 city employees were working a four-day week, and another 150 had a nine-day fortnight, but few private-sector employers followed the city's lead. In fact, apart from minor scheduling and internal communication problems, the main argument raised against the four-day week was that private business was upset by the precedent. According to a 1998 City Manager's report, "Most people and businesses work a five-day week and expect their government counterparts to do so also." In contrast, municipal employees argued that reverting to five days would reverse the gains in morale and productivity, make recruitment and retention of key staff more difficult, deprive communities of volunteers, cost individual employees thousands of dollars in additional work-related expenses for commuting and child care, and ultimately lead to higher taxes. The city's engineering department estimated that returning to five days would mean an additional 700 extra vehicle trips and 17,500 kilometres of auto travel per day, generating an additional 1,240 tonnes of pollutants annually. Yet City Council voted in 1999 to end the four-day week—on Clean Air Day. However, city workers said they would push for the return of the measure in their next round of collective bargaining.[37]

Private-Sector Experience

• In the auto industry, the Canadian Auto Workers (CAW) bargained in 1993 for five Scheduled Personal Absence (SPA) days per employee per year at each of the Big Three automakers. Then, in 1996, CAW members gained an additional ten SPA days over three years. Under the agreement the average auto worker got one week of paid absence every seven or eight months in addition to vacation entitlements. This achievement, which represents a deliberate decision by workers to capture part of their share of productivity gains in the form of more leisure time, made possible 1,200 new jobs in 1993 and an additional 800 jobs in 1996.[38]

In September 1993 Chrysler and the CAW negotiated WTR and new hiring at the minivan plant in Windsor, Ontario. The company cut regular daily hours from 8 to 7.5 with no reduction in pay, reduced overtime hours for existing workers, and added a third shift. The result was 800 new hirings, though these were due not just to the reduction of hours but also to an increased demand for minivans. At first some workers resisted the reduction of overtime, but the commitment of the union leadership helped create majority support within the local. For its part, Chrysler gained from the ability to operate its plant for more hours each week. This example illustrates how, in capital-intensive sectors of the economy, shorter work time without loss in pay can be exchanged for changes to the organization of work time that benefit the company. The approach was later copied by the Chrysler car plant in Brampton and the GM truck plant in Oshawa, both of which moved to three-shift operations while cutting workdays to 7.5 hours.[39]

The Windsor example is often cited as one of the main WTR achievements in Canada, although the plant still has high levels of overtime—in the form of regularly scheduled, mandatory, 48-hour weeks. In 1998 many of the workers had difficulties financially and mentally adjusting to a temporary slowdown that meant an end to Saturday work. This led Kevin Wilson, a young worker who owed his job to the 1993 agreement, to comment that overtime was both a "job killer" and a form of "crack" for workers. Wilson advocates making all overtime after 40 hours voluntary (a long-time demand of the CAW), as a first step towards a 30-hour week.[40]

• Polysar Rubber (now Bayer) in Sarnia, Ontario, is one of a number of workplaces in which members of the Communications, Energy and Paperworkers (CEP) have negotiated WTR. In 1974, after a strike vote, the union and company reached an agreement to move from a 40-hour week to an average 37.3 hours with no loss in pay. Workers continued to work eight hours a day, taking the extra time off every third Friday. These "Happy Fridays," and the long weekends they created, became extremely popular, spreading to six CEP plants in Sarnia. Non-union plants followed suit, along with some public-sector workplaces. The days have become a focus for community events: picnics, fishing derbies, golf tournaments, and other activities.[41]

• In the Quebec pulp and paper industry, 16,000 workers have a 37.3-hour week, an arrangement reached in the mid-1970s following a four-month strike. CEP researcher Julie White says that the measure created additional jobs at the mills and resulted in "a better shift schedule that was a huge improvement for workers' family and social lives."[42]

• La Presse newspaper in Montreal first went to a 32-hour week over five days in 1971 and later, in 1977, moved to 32 hours over four days. Some journalists and editorial staff have a 32-hour shift over three days to cover weekends. The shorter workweek applies to 1,000 unionized workers at the paper.[43]

• Bell Canada introduced a four-day, 36-hour week for 12,000 technicians in 1994 as an alternative to 5,000 planned layoffs. Workers, who had previously put in, on average, 38-hour weeks, disliked the idea at first. For one thing, they felt it was imposed on them. They also resented the 5 per cent pay cut for the two-hour weekly reduction—at a time when Bell was highly profitable. Yet they voted 70 per cent in favour because of the no-layoff guarantee. Once the new schedule was in place, their opinions changed dramatically. Workers enjoyed their three-day weekends, found that the loss of two hours' pay was only about $30 per week after tax, and had plenty of opportunity for overtime if they wanted it. But management's views also changed due to unexpected and costly difficulties. By the end of 1994 the company had terminated the four-day-week agreement, despite overwhelming support by workers to continue it in some form.

Some critics have used the Bell case to argue that a shorter workweek is unlikely to succeed in Canada. Julie White and another CEP researcher, Diane Goulet, offer a more convincing take. According to them, upper-level Bell management made serious scheduling errors. Management allowed days off to be scheduled mainly on Monday and Friday, the company's two busiest days. With four days of nine hours, workers put in an additional daily hour from 5 to 6 p.m., which proved unproductive for reasons such as lack of access to customer premises after five o'clock. One result was a dramatic and costly increase in overtime. White and Goulet ascribe these and other problems to a failure to plan and consult adequately with front-line managers and workers. More positively, the case illustrates, again, how workers may be anxious about shorter hours and even initially oppose the idea, but can end up appreciating the additional free time in practice. It also shows that workers will consider supporting WTR when it is clearly linked to the creation or preservation of jobs, even if it involves a loss in pay. According to White and Goulet, "Canadians have every reason to consider shorter hours of work as one tool in the struggle to deal with unemployment and inequality. Nothing that occurred at Bell suggests otherwise."[44]

• Air Canada and Canadian Airlines have an early retirement phase-in program, negotiated by the CAW, that gives customer-service agents the chance to phase out of their careers. Workers over the age of 55 can move to part-time and start collecting a portion of their pensions, allowing the companies in turn to maintain access to their skills while rejuvenating the workforce by hiring younger workers. Many of the hours freed up are used to allow part-timers with less seniority to move to regular full-time hours.[45]

• The Royal Bank of Canada introduced a broad-ranging flexible work arrangements initiative in 1990. An estimated 30 per cent of Royal Bank employees—more than 13,000 people—use these arrangements, which include job-sharing, "flexiplace" (working outside the office or from home), "flextime" (flexible start and finish times), compressed workweeks, and variable hours (working less than 37 hours per week). Although not all of these provisions are forms of WTR, the bank does have over 1,100 job-sharing arrangements. A review of the policy found high employee satisfaction (94 per cent), largely because the arrangements were helping with "the struggle to juggle" work, family, and life responsibilities. Some 63 per cent of managers said they would highly recommend flexible work arrangements after seeing the benefits in employee performance.[46]

• At Alcan in Jonquière, Quebec, union and management reached an agreement in 1995 for the banking of unpaid hours. On a voluntary basis, workers could continue to work 40 hours per week, but were paid for 38. The remaining two hours per week accumulated in a time bank, to be taken as extra vacation—an additional 11 days a year. Wages were

Box 6.1   The United States and Japan

From "Free and Lazy" to the "Overworked American"
In his 1883 denunciation of the ideology of work, Paul Lafargue favourably compared "the American, free and lazy" to the oppressed and work-obsessed European labourer. Today the United States is surpassing Japan to become the long-hours champion among major industrial nations.

The 1938 Fair Labor Standards Act introduced a 40-hour standard work-week, long before most European nations reached the same standard. There has been no reduction of the legislated federal standard since then, despite occasional introductions of shorter-hours bills in Congress. A 30-hour work-week bill was passed by the U.S. Senate in 1933 in response to the mass unemployment of the Great Depression and was close to becoming law before President Franklin Delano Roosevelt was dissuaded by business opposition. Since then there have been occasional, unsuccessful efforts to raise the issue of shorter work time in Congress, the most recent being a 35-hour bill in 1979.

U.S. work hours increased substantially in recent decades. Economist Juliet Schor estimates that average hours of work began rising slowly in the 1970s and accelerated rapidly in the 1980s. The result is that the average U.S. worker was toiling for 138 hours longer per year (3.5 weeks) in 1989 than in 1969. The OECD estimates that average annual hours rose by 5.4 per cent from 1983-97 to reach 1,967 hours per employed person in 1997. The Families and Work Institute found in 1997 that U.S. men worked an average of 49.4 hours per week versus 42.4 hours for women.

In 1998 citizens in Berkeley, California, gained enough signatures to put the question of a 35-hour workweek—with no loss in pay and double pay for overtime—on the November municipal ballot. The effort, although ultimately unsuccessful, was a sign of resistance to the growth of long hours and income disparities.

Similar resistance has shown itself in a number of other places:
- labour disputes—for example, Bell Atlantic employees winning limits on mandatory overtime; U.S. West workers rebelling against 60-hour work weeks;
- opinion surveys—64 per cent of U.S. workers said they wanted to work fewer hours in 1997, way up from 47 per cent in 1992;
- skyrocketing absenteeism—unscheduled absences up 25 per cent in 1997-98;
- and even corporate advertising—"Why work a twelve-hour day, when you can do it in eight?" asks Microsoft.

Unfortunately, such ideas tend to be more easily understood by the marketing departments of major corporations than the human resources departments. But some positive cases do exist, such as SAS Institute Inc., a North Carolina software company with a strikingly European work schedule. Full-time workers, including the CEO, clock in for 35 hours per week.

Previously rejected as "freakish" by other software firms, SAS was by 1999 attracting attention because of its millions of dollars in annual savings due to low employee turnover and more alert, less error-prone programmers.

The "Lifestyle Superpower"

Although North Americans tend to stereotype Japan as a nation of workaholics, that country's government has undertaken one of the most ambitious attempts to reduce work hours in recent decades. In 1992 the Japanese cabinet approved "The Lifestyle Superpower Five-Year Plan." The goals include improvements in social infrastructure and housing, as well as a reduction of average annual work time by 2.2 per cent per annum (from 2,008 to 1,800 hours over the life of the plan). The plan advocated a legislated standard 40-hour week, a change introduced between April 1994 and April 1997, depending on the sector.

Significant reductions in work time occurred in Japan both before and after this plan was announced. From 1983 to 1994 Japan had the largest average decline in annual work hours per person of any OECD country: an average reduction of 19.7 hours per year. From 1990 to 1997 average annual hours per employee were reduced from 2,064 to 1,891, an 8.4 per cent decline in seven years. This included the second-largest annual reduction ever in Japan, in the year after the "Lifestyle Superpower" plan was introduced, although hours reductions slowed after that. By 1994 the average workweek was estimated at 39 hours.

While Japanese hours were falling, U.S. hours were rising. Although work hours statistics are calculated differently in each country, the available figures suggest that Japan no longer has the dubious distinction of being the developed world's long-hours capital.

The recent decline in hours in Japan is arguably one reason why, despite a severe economic crisis due to the bursting of a speculative financial bubble in the early 1990s and the Asian crisis of 1997-98, unemployment was held at relatively low levels (4.8 per cent in April 1999).

Sources:Paul Lafargue, *The Right to Be Lazy* (Chicago: Charles H. Kerr, 1989), p.60; Benjamin Hunnicutt, *Work without End* (Philadelphia: Temple University Press, 1988), pp.153, 246-47, 311; Juliet B. Schor, *Beyond an Economy of Work and Spend* (Tilburg, Netherlands: Tilburg University Press, 1997), p.9; Organisation for Economic Co-operation and Development, *OECD Employment Outlook: June 1998* (Paris: OECD, 1998), p.207; James T. Bond, Ellen Galinsky, and Jennifer E. Swanbert, *The 1997 National Study of the Changing Workforce* (New York: Families and Work Institute, 1997), pp.72, 74; Abraham McLaughlin, "Long Workdays Draw Backlash," *Christian Science Monitor*, Aug. 28, 1998; Sue Shellenberger, "Overloaded Staffers Cope by Calling in Sick, *The Globe and Mail Report on Business*, Sept. 24, 1998; Leslie Kaufman, "Some Companies Derail the 'Burnout' Track," *The New York Times*, May 4, 1999, p.A1. Information on Japan from Roche, Fynes, and Morrissey, "Working Time and Employment: A Review of International Evidence," *International Labour Review*, 135,2 (1996), p.139; OECD, *OECD Employment Outlook: June 1998*, pp.156, 167, 169, 207; "Economic Indicators," *The Economist*, June 12, 1999, p.96.

RICARDO LEVINS MORALES, NORTHLAND POSTER COLLECTIVE

In the United States, where hours of work have been on the rise, labour activists find themselves refighting past struggles.

increased somewhat (by 25 cents per hour) to cushion the financial impact. Some 70 per cent of workers signed on to the 40-38 plan. Overtime hours for all workers were also banked to be taken as time off. As a result the company rehired 112 laid-off workers.[47]

WORK TIME IN THE SOUTH

Discussions about a 32-hour or 35-hour week may seem far from everyday reality in the poorer nations of the South. But they are still relevant on two levels. If the North were to opt for a model of non-material growth, focusing on WTR rather than infinite consumption growth, much more "ecological space" would be available for the future growth in the South that is legitimately needed to reduce poverty. More directly, the South has its own struggles for WTR—from shortening the workday to putting bounds on work hours over the life cycle through controls on child labour and the introduction of retirement and pension rights. These Southern struggles are also a matter of concern for those of us in the North—both out of solidarity and self-interest in not having our labour conditions eroded through low-standards competition.

Workers in the South are often victims of appalling work-time abuses reminiscent of 19th-century standards in the North. The abuses result in damage to health, increased likelihood of industrial accidents, and a lack of time for a decent human life. In some cases workers receive such low wages that they actively seek extremely long hours to survive—illustrating that a wage increase can in some cases be the most effective form of WTR policy. In other cases overtime is forced on workers who have no say in the matter. For instance, in 1998 Mohammed, a young Bangladeshi garment worker, told a researcher for CAFOD, the aid and development agency of the Catholic Church in England and Wales:

> I didn't go to work today because I'm not feeling well. I'm ill because I haven't had a day off in two months. My head feels heavy and sore. I have no energy left. There's no doctor or medicine at work. Normally, I only get one day off a month. I won't get paid today. I told my supervisor, and he said that if I don't go in tomorrow they'll dock three days' salary. The hours are long, 8.00 a.m. to 9.00 p.m. or 10.00 p.m., and sometimes until two in the morning or all night. The management decides on overtime; we do what we're told. I'm not happy about the hours, but there's nothing I can do. If I complain, the managers say, "if you don't want to work overnight, you won't work here anymore."[48]

Similar conditions are found in many countries of the South, often in plants that act as subcontractors for large Northern corporations. In Haiti a 1996 investigation found that workers at Quality Garments—a subcontractor making dresses for K-Mart and Mickey Mouse pyjamas for Walt Disney Co.—routinely put in eight to ten hours per day, Monday through Saturday. When the company had orders to fill, they were required to work Sundays as well, resulting in one case of more than 50 workdays without a day off, up to 70 hours per week, during Haiti's hottest season. While CEO Michael Eisner of Disney earned $203 million from salary and stock options in 1993, a Haitian minimum-wage worker sewing clothes

for Disney would have had to work approximately 1,040 years to earn what Eisner pocketed per day. Meanwhile, workers at the Alpha Sewing plant, which produces industrial gloves for Ansell Edmont of Ohio, were working from 6 a.m. to 5:30 p.m., Monday through Saturday, and often from 6 a.m. to 3:30 p.m. on Sunday as well—a 78-hour workweek. Not only did 75 per cent of the workers make less than Haiti's minimum wage, but they were also exposed to dangerous chemicals, such as polyvinyl chloride, without any protection, even though they were making gloves for the world's largest manufacturer of protective industrial clothing.[49] These examples bring to mind the time when Gandhi was asked what he thought of Western civilization. "It would be a good idea," he replied.

China announced new work-time regulations in 1995 that stipulated a standard 8-hour day and 40-hour week, with a maximum 3 hours of overtime per day and 36 hours per month. These standards are advanced by international comparison—stronger than those in many Canadian provinces—but they are routinely abused. A 1997 investigation into the conditions in toy factories found that workers were frequently subjected to forced overtime until two or three in the morning, and sometimes even overnight. Many toy factories gave their workers only a half-day off per week; some gave none at all. A study of the Chinese garment industry in the same year found that work hours in the enterprises investigated averaged 69 hours per week. A 1998 report found similar abuses. At one plant producing "Kathie Lee" items for Wal-Mart, workers were paid between 20 and 35 cents an hour for an 84-hour workweek, with severe fines for refusing overtime, often in the form of mandatory 24-hour shifts during rush times.[50]

The irrationality and brutality of the world economic order are evident in the conditions that workers in the South face in their efforts to take home what amounts to less than a living wage, while producing goods designed to serve the status of consumers in the North as much or more than real need. For instance, in 1997 Nike CEO Phil Knight made U.S.$80 million in the fourth quarter alone from dividend "earnings," while a Nike contract employee making Air Jordan shoes in Indonesia working 60 hours per week made U.S.$811 for the entire year.[51]

These abuses are also products of specific production regimes in which the factory owner is not necessarily the guilty party. One observer of sweatshops in El Salvador points out, "Local factories producing under contract for big US retailers like the GAP or Eddie Bauer have set deadlines they have to meet to fulfill their orders. Profit margins are very low. For the maquiladora owners to survive under this system, they try to keep the pace of production up. They keep a small workforce and demand a lot of overtime when orders are heavy."[52]

These kinds of conditions are found not only in the sweatshops of the "least developed" nations. In the mid-1990s in Chile, Latin America's model student of neo-liberalism, seasonal workers in the building sector and in the key export sectors of farming and forestry experienced working hours of at least 10 hours a day, more often 12 or 14, in hard and dangerous conditions.[53]

South Korea has been hailed for having made the "leap from poverty to affluence in one generation." But it did so with an economic ideology of growth through sacrifice, of non-stop work justified by the need to "stand firm" against the communist North. (This Cold War argument against WTR was heard in other parts of the "free world" as well.) According to *The Economist*, "The country was built by men who worked appalling hours, led by obsessive bosses who, along with their workers, slept on the docks and construction sites." For instance, Kin Woo Choong, who founded the Daewoo industrial group in 1967, never took a day off until his son was killed in a car crash in 1990. He expected his employees to work six days a week, 12 hours a day, until the mid-1980s. Anybody who protested was fired or jailed. Along with the hyper-exploitation of labour came massive environmental degradation, due largely to an obsession with the rapid growth of heavy industry.[54]

The strikes of 1987 were a turning point for South Korea, as its military rulers had to concede democratic reforms. Trade unions took advantage of the democratic opening to campaign—successfully—for higher pay and shorter work hours. The idea of leisure was no longer taboo. In 1983 average annual hours per employed person stood at 2,736. By 1997 they had fallen to 2,434—still high by international comparison, but a significant 11 per cent reduction all the same.[55]

Things were looking better for South Korean workers until the great Asian crash of 1997-98. As companies sought to slash costs by throwing people out of work, Korea's trade unions pushed instead for job-sharing and reduced work time in return for pay freezes, but no loss in pay. Their efforts could not stop unemployment rising from below 3 per cent to 9 per cent in less than one year. Some Korean firms abused the idea of shorter work time. For instance, Cheil Communications, a subsidiary of the Samsung group, made some of its workers—women as well as men— take unpaid "paternity" leave for up to three years. Many Koreans who kept their jobs found themselves working longer hours, but earning 20 per cent less. By early 1999 the unions were renewing their calls for WTR—by reducing the workweek from 44 to 40 hours with no loss in pay—as an alternative to job losses.[56]

In Brazil shorter work time was an important item in the 1998 platform of Workers' Party (PT) presidential candidate Luiz Ignacio da Silva, a former metalworker better known as "Lula." Some eight years earlier the first congress of the PT recognized the linkages between technological development and automation within capitalism and the generation of technological unemployment as well as exploitation of labour and the environment. The congress argued that if workers were to gain control of new technologies they could be a force for liberation, through the reduction of the workday, a decrease in inequalities, and the increase in time available for leisure and political activity. The PT recognized that the Northern model of development could not be equalled by the South, both because of social contradictions within capitalism and because of ecological limits to its universalization. Mixing Marxist analysis with an advanced environmental awareness, the PT called for new criteria for national accounts that, unlike GDP, take into account environmental degradation and non-material forms of wealth like leisure. According to the Congress, "For us the development of free time and the cultural advance of the people are indicators of development, and for this it is fundamental to return to the struggle for the reduction of work time. There is no natural limit to the workday. It is clearly political and a result of class struggle."[57]

One positive example in the South is the new employment standards law approved by South Africa's ANC government in 1998 despite stiff business opposition. The law introduced a 45-hour workweek (to be cut gradually to 40 hours), a limit of 10 hours of overtime per week, time and a half for overtime work, and double pay for Sunday labour. It also included four months' paid maternity leave and a ban on the employment of children under 15. According to the COSATU trade union confederation, "To us the right to have our working hours regulated, including the right to spend adequate time with our families, is a basic freedom and cannot be separated from our struggle for liberation from apartheid oppression."[58]

Meanwhile, the idea of granting time off to better distribute available opportunities took a surreal turn in the land of Gabriel García Márquez. A controversial bill introduced in 1998 in Colombia would allow inmates to take a vacation from jail. The goal was to relieve the crisis of prison overcrowding, with some prisons at 300 per cent occupancy. Prisoners would be eligible for a maximum 60 days off per year if they had behaved well and never tried to escape.[59]

Canadian work-time standards compare favourably to those in the United States and Japan, and very favourably to those in the South, where many workers find themselves at the bottom of the international capitalist pecking order. Yet Canadian work-hour policies in the 1990s remained, at best, a mixed bag ranging from positive, albeit moderate tinkering (Quebec, British Columbia) to highly regressive reforms and proposals (Ontario under Mike Harris), while the federal Liberal government took no significant positive action. Public-sector and private-sector workplaces have generated a small number of positive WTR initiatives in practice. The existing examples illustrate that WTR is possible in Canada, and that there can be important benefits in terms of improved quality of life for workers, job creation for the unemployed, and better employee performance in the interest of firms. Yet the examples remain few in number. If Canadians are to build on these experiences and create a much broader shorter work-time movement, they would do well by trying to learn from the pacesetters in Europe.

Europe's New Movement for Work-Time Reduction

Lavorare meno, lavorare tutti. (Work less, everyone works.)

Italian shorter work-time movement slogan

People are rather jealous when I tell them I have Fridays off.

Foppe Hoogeveen, Dutch economics professor with a four-day week, 1999

In Europe, where for some time now the examples of shorter workweeks, lengthy vacations, and other work-time measures have compared more than favourably to standards in North America, a wide range of WTR options and innovative combinations of policy tools are at work. In the late 1990s many European countries were poised to widen the gap even further. The 1997 French decision to legislate a 35-hour workweek was not only one of the most important work-time developments in recent history, but also set off a significant new wave of demands for WTR across the continent.

FRANCE: LEGISLATION + FINANCIAL INCENTIVES + COLLECTIVE BARGAINING = 35 HOURS

The 1997 announcement of a 35-hour plan was not the first bold WTR initiative in France. In 1936 Leon Blum's Popular Front government cut the basic workweek from 46 or 48 hours to 40 hours with no loss in pay and introduced two weeks' paid holiday. (The concept of paid vacation was so radical at the time that it took a year or so for the idea to sink in and for workers to begin taking full advantage of the new right.)[1] Years later, in 1982, François Mitterand's Socialist government legislated a reduction of the workweek from 40 to 39 hours, as well as adding a fifth week of paid vacation. However, a campaign promise to further reduce the workweek to 35 hours was never implemented. The small reduction in work time had a relatively disappointing effect on employment (estimated at 14,000 to 28,000 new jobs created, or 50,000 to 100,000 jobs including layoffs avoided).[2] Critics also made much of the legislated imposition of a single model on all firms.

WTR largely disappeared from French public policy debates until 1993, when it re-emerged as an option to deal with skyrocketing unemployment. Advocates now emphasized taking the government savings that resulted from the hiring of new workers and using those savings to lower the payroll taxes of companies that reduced hours and hired more people.[3] A small financial incentives package, introduced by the right-of-centre parliament in 1993, was greatly expanded in the 1996 Robien Law, named after the conservative parliamentarian who sponsored it. The legislation provided significant reductions of social security payroll taxes for firms that reduced work hours and increased employment by at least 10 per cent, and even greater incentives for firms that reduced hours and increased employment by 15 per cent.[4]

Within two years 2,000 firms had taken advantage of the Robien incentives to introduce 35-hour or 32-hour weeks (with one in four agreements leading to a 32-hour week). Some 355,000 employees had their work hours reduced, 25,000 jobs were created, and a further 17,000 layoffs were avoided.[5] Like the 35-hour law that followed, the question of wage levels was left to negotiations between employers and employees. The payroll tax incentives, combined with the opportunities created to reorganize production and increase productivity, made it possible for work time to be reduced with little or no loss in pay. Of the first 1,500 Robien accords, 44 per cent led to shorter hours with no loss in pay; 18 per cent maintained pay levels, but with a temporary salary freeze; and 37 per cent saw a less than proportional loss in pay. In only 1 per cent of cases did shorter hours come with a proportional loss in pay.[6] Although the French Democratic Labour Confederation (CFDT) praised the law, the more left-leaning General Confederation of Labour (CGT) criticized it for being too generous to employers. The president of the Employers Group of the Port of Marseilles called the Robien Law "the best law that we have known in recent years."[7]

The Robien Law experience was of great importance in creating a climate of public opinion favourable to a more ambitious work-time initiative. The 2,000 applied cases demonstrated that WTR could indeed create jobs, that neither employers nor employees had to make unacceptable financial sacrifices, and that WTR was possible in different sectors, professions, and firms of all sizes—half the deals were reached in firms with less than 50 employees. The experience also generated valuable learning about how to reorganize work in response to shorter hours in different types of firms.[8]

On June 1, 1997, a Socialist-led government, in coalition with the Communist Party and Greens, came to power in France on a platform highlighting a 35-hour workweek with no loss in pay. That October Prime Minister Lionel Jospin made good on the commitment with the historic announcement of the plan. The initiative combined legislation and financial incentives, and collective bargaining on the sectoral and workplace levels would adapt WTR to the realities of business and the preferences of workers. The decision had a ripple effect, helping to push WTR towards the top of policy and collective bargaining agendas in other European countries.

The French parliament passed the first of two 35-hour laws, the Aubry Law, in June 1998.[9] Its main points:

• A 35-hour workweek would become the legislated standard on January 1, 2000 (2002 for firms with fewer than 20 employees). Hours above 35 would be considered overtime.

• Companies that reduced hours and hired more workers would be provided with financial incentives in the form of lower employer payroll taxes. The sooner a firm reduced hours, the more generous the aid. For instance, a company that reduced hours before July 1999 by 10 per cent (for example, from 39 to 35 hours) and hired 6 per cent more workers would receive 9,000 francs (C$2,108) per employee in the first year and 8,000 francs (C$1,874) in the second, declining gradually to 5,000 francs (C$1,171) in the fifth year.

• An additional 4,000 francs (C$937) per worker would be provided to firms that reduced hours by 15 per cent and hired at least 9 per cent more workers.

• Additional aid would be provided to firms that were labour-intensive, had a high percentage of low-wage workers, or took on a high percentage of young people, disabled, or long-term unemployed.

• After five years the government would provide a permanent "structural aid" of 5,000 francs (C$1,171) per worker to firms that reduced hours to 35 or less, without any hiring conditions.

• "Defensive" company-union agreements that saved jobs in firms with economic difficulties would also make a firm eligible for the financial incentives.

• Despite the Socialist electoral campaign slogan of "35 hours, paid 39," the law did not specify wage levels. Details like wages and linking shorter hours to more flexible work organization were left to collective bargaining.

• Workplaces could implement WTR in a way to best meet their needs. For example, a 35-hour week could be spread over four or five days, with alternating four-day and five-day weeks, or it could mean "annualized" reductions, such as additional days off (roughly 23 per year) and extended vacations.

• In autumn 1999, after a review of workplace negotiations up to that point, a second law would determine important remaining details such as the treatment of overtime hours.

The plan's financial incentives were designed to allow WTR to be implemented with little or no loss in pay for workers and without creating excessive costs to business. However, salary moderation, in the form of diminished pay increases or wage freezes, was expected as productivity gains over a number of years were to be used to finance the reduction in hours. Efficiency gains from greater flexibility in work-hour scheduling and the reorganization of work were to be another possible way for business to limit cost increases.

The French National Employers' Confederation (CNPF) bitterly opposed the 35-hour law, claiming that it would create new costs for business, deter investment, and hinder job creation. Despite the apparent flexibility of the 35-hour law, the CNPF made full use of its rhetorical arsenal, calling the legislation "anti-economic," "archaic," and "ideological." The CNPF president, Jean Gandois, resigned after the law was announced, saying he had been "duped" and should be replaced by someone with more of a "killer" instinct. (Interestingly, Belgian steelmaker Cockerille Sambre, whose CEO was the same Jean Gandois, moved from a 37-hour to 34-hour week without loss in pay in 1997.)[10] The CNPF later softened its stance somewhat, resigning itself to dealing with the law and leaving its member firms and sectoral employer organizations to negotiate as they saw fit.

In some cases companies followed up with aggressive campaigns, threatening to terminate existing collective agreements to "neutralize" the effects of the law. Other French firms found that they could derive benefits from shorter work time by linking it to company reorganization and modernization. The CNPF's new president, Ernest-Antoine Sellière, admitted in 1998, "There can even be cases, I don't deny it, where, thanks to the 35-hour week, the organization of work, working conditions or productivity will improve."[11]

France's labour unions have generally been supportive of the 35-hour initiative, with some differences of opinion on key issues. The French Democratic Labour Confederation (CFDT), the labour organization most strongly behind the government's plan, has tended to echo the government's position, emphasizing the potential for "win-win-win" solutions benefiting employees, employers, and the unemployed. The CFDT supports 35 hours as a first step towards a 32-hour week and has been open to salary moderation and possibly even some reduction in pay for those with above-average incomes, if WTR could be linked to new hiring.[12] It sees a loss of pay for workers as "neither automatic, nor excluded." The CFDT has been more willing than other unions to put employment creation ahead of wage gains for its members. It has also been relatively open to greater work-time flexibility in return for shorter hours.

The General Confederation of Labour has also supported the 35-hour initiative, which it believes could be a "rejuvenating experience" for the union movement and an opportunity for a major social advance. However, the CGT, with links to France's Communist Party, went into the 35-hour project rejecting wage and flexibility concessions in return for shorter hours. It aimed to "create jobs, raise pay, and transform work" through the implementation of the 35-hour week. In 1998 the CGT stated, "The reduction of work time cannot be done to the detriment of workers. There is no question of the CGT accepting any wage freezes, especially for firms making profits."[13] As implementation of the 35-hour law progressed, however, a convergence between the CFDT and CGT was increasingly evident, including joint action in negotiating with employers. The CGT also began moving from a unionism of "protest" to one of "proposal" and acknowledged that it was prepared to discuss certain forms of flexibility, like the calculation of work hours on an annual basis.[14]

Force Ouvrière (FO) has been the least committed of the major union federations to the 35-hour project. The FO has supported a 35-hour week without loss in pay, but its leader, Marc Blondel, stated that the shorter workweek was not a top priority and would not likely be a major job creator. His union preferred Keynesian expansionary measures and wage increases to increase demand and reduce unemployment.[15]

Conflict and Consensus in 35-Hour Negotiations

With the first phase of legislation in place, attention turned to negotiations at the sectoral and workplace level. In May 1999 the French government released an assessment of the first 11 months of negotiations. A total of 4,076 workplace agreements had introduced workweeks of 35 hours or less, reducing the work hours of 1,142,427 employees and generating a positive employment effect of 56,767 jobs—42,834 new jobs created, 13,933 layoffs avoided. (By August the job-creation total had grown significantly, to 118,433 based on 14,615 agreements.) Employers and employees had opted for a diverse range of options, from shorter workdays to additional holidays on an annual basis. Most agreements also covered managers, who often saw work time above 35 hours per week accumulate in "time banks," to be taken later as time off. In a number of agreements, WTR helped to reduce the precariousness of employment by opening up opportunities for temporary contract workers to gain permanent positions or by creating jobs for youth. In 85 per cent of cases worktime was reduced with no loss in pay, but this generally came with salary moderation or wage freezes, usually over two years.[16]

The process has been widely credited with revitalizing "social dialogue" between management and labour in firms—the most "revolutionary" change brought on by the law, according to some observers. Agreements were signed in all types of sectors and in all sizes of firms, with a surprisingly large number of small firms taking action.[17] Some critics considered the initial employment results to be disappointing. However, advocates of the law pointed out that the pace of 35-hour negotiations was accelerating rapidly, with many more jobs to come— conservative estimates were for at least 250,000 jobs by 2002, while the Minister of Employment aimed for 450,000. Furthermore, critics originally claimed the 35-hour law would scare away investment and actually destroy jobs. As it turned out, 1998—the year following the announcement of the law—was the best year for job creation in France out of the last 30, with 350,000 private-sector jobs created, including those due to WTR, and an additional 100,000 youth jobs funded by the left-of-centre government.[18]

In many cases, agreements reconciled the needs of employers and employees while creating jobs for the unemployed. In some cases, however, employers took a hardline negotiating stance, blocking the potential benefits of the plan. For instance, in July 1998 the Union of Metallurgy and Mining Industries (UIMM) reached an agreement with some of the smaller unions and the FO that increased allowable overtime from 94 hours per employee per year to 180 hours, despite the prevailing legal standard of 130 hours. The deal also increased work-time flexibility (by allowing the workweek to rise for limited periods up to 48 hours instead of the current 46) and extended "flat-rate" salaries, without reference to work hours, from managers to more employees. As a result the 35-hour law could be implemented without any new hiring and without any real reduction in work time. There would be a small increase in pay for workers due to the increase in overtime. Rather than "35 hours, paid 39," as the rallying cry put it, this deal was labelled "35 hours, worked 39." The deal ran counter to the spirit of the law and did not conform to the existing labour code, and the government decided not to "extend" it, which meant that it would not be obligatory for firms in the sector. Nor would any similar deals be "extended."[19]

Another controversial deal at automaker PSA-Peugeot-Citroën cut two paid breaks from the calculation of work time, resulting in a minimal real reduction of hours, and linked 35 hours to more obligatory Saturday work without overtime pay. A front-page article, "The Weekend Will Start Sunday," in the daily *Libération* reflected concern over this erosion of established time rhythms.[20] In the early stage of 35-hour negotiations, work-time flexibility measures of this sort were a greater source of controversy than questions about salary levels. Yet despite such concerns, support for the 35-hour week among labour unions and workers remained strong, mainly due to its contribution to job creation. A poll commissioned by the French government in April 1999 found that 81 per cent of employees in firms that had moved to 35 hours said the agreement had responded "well" or "very well" to their wishes, while May Day 1999 saw the CGT and CFDT marching together in favour of 35 hours.[21]

In October 1998 companies and unions in the textile sector reached a deal to reduce effective work time by between 98 and 148 hours a year, guarantee the maintenance of employees' purchasing power, and favour employment creation.[22] Small-scale construction firms introduced 35 hours with no loss in pay, job creation, and limited flexibility in the workweek up to 42 hours. At Credit Mutuel de Normandie, 440 employees moved to a 4.5-day week without a loss in pay, although with a wage freeze, and 40 new jobs were created. At the newspaper *Parisien*, a June 1999 accord called for 24 new jobs and an additional 22 paid days off (4.4 weeks in total) for journalists—in addition to their existing nine weeks' vacation. A number of foreign-owned multinationals have reached 35-hour deals, including Toys R Us, DHL France, and Packard Bell NEC. At

Eurodisney, Mickey Mouse gets a shorter workday with no loss in pay along with 608 new jobs created—a rather better deal than Disney's sub-contract employees in Haiti were getting. New examples were emerging on a daily basis in 1998 and 1999 and seemed likely to continue coming up to and beyond January 1, 2000, when the 35-hour standard would become legally binding.[23]

Some firms began reducing hours even without the benefit of financial incentives. Eurocopter, the largest helicopter manufacturer in Europe, introduced an average 35-hour week, with alternating four-day and five-day weeks and scheduling based partly on peaks in demand. Employees would still be paid for an average of 60 per cent of the hours no longer worked, on a sliding scale to protect low-income earners. The deal would lead to the creation of 360 jobs. Because hours were being reduced by less than 10 per cent, there would be no payroll tax reductions from the government, but the company would gain significant benefits from the increased flexibility of work time and longer operating hours for its machinery.[24]

Although the 35-hour law did not apply to civil servants, the public sector also began the shift towards shorter hours. For example, 6,000 employees of the urban community of Strasbourg would go to 35 hours by December 31, 2000, in a move that would take in 260 different professions in 300 workplaces. Between 120 and 150 jobs would be created. The municipality aimed to link shorter hours with improved service to the public by increasing the opening hours of services, increasing productivity, and reducing absenteeism.[25]

One of the most significant 35-hour deals in the first year of implementation was at EDF-GDF, the publicly owned electricity and gas firm. Some 142,000 employees were to move to 35 hours with no loss in pay, along with a voluntary 32-hour option for 37 hours' pay. An expected 18,000 to 20,000 young people were to be hired—with 20 per cent of the jobs reserved for youth from disadvantaged backgrounds. With retirements and other departures, a net job creation of 3,000-5,000 jobs was expected. In contrast, the firm had previously been cutting 2,000 jobs per year.[26]

France also began getting serious about cracking down on the unpaid overtime of salaried workers—an abuse common in many countries. In June 1999 a court in Versailles found Bernard Rocquemont, ex-CEO of the defence-electronics firm Thomson-RCM, guilty of breaking the law against clandestine work for subjecting his management employees to 45,000 hours of unrecorded, unpaid work in 1997. He was fined 50,000 francs (C$11,710). Managers in France, who work on average 45 hours per week, have been surprisingly vocal in their demands for the 35-hour week to apply to them, too. Some observers see this as a sign that the 35-hour week has already generated fundamental social changes. In the words of one editorialist, "The French have never before questioned their relationship to work to the same degree."[27]

In France much of the passion and heated rhetoric on all sides of the 35-hour issue have been due to the strong symbolic importance of the measure. For proponents, WTR represents a "symbol of hope" in the fight against unemployment, a sign of solidarity between those with and those without jobs, and a "key to a social Europe" that avoids U.S.-style inequalities and erosion of social cohesion. Some employers reacted angrily because the government's move symbolized a loss of their authority over economic policy. For the government the 35-hour week symbolized a commitment to its campaign promises and was a sign of being "anchored on the left"—an important factor politically during a time when many of its other policies, like meeting the restrictive 1991 Maastricht Treaty criteria on the single European currency, and the privatization of state firms, were similar to the previous right-of-centre government.

Jumping a Chasm in Two Leaps?
In June 1999 the French government revealed its intentions for the second law on 35 hours, based on a review of the negotiations until that point. It announced a one-year transition period to give time for successful negotiations. In the year 2000, hours between 35 and 39 would cost employers only 10 per cent more, with the full 25 per cent overtime premium applied only in 2001. It would also be two years before the annual overtime maximum of 130 hours per worker would take into account all hours beyond 35.

The package included a number of other measures. For purposes of work-time regulation, three categories of managers were announced. Executives (dirigeants) were exempted from the 35-hour law. Managers integrated into work teams would be covered by the regular 35-hour provisions. A third group with autonomy in the management of their time would see a new maximum of 222 days worked per year on the condition that they received at least 5 additional days off—a standard much lower than the 20 or more days off that many 35-hour agreements have delivered. In workplaces with work time averaged on an annual basis, 35 hours would be the new average reference point, resulting in a 1,600-hour maximum over the year. Workers getting the minimum wage received a double guarantee: no loss in pay with the move to 35 hours and continued increases in the minimum wage above the rate of inflation (although minimum wage increases would not grow as quickly as they might have without the move to 35 hours). The government confirmed its commitment to link the 35-hour week to a reduction of payroll taxes for low and medium salaries, announced new rules for the use of "time-savings accounts," and specified that agreements could allow some of the hours liberated by WTR to be devoted to training—raising some concerns about the "free time is for training" phenomenon.[28]

Initial reactions to the government's "go-slow" approach in the second law were somewhat less than positive. Many on the left denounced the measures, particularly the transition period, for their lack of ambition. The CGT and the French Communist Party called it a victory for employers. The CFE-CGC, a union representing managers, called the guarantee of only five additional days off for managers a "provocation." Alain Lipietz of the Greens went as far as calling the proposal "a horror," because, in his view, rapid WTR was needed to create jobs and bring employers to the bargaining table. Yet the approach was still too rapid for some. The president of the small business employers' confederation said the one-year transition was like having your hanging delayed ("*un delai de pendaison*"). The CFDT was one of the few voices of support, saying that time was needed for proper negotiations to achieve a real and effective reduction of work time. It remained to be seen if annoying just about everyone meant that the 35-hour project was going off the rails or, paradoxically, if it was a sign that the government had found the right balance. Parliament was expected to debate the measures in autumn 1999.[29]

From a North American perspective, 35 hours at any speed sounds radical. But French proponents of WTR have somewhat higher expectations. In a 1998 book called *35 Hours: The Double Trap*, Pierre Larrouturou, a workplace consultant with Arthur Andersen and proponent of a four-day week, harshly attacked the timidity of the government's plan. During a time when persistent mass unemployment was destroying lives, eroding social cohesion, and feeding the growth of the far-right National Front, Larrouturou saw it as "scandalous" and "morally unacceptable" that the government had opted for 35 hours. He pointed to statistics showing that the 35-hour plan would only create between 200,000 and 280,000 jobs, compared to 1.6 million jobs with a 32-hour week. (The difference comes about because small reductions in work time are compensated for largely by increased productivity, while larger reductions require proportionately greater hiring.)[30] "When you're trying to jump a chasm, going in the right direction is not enough," Larrouturou commented. He was joined in his criticism by former socialist prime minister Michel Rocard, who said the 35-hour plan only went part of the way in the right direction.[31]

Larrouturou called for much more significant financial incentives for firms that reduced hours and created jobs, along with stronger controls and penalties for overtime. His 32-hour plan would also involve greater financial sacrifices on the part of the employed. He estimated that a 32-hour week (an 18 per cent reduction in hours) could be implemented with an average 3 per cent reduction in pay, with no loss in pay for those earning less than 8,500 francs per month (C$1,991) and a maximum 5 per cent reduction for high-income earners. (The figures are based on making full use of the savings from lower unemployment to finance the process, in addition to induced productivity gains.) Larrouturou maintained that politicians and union leaders who said that such relatively small reductions in income would not be accepted were underestimating both the economic realism and the solidarity of employed workers with the unemployed.

The debate over the 35-hour week in France has been dominated by employment concerns and the related issue of maintaining a cohesive society. Secondary issues have been the linkage of WTR to more flexible hours and increased productivity through work reorganization, and the generation of more free time for workers. Ecological issues have not been at the forefront of the discussion—even though the Green Party and green intellectuals have long been among the most persistent supporters of WTR, keeping the flame alive in the late 1980s and early 1990s when many, including the Socialists, had abandoned the idea.[32] The Greens also played an important role within the Jospin government in pressing for the honouring of the 35-hour election promise, and they have called for a further reduction to 32 hours early in the new millennium. They have also worked with Green parties in other countries to apply WTR across the continent, in parallel to the efforts of trade unions to generate a European-wide movement.

GERMANY: LABOUR'S COLLECTIVE BARGAINING PUSH

Germany provides the best example of significant WTR achieved exclusively through collective bargaining. Beginning in the 1980s, labour unions embarked on impressive work-hour campaigns. The leading force was the metalworkers' union IG Metall—the world's largest independent trade union. In 1984 a seven-week IG Metall strike ended with an agreement on a systematic reduction of weekly work hours from 40 to 35, starting with 38.5 hours in 1985. The 35-hour target was finally reached in 1995, without loss in pay, though workers experienced lower wage increases than they might otherwise have achieved. By 1996 the 35-hour week was also in place in printing and iron and steel, while the average workweek in West Germany was 37.5 hours (39.4 in the East). In the West, average annual hours per worker fell from 1,732 to 1,644 in 1987-97, mostly during the first half of the period. All this was despite the legislated standard workweek remaining unchanged at 48 hours—the standard since the 1930s.[33]

Although the general reduction of work time without loss in pay slowed during the difficult economic years of the early 1990s, an increasing use of hours and incomes reductions avoided layoffs in many struggling companies. The most prominent example was Volkswagen, which cut weekly hours from 36 to 28.8 in 1993 to save roughly 30,000 jobs. This reduction of hours by 20 per cent came with pay cuts of between 11 and 15 per cent, depending on the job category. The agreement also gave employers greater work-time flexibility in response to fluctuations in demand.[34] More generally, it became increasingly common in the 1990s for collective agreements to give employers the right to temporarily reduce hours, with proportional cuts in pay, in return for no-layoff guarantees. Unions have tended to see the approach as a better way to deal with economic slowdowns or loss of contracts than throwing people out of work, while companies have benefited by keeping workers' skills in the firm and thereby maintaining production quality.[35]

By 1998 the idea of WTR as a solution to Germany's stubbornly high unemployment appeared to be on the upswing again. At its May 1998 conference, IG Metall proposed a bold new initiative: a 35-hour week in East Germany, a reduction of overtime, and the encouragement of part-time work and partial retirement, followed by further WTR of 10 per cent, through either a 32-hour week or a reduction of annual hours to 1,400 after the year 2001. (The average in metalworking in 1997 was 1,532 hours.)[36] In February 1998 the president of the main public-sector union (ÖTV) pointed to a 30-hour week as an important goal. Dieter Schulte, chair of the DGB union confederation, even spoke of an average 25-hour week as a medium-to-long-term goal.[37] However, some sectors of the labour movement questioned whether further WTR was the best strategy for creating jobs, and it remained uncertain as to whether wages or further WTR would in practice gain top priority in the years ahead.

One new twist has been the debate within labour on wage compensation. In the past German unions always fought for WTR with no loss in pay. The 1990s saw many cases of WTR without full wage compensation, as in the precedent-setting Volkswagen deal. A debate emerged over whether to reaffirm the traditional stance of shorter hours without loss in pay or to embrace a "solidaristic wage policy" involving some pay loss for upper-income workers in return for job creation. Klaus Zwickel, president of IG Metall, has called for a solidaristic policy as part of his 32-hour proposal, with lower-income workers receiving a higher proportion of wage compensation for the cut in hours, and companies that create more jobs through WTR paying a lower wage compensation rate. Zwickel has also pointed to a three-way sharing of the costs of reducing the week from 35 to 32 hours: one hour paid for by the employees, one hour paid by employers, and the third paid by the federal government through wage subsidies.[38] Other union leaders have expressed a similar openness to accepting some loss in pay for WTR if employers commit to creating new employment.[39] Some have maintained that with rapid labour productivity growth and high profitability, workers have no reason to accept lower pay with shorter hours. If real incomes are reduced in return for shorter hours, they say, worker support will soon evaporate.[40]

German employers have generally been resistant to any further WTR, calling instead, as in the rest of Europe, for greater flexibility in work-time scheduling in response to the needs of firms. They have sought "work-time corridors," which allow firms to alter the workweek between, say, 30 and 40 hours to match fluctuations in demand. Some employers have also called for a return to a standard workweek of 40 hours. They have in some cases pushed for "pacts for jobs," which would increase work time by two to three hours per week, without additional payment, to keep plants open under the threat of shifting production to Eastern Europe.[41] Yet one union leader maintains, "Employers aren't against shorter work time per se, but it's a debate about the conditions."[42] For example, German employers have seen the benefits of temporary reductions in hours as an alternative to layoffs. Employers have generally been more willing to reduce hours for low-skilled workers, but more concerned about cutting back hours for highly skilled workers. In some cases they have pushed for split-level contracts, with different work hours for different skill levels.

The Christian Democrat government of Helmut Kohl was not supportive of WTR, but the September 1998 victory of the Social Democratic
Party, in coalition with the Greens, seemed likely to give a boost to the
idea. Although shorter workweek legislation along French lines was not
on the agenda, the new chancellor, Gerhard Schroeder, quickly organized
a tripartite summit of government, business, and labour to begin developing a new "pact for employment." IG Metall made it known that no
employment pact would be possible unless the WTR item was addressed.
Unions called for a dramatic reduction in the 1.8 billion hours of overtime worked in 1998—a "social scandal," in their view, at a time when
four million people were unemployed. Labour also proposed a "pact
between generations" that would allow employees to voluntarily retire at
age 60, with a full pension, to create opportunities for younger workers.
Employers were less than enthusiastic about most of the labour proposals,
but more voluntary part-time work and greater use of work-time "savings
accounts" stood out as potential areas for common ground.[43]

The Making and Saving of Jobs
Studies show that WTR in Germany has had a positive employment effect.
German employers tend to downplay this success, although their studies
count only new jobs created and leave out jobs saved. In contrast, labour
union studies show significant employment benefits.[44] Union researchers
estimate that from the mid-1980s to the mid-1990s one million jobs were
saved or created through a range of WTR measures in all sectors.
Economists Marcus Rubin and Ray Richardson point out that all 12 studies of the 1985 move to a 38.5-hour week in metalworking found positive
employment effects.[45] IG Metall calculates that its reduction of weekly
hours from 40 to 35 helped to save or create 294,700 jobs in the metalworking sector in 1985-95.[46] Another study shows that 43 per cent of all
full-time jobs created in West Germany in 1983-92 were due to WTR.[47]
Still, not all of the reduction in hours can be translated into jobs—some
of it is absorbed by productivity gains. Research in Germany shows that
between half and two-thirds of the hours freed go to job creation, with
the greatest effect generally experienced in blue-collar production.[48]

   This positive employment effect can take two forms: new jobs created
and layoffs avoided. The main effect in Germany appears to have been
saving rather than creating jobs. The 1980s and 1990s saw dramatic
increases in manufacturing productivity, in the 6-8 per cent range in some
sectors. In the face of this, WTR has been essential in minimizing labour-
shedding.[49] The effect has been increased job security for many workers

and the prevention of much higher unemployment, but no major dent in existing unemployment.

One option being explored to increase the employment effect of WTR is the expansion of the personal right to choose part-time work. While collective reductions of standard work hours in Germany and the Netherlands since the 1980s have been similar, in spring 1999 German unemployment stood at 10.5 per cent versus 3.4 per cent in the Netherlands. One major difference is that the Dutch have also encouraged a dramatic increase in individualized part-time options. There is now wide agreement in Germany on the need for more part-time work, as long as it comes with sound social protections.[50] An interesting example, which may signal things to come, is an experimental July 1998 deal in Lower Saxony's metalworking sector. Workers will be able to voluntarily choose to reduce their hours in return for an employer commitment to new hiring. For example, one new 30-hour job will be created for every six workers who choose to go from the standard 35 hours to 30. Up to two-thirds of the income loss will be compensated through bonus payments from a common fund paid into both by employers and workers. Similarly, in 1998 the municipality of Wuppertal gave its 5,000 employees the right to choose shorter hours of work—with guarantees that the city would replace the hours with new hiring—in addition to a drastic reduction of overtime and the promotion of part-time retirement.[51]

Flexibility versus Quality of Life?

One of the main concerns about WTR in Germany has been the corresponding increase in work-time flexibility. Flexibility measures have included "work-time corridors" allowing companies to reduce or extend work time within certain limits; more weekend and evening work; the accumulation of overtime hours in work-time accounts; the possibility of longer work hours for part of the workforce (usually skilled workers); and the calculation of hours on an annual basis. Both employers and employees want more flexibility, but these measures have usually been introduced on employers' terms. Some critics wonder whether the benefits to workers of shorter hours have been worth the price paid in flexibility.

Eckart Hildebrandt, after extensively researching the VW case, argues that workers have gained shorter hours at the cost of a greater dependence on the company's time logic. For example, when employers gain more freedom to schedule Saturday work, it becomes harder for workers to coordinate family activities. Friendships at work become increasingly difficult to build, because workers have such varying schedules. More variable hours at the whim of the company erode employees' ability to participate regularly in activities outside of work. For instance, soccer teams disappear when it is no longer possible to find 11 players available at the same time each week. Hildebrandt maintains that these trade-offs have destroyed much of the potential promise of more autonomy and higher quality of life—the very ideas at the core of a green vision of working less and living better. "Shorter work time combined with extreme flexibility means less time welfare than before," Hildebrandt warns. "You get more time, but more time you can't use."[52]

Although this critique is not universally shared—some people point to examples in Germany of flexibility that meets the needs of both employers and employees—it highlights the need for more reflection on the conditions necessary for WTR to genuinely improve employee welfare. Hildebrandt found the example of the "Happy Fridays" resulting from WTR in Sarnia, Ontario, to be a positive example of a new collective time rhythm that could improve the lives of workers, in contrast to much of what he has seen in Germany.

Whither the German Work Ethic?

The combination of shorter workweeks and long vacations means that German work hours are considerably lower than in North America, and still there are strong pressures for further hours cuts. Even the German jobless are demanding more leisure. An unemployed person can officially only be off the scene—that is, unreachable—for three weeks each year and still receive benefits. In 1998 an association of the unemployed began pushing for six weeks' holiday for the unemployed, just like Germans with jobs, to recover from "the frustrating experiences of trying to find a job" and "the fight with bureaucrats."[53] The very capability of the German unemployed to think such thoughts, let alone make their demands public, illustrates the differences in attitudes about work in Germany and North America. Yet the differences once operated in the other direction. For instance, not until the mid-1950s, when normal work time was 48 hours over six days, did IG Metall begin a campaign for a 40-hour week and "free weekend." It finally reached the 40-hour week in 1967, 41 years after Henry Ford first did the same in his U.S. plants.[54] A study on employee preferences for more money versus more time found that the positions of German and U.S. workers had reversed since the 1970s, with Germans both working longer hours and indicating a greater desire for longer hours at the beginning of the period.[55]

As in France, WTR in Germany has had great symbolic importance. The work-time campaigns of the 1980s were an important symbol of the labour movement's resiliency, showing that it could still offer fresh solutions to the pressing issue of unemployment. The debate around IG Metall's 32-hour initiative has largely been about finding a symbol that will help revitalize the labour movement, and the business resistance has in part been linked to the role of WTR as a symbol of trade union power. At the same time, some critics see WTR as a symbol of a declining German work ethic. Chancellor Kohl, for instance, maintained, "A successful industrial nation—which means a nation with a future—does not organize itself as a collective amusement park."[56] Yet with his 1998 defeat at the polls it now appears that Kohl is the one without a future.

THE NETHERLANDS: WORK-TIME REDUCTION IN EUROPE'S NEW ECONOMIC MODEL

Share your jobs. There's so much to do in life, apart from work.

Henk Krull, Dutch trade union leader

By the late 1990s the Netherlands was being widely hailed as a new economic model for Europe due to its unemployment rate (3.4 per cent in April 1999), low inflation, sound public finances, competitive firms, low inequality, and preservation of social protections.[57] This stood in marked contrast to the early 1980s, when the expression the "Dutch disease" was common and one observer called the Netherlands "perhaps the most spectacular employment failure in the advanced capitalist world."[58] WTR has been a key part of the Dutch turnaround, both through collective reductions of standard hours and an increase of individualized "part-time" options. Employees in the Netherlands now have, by some estimates, the shortest average annual work hours in the industrial world. In 1970 Dutch employees worked an average of roughly 1,800 hours per year, decreasing to 1,530 hours in 1983 and 1,397 hours in 1995.[59]

Compared to France and Italy, where employers' groups reacted angrily to 35-hour initiatives, the Netherlands has experienced a relatively co-operative WTR process. Since the economic crisis of the early 1980s, government, business, and labour have reached a broad consensus on most elements of economic policy. WTR has been a central part of this consensus, although the work-time debate has changed considerably. Most noticeably, the emphasis has shifted from collective reductions of work time towards individualized, flexible work-time options.

The 1982 Wassenaar agreement was the turning point for the Dutch economy, which was caught in an economic vicious circle: rapidly rising unemployment, skyrocketing demands on welfare state programs, ballooning government deficits (reaching 10 per cent of GDP), rising taxes, escalating wage demands as workers sought to maintain after-tax real wages, a profit squeeze on employers who then cut workers to reduce costs, leading to yet more unemployment—eventually peaking at 12 per cent.[60] A key element of the Wassenaar consensus was wage moderation aimed at restoring profitability. To make this acceptable to workers, companies agreed to a shorter workweek—a labour demand they had bitterly opposed. From 1983 to 1986 the workweek was reduced from 40 to 38 hours (a significant 5 per cent drop in hours, often taken as an additional day off per month). The shift generally came without a decline in nominal wages, but due to inflation real wages did fall over the period by about 9 per cent on average. One result was a significant increase in the profitability of Dutch firms—which was, in fact, the intention, one that the labour unions had also accepted as necessary.[61]

A second phase of workweek reduction began in 1993. By 1996 half the sectors in the economy—and about half the workforce—had moved to a 36-hour week. During this phase WTR had less to do with creating jobs and more to do with giving employers greater flexibility and workers more free time.[62] Some sectors and firms have gone further, to 35 or 34 hours. It also became common in both the public and private sectors to hire workers under age 26 for 32 hours per week to maximize youth hiring.[63]

Alongside collective reductions in standard work hours came a dramatic increase in part-time work. Between 1983 and 1996 the percentage of employees working part-time increased from 21 per cent to 36.5 per cent, giving employment rates a substantial boost. This high rate of part-time labour will undoubtedly alarm many progressives in North America, who tend to see part-time as a reflection of inadequate employment opportunities. The part-time work is also highly concentrated among women—75 per cent of the part-time jobs are held by women—raising concerns about gender inequity.[64]

"Part-time" in the Netherlands, however, is very different from "part-time" in North America. The Dutch consider 35 hours or less per week to be "part-time." In Canada, where 30 hours a week divides full-time and part-time work, many people holding "long part-time" jobs—

such as a four-day, 32-hour week—are considered "full-time." Also, a 1996 Netherlands law makes employer discrimination between part-time and full-time employees illegal: employers have to provide equal treatment—in pay conditions, benefits, and employment opportunities.[65] Individuals have also gained expanded rights to choose part-time work. A majority of collective agreements now give individual workers the right to reduce their hours.[66] These measures have contributed both to the growth of part-time work and the low level of involuntary part-time. A 1996 study found that only 6 per cent of Dutch part-timers said they wanted a full-time job but could not find one, versus 37 per cent in France.[67] There has been much discussion in France about *"temps-partiel choisi"* (chosen part-time), but the Netherlands has done a much better job of ensuring that part-time is really *"choisi"* and not *"subi"* (imposed).

Compared to employers in other nations, Dutch firms have been relatively open to WTR. While pointing out that the "reduction of working hours is no 'panacea,'" the Confederation of Netherlands Industry and Employers (VNO-NCW) reckoned in 1998 that the "reduction of work hours might be one of the ingredients in a mix of policy measures."[68]

From Collective to Individual Reductions of Work Time

After the reduction to 38 hours in the 1980s, Dutch employers increasingly resisted further collective WTR. In the 1990s, as unemployment fell, employers' fears of labour shortages for certain jobs rose. Firms also became concerned about organizational problems if greater work-time flexibility and the extension of operating hours did not accompany further work-time cuts. In some cases employers tried to undo previously agreed reductions of work time. While resisting further collective reductions of the workweek, employers remained relatively open to the idea of a voluntary, individual choice of shorter hours, which they maintained could respond to employee's desires for more free time while giving them the work-time flexibility they want.[69]

The labour movement also shifted its emphasis towards individualized WTR. It put demands for further collective cuts to work time on the backburner in favour of extending voluntary individual options—a change partly due to increasing employer resistance to collective reductions and the increasing desire of both employers and employees for flexibility in work-time arrangements. Another factor has been the growing pressure from some workers for wage increases after years of salary moderation. In response, one 1997 collective agreement gave workers the choice between an additional eight days off (twelve if the employer decided on the timing) and a 3.2 per cent wage increase. Lower unemployment has also made it more difficult to achieve rank-and-file consensus on the need for WTR.[70]

In the late 1990s the Netherlands' "purple coalition" of social democrats and free-market liberals had no plans to follow France and Italy by legislating further WTR. But in April 1997 the government did introduce a new career breaks bill, similar to leaves policies pioneered in Denmark. The bill would give any Dutch employee the right to unemployment benefits while taking a caregiving or study leave, on the condition that the employer consented and hired an unemployed person for the same period. The net cost to the government budget would be kept to zero, due to the savings created through hiring the unemployed and a 900 guilder (C$630) per month limit on benefits.[71]

Another proposal before parliament for "Right to Part-Time" legislation would guarantee all workers the choice of reducing their work hours, with a proportional reduction in pay. An employer could only refuse the request based on strong organizational grounds. The bill would also make it easier for part-time workers to extend their hours, if they want to do so. The measure was originally proposed by the opposition Green-Left party, but was later integrated into the government's "work and care bill," which would also include the right to ten days of paid leave per year for the care of family members. Despite opposition from employers and divided opinions among labour, the bill was expected to become law in 1999 or 2000.[72]

The Green-Left's promotion of the right to shorter work hours has been motivated by two main concerns—employment creation and gender equality—and with falling unemployment, gender issues have become increasingly prominent in the discussion. After years of persistent calls by feminists for a more equal distribution of household tasks, it has become increasingly "fashionable" for men to play a greater role in the raising of children—although women continue to be mainly responsible for unpaid household labour. Indeed, in 1997 the Minister of the Economy took pains to excuse himself from a parliamentary debate to get home for his daughter's birthday. The Green-Left has hoped that the "right to part-time" would further this trend by creating opportunities for men to participate more fully in family and household duties, while at the same time helping to meet the work-time needs of women.[73]

Since the mid-1990s the government has promoted a "combination" scenario in which both parents with young children would work roughly 75 per cent of their normal hours, allowing both to participate in child care and reducing the need for day care. These "1.5-job" arrangements have become increasingly common—supported by the explicit promotion of "long part-time" jobs between 28 and 32 hours for both men and women, and regardless of the level of skill and function.[74] By the late 1990s one in five Dutch men was working part-time—still far less than the rate for women, but high by international comparison. The FNV labour confederation launched a campaign at the beginning of the decade to encourage men to consider working part-time, with slogans like, "Good morning, I'm your father." These efforts appear to have been successful in breaking the stigma attached to male part-time work. Richard Wieland, a Dutch doctor with three children and a four-day week, was asked if part-time work and less money made him less of a man. "No, not less of a man, but maybe more human," replied Dr. Wieland.[75]

Surprisingly, the Green-Left has not emphasized the ecological side of its WTR proposals. Although some party members have been interested in that link, the complexity of the issue makes it more difficult to communicate than a focus on jobs and gender issues. Nevertheless, ecological values have been, at least indirectly, at play. One factor in the acceptance of significant WTR in the Netherlands has been a rejection on the part of many people of consumerist values. In the 1990s the Netherlands, along with Denmark, topped the ranks of countries with the greatest presence of "postmaterialist values." Employees in those same two countries not only had among the shortest work hours, but also showed the greatest preference among EU nations for even fewer work hours rather than more income.[76]

The Threat of the 24-Hour Economy

A wide consensus exists among government, business, and labour in the Netherlands that increased work-time flexibility can benefit both employers and employees. However, some people have warned of the costs to workers and society.

In 1998 Dutch churches, supported by a wide coalition including environmental organizations, launched a high-profile "Action Against the 24-Hour Economy" to prevent the further extension of business opening hours and the loss of collective time rhythms. The churches pointed, for example, to the damage to family life that occurred when it was no longer possible to bring all members of a family together at the same time because of evening and weekend work. With a slogan of "Take Time to Live," the campaign sought to resist the increasing domination of economic logic over other values.[77] The effort highlighted, once again, the importance of the quality of free time, and of when that time is available.

The concern over flexibility and longer business hours, along with the high levels of (largely female) part-time work, indicates that the Dutch model is not without its controversies. Some critics, on both left and right, question the official unemployment numbers and Dutch success more generally.[78] The official numbers ignore, for instance, the extremely high numbers of people receiving "disabled" benefits—although as disguised forms of unemployment go, this is certainly preferable to the U.S. model of stockpiling people in prison. Yet no one can seriously doubt that impressive employment creation has occurred since the 1980s. The job-creation rate averaged 1.8 per cent per year in 1985-95, higher than the 1.5 per cent rate in the United States and much higher than the 0.4 per cent average in the European Union.[79] Perhaps the greatest concern is that the combined package of wage gains and WTR has not kept pace with increases in labour productivity. The result has been a shift in income shares from labour to capital and some "export" of unemployment to other European countries where combined wage and work-time gains have been greater. In 1998, however, Dutch labour unions, in a positive change of course, joined others from Germany, Belgium, and Luxembourg in a commitment to bargain for a combined package that keeps pace with productivity.[80]

Despite its flaws, with its innovative WTR measures—such as the emerging right to shorter work hours—and its high rate of postmaterialist values, the Netherlands could be well-positioned as a trailblazer for a green vision of working less, consuming less, and living more.

DENMARK: LEADING THE WAY ON LEAVES FOR SOCIAL AND FAMILY NEEDS

By the late 1990s Denmark had one of the lowest average annual work hours per employee in Europe—1,568 versus a European Union average of 1,671—and one of the lowest unemployment rates, at 4.6 per cent in July 1998. The standard workweek, regulated by collective agreements, was 37 hours, while all employees had won the right to five weeks' paid holiday.[81]

But Denmark stands out mainly for being a pioneer in leave policies. Since 1994 all employees have been able to take educational, parental, and personal sabbatical leaves of up to one year, subject to the agreement of their employers. While they are away employees can receive unemployment benefits: 100 per cent of regular benefits for educational leave, 60 per cent for parental and sabbatical leave. The parental leave option gives both mothers and fathers the choice of spending up to a year at home for each child under eight, in addition to a relatively generous regular maternity and paternity leave. A worker can also take a sabbatical for any purpose, as long as the company hires an unemployed person as a replacement. That policy, in

A cartoonist's view of the 1998 Danish strike for a sixth week of vacation.

effect, amounts to an exchange of wages and unemployment benefits between someone with and someone without a job. These programs have proved popular, with 121,000 people taking leaves in 1996. Rather than simply paying people to be unemployed, the programs use government funds to create new job openings for the unemployed while establishing learning and living opportunities for the already employed. Since the introduction of these "job-rotation" measures, the number of long-term unemployed has been cut in half.[82]

In spring 1998 Denmark was rocked by a nationwide general strike (and lockouts) over worker demands for a sixth week of paid vacation. The dispute, which lasted 11 days and closed down transportation, food, and fuel systems before the social-democratic government imposed a settlement, cost the Danish economy an estimated $200 million per day. With fuel in short supply, bikes were suddenly more numerous on the road than cars. In the end each worker was granted two more days off per year, while those with children under 14 gained an additional two days in 1998 and one more in 1999. The full introduction of a sixth week of paid holidays remained a key union bargaining demand.[83]

Although to some critics striking for a sixth week of vacation may seem excessive, the Danish workers' demands for more free time were not only a justifiable attempt to share in the country's recent economic success but also an enlightened choice of putting time over money as the way to take that share. As Kete Persson, a 24-year-old lab assistant, put it, "Everyone is talking about the good economic results in Denmark. As for me, I want my share in the form of free time." Denmark's progressive tax system may have contributed to making time a more attractive choice than money. According to Persson, "I'm satisfied with my salary. We have enough to live on without problem. And if I got more money, that would mean paying more taxes."[84]

Family and gender issues have also been a key part of the Danish work-time debate. A main force behind the demand for more free time in the 1998 strikes was the federation of female labourers (KAD), a century-old, all-female union with 100,000 members. While the strikers called for an additional week's vacation, KAD wanted 20 more days. The demand for more free time is an "absolute priority," according to one KAD member.[85] Denmark has a high labour-market participation rate for both women (75 per cent) and men (83 per cent), and Danish men, it is said, participate more in family life than in most countries. These factors contribute to the widespread support for more time away from the job. Although existing family-leave and child-care policies in Denmark are far more advanced than in countries like Canada, "More free time and time off to spend with children are at the top of the Danish agenda."[86]

The Danish government announced a new "family-friendly" policy initiative in June 1998. Along with business and labour, the government planned to explore issues such as creating more flexible and family-friendly workplaces, expanding access to part-time work, making it easier for individuals to shift back and forth between full-time and part-time work, improving part-time conditions, and making family considerations an integral part of company personnel policy.[87] One option is to add flexibility to parental leaves. Workers have only had a choice between full-time work and full-time leave. One trade union proposal would give parents the option of full-time leave or varying degrees of part-time work combined with partial paid leave. This wider range of options could increase the number of men—who now account for only 8-10 per cent of those on parental leave—choosing to take time off for parenting. More flexible parental leave would represent an example of flexibility in the interests of workers, or "time sovereignty."[88]

Unlike the debates in many other European countries, Danish work-time discussions do not include job creation as a major theme. Despite having both low work hours and low unemployment, the country has seen relatively little support for WTR as a job creator. This is the case even among the labour unions, which favour growth-oriented strategies to create jobs. Instead, they value WTR as a way to improve the quality of life of workers and to meet social and family needs.[89] On the one hand, the emphasis on more free time reflects Denmark's relatively strong "postma-terialist" values[90] and is very much in line with an alternative, green vision of progress. On the other, Denmark does not seem to have made a clear break with productivist growth strategies as the way to maintain high levels of employment.

OTHER EUROPEAN NATIONS

Belgium

Belgium has perhaps the greatest variety of WTR policies. In 1995 its public-sector workers were given the right to choose a four-day week to create openings for new hiring. Their four days' pay is topped up with a flat-rate allowance, so that they continue to receive roughly 90 per cent of their former pay. Some 7,000 employees, 8 per cent of the public work-force, were participating by the end of the first year of the program.[91] New recruits to the public service also work a four-day week in their first year of employment. To encourage the shift to part-time work, part-timers are entitled to the same social security rights as full-time workers. The government has encouraged phased-in retirement by allowing employees over 55 to work half-time and receive half their pensions.[92]

Private-sector employers and employees are encouraged to choose shorter hours through financial incentives. For instance, for the 1997-98 collective bargaining round the government reduced employers' social security payroll taxes by 150,000 Belgian francs (C$5,712) to help offset the cost of each newly created job, if two of the following conditions were met in negotiated agreements: collective reduction of work hours, part-time work on a voluntary basis, partial retirement, flexible work sched-ules, additional training, and temporary leave or career breaks.[93]

Like employees in Denmark, Belgian workers are encouraged to take career breaks of between three months to one year. The employee on leave receives a payment of roughly 12,066 Belgian francs (C$460) per month, while the employer gets a payroll tax reduction if an unemployed worker is hired as a replacement. Employees can also take part-time career breaks, with full-time workers moving to part-time and receiving a monthly income top-up from the government. As of December 1996, 19,973 employees were taking full-time leave, while 32,470 had opted for the part-time option.[94]

Under the "Vande Lanotte plan," firms in difficulty became eligible for a reduction of payroll taxes for two years if they brought in a 32-hour week to avoid planned layoffs. The firms have to compensate workers for at least part of the loss of earnings. The plan was extended to allow "healthy" companies to draw on it when they created jobs through shorter hours. The first company to take advantage was Labatt's parent company Interbrew, which cut the workweek at one of its breweries from 37 to 32 hours in spring 1998 to avoid layoffs.[95]

Belgium's first sectoral agreement on a 35-hour week came in December 1997 in electricity. According to the agreement, by 2002 the industry would introduce a standard of 35 hours. Some 300 new jobs would be created and a planned hiring of 1,000 workers sped up. In return wages would be frozen until 2002. One union leader praised the deal for taking workers "one train-stop nearer the 32-hour station." The difficult choice of a wage freeze in return for shorter hours and new hiring was supported by 88 per cent of the workers.[96] Also in 1997, Volkswagen's Brussels factory reduced its weekly hours from 36 to 35 with no loss in pay, along with introducing a 32-hour week—with an 8.5 per cent cut in pay—on a voluntary basis for night-shift workers. A spring 1999 agreement at the Bayer chemicals plant in Antwerp brought a major breakthrough: a 33.6-hour workweek with a five-shift system, enabling 160 jobs to be saved. Unions hoped to introduce the system sector-wide, with the goal of creating up to 1,000 jobs.[97]

After neighbouring France announced its 35-hour legislation, Belgium's debate on WTR grew more intense. In October 1997 prominent trade union and academic figures launched an appeal, "35 hours in Belgium too." The main trade union confederations and francophone Socialist Party were even more ambitious, endorsing a four-day, 32-hour week. Employers, in contrast, resisted a general reduction of work time and urged greater work-time flexibility.[98]

Finland
By the time the demand for 35-hour legislation spread to Finland in 1998, some innovative work-time policies were already in effect. Some 20 municipalities, and a number of private firms, were experimenting with six-hour days, with second shifts added to increase service to the public. Experience showed that extra costs for recruitment and wages were offset by increased productivity.[99] Since 1994 a "part-time supplement" has compensated employees for half the wages lost when they reduce their work time from anywhere between 40 to 60 per cent for one year, so long

as the employer in question agrees and an unemployed person is hired to the same position. In 1996 the country launched a sabbatical program similar to the Danish approach, with positive results. In 1998 Prime Minister Paavo Lipponen put work in its place and made history at the same time, becoming the first man in a Finnish government to take a week's parental leave to care for his newborn child.[100]

Italy

In October 1997, only a few days after the French announcement, Italy too declared that it would legislate a 35-hour week. The draft legislative package unveiled in March 1998 was more of a package of incentives and disincentives than a legislated imposition of shorter hours. The "normal" workweek would be reduced from 40 to 35 hours by January 1, 2001, for all firms with more than 15 employees. Payroll taxes would be trimmed for firms that reduced hours, with additional incentives for creating jobs or avoiding layoffs. Firms would be able to keep an "ordinary" workweek of up to 40 hours, but payroll taxes would be increased on hours above 35. Only the hours over 40 would be considered overtime and require premium pay in addition to the higher payroll taxes. The incentives for shorter hours would be offered to all firms, regardless of size, starting in 1998, while the penalties for long hours would apply only to firms with more than 15 employees after 2001. The effect of the "experimental" incentives would be evaluated by November 2000, with revisions following if necessary.[101]

Under this proposal, a 35-hour week would not be legally binding. The 35 hours would simply serve as a reference point for applying incentives and disincentives. As in France, the law left the key issue of salary levels up to negotiations between employers and employees. The design of the law indicated the government's goal of not undermining its dialogue on economic policy with business and labour, while at the same time trying to maintain its parliamentary majority. It was due to pressure from the far-left Rifondazione Comunista, which demanded a legislated 35-hour week with no loss in pay as the price of parliamentary support, that the centre-left government originally made its 35-hour commitment. The French move, which opened up the possibility of a European-wide WTR effort, was another factor in convincing Italy's government to act.

By mid-1999 the Italian parliament had yet to give final approval to the 35-hour law, and it was unclear if and when this step would take place. But the government did enact new limits on overtime in November 1998: upper limits of 80 hours every three months and 250 hours per year,

Workers in Brescia, Italy, demonstrate for shorter
work hours, 1997.

along with a provision to make all overtime work voluntary for employees. The government has aimed to respect the autonomy of collective bargaining as much as possible, so these measures only apply where collective
agreements do not cover these issues. Managers must also inform local
labour offices within 24 hours if weekly work hours exceed 45. Firms
violating the standards face increased fines, paid into a jobs fund used to
create financial incentives for shorter work time. The government also
proposed financial incentives to promote "relay part-time," whereby
workers nearing retirement shift to part-time work and the hours freed up
are used to hire a young worker under the age of 32.[102]

Italian business leaders have been hostile to the 35-hour project,
despite the mildness and flexibility of the proposed law. The labour
unions have supported the objective of WTR and legislation that would
promote the negotiated reductions of hours, but have resisted any law
that would take decisions over work hours out of the realm of collective
bargaining.[103]

Away from the confrontation of "political theatre," a number of Italian firms reduced work hours in the 1990s, often by linking shorter hours for individuals with longer operating hours for capital. An important example came in June 1998, when a new collective agreement was reached in the chemicals industry. The deal cut the workweek from 40 to 37.75 hours, while allowing weekly schedules to vary between 28 and 48 hours according to the firms' requirements. An "hours bank" was introduced in which workers could accumulate overtime, with 50 per cent of overtime to be paid and the other 50 per cent used for days off or attending training courses. Weekly hours between 28 and 32, with an equivalent reduction in pay, could also be applied to newly hired workers to maximize job creation in regions with high unemployment. Both labour and employers in the sector welcomed the agreement, but the national employers' federation was highly critical and hoped to prevent the idea of WTR from spreading.[104]

In July 1998 new collective agreements were reached for employees of Italy's ministries and state-controlled bodies. A 35-hour week without loss in pay was announced for certain categories of employees—shift workers, counter staff dealing with the public, and museum employees, for instance. In return, public services and facilities such as museums and art galleries would extend their operating hours into evening—travellers who have found themselves repeatedly locked out of closed Italian museums will appreciate the revolutionary nature of this change. Although the shorter workweek would cover only a limited number of workers, it was a further sign of movement towards 35 hours as a new norm.[105] Italy's commitment to a 35-hour week has not been as strong as France's, but Italy has nevertheless taken some important steps forward.

Sweden

WTR policies in Sweden have focused mainly on meeting the social and family needs of working people, rather than on job creation. As one review pointed out, "Hours cuts are seen primarily as a means of furthering workers' well-being and indirectly also a means of furthering equality between the sexes, as it makes it easier for both men and women to combine gainful employment and parenthood."[106]

Sweden has among the lowest annual work hours of any major industrialized country. Like many other European countries, Swedish workers are entitled by law to at least five weeks' paid vacation, but, like its neighbour Denmark, Sweden especially stands out in the areas of parental and educational leaves. Parental-leave provisions entitle both parents to full-time leave from work until the child in question is 18 months old. Parents also have the right to choose to work 75 per cent of their normal hours until children are eight years old or have completed the first year of school, with partial compensation for the loss of earnings. In 1998 the government proposed a new law guaranteeing parents the right to leave for urgent family reasons such as sickness or accident.[107]

Since 1975 all Swedish employees have had the right to full-time leaves of absence or part-time work to pursue educational opportunities. Upon their return employees are guaranteed the right to take up a position that has the same working conditions and employment terms as in their previous job. This has greatly encouraged skills upgrading, because employees have job security while they leave to study. To further enhance access to education, widespread agreement exists on creating educational accounts that workers can draw on during leaves, although business and labour disagree on the form those accounts should take.[108]

Swedish work hours began increasing gradually in the 1980s. They had previously been, by some estimations, the lowest in the OECD.[109] The trend may now be starting downward again. Collective bargaining in 1998 led to important WTR breakthroughs. In addition to pay increases averaging 3 per cent per year, almost all agreements contained new provisions on the length and organization of work time. In engineering, Sweden's largest industrial sector, the workweek was reduced by 30 minutes—an apparently small amount, but the kind of annual change that can make a big difference over a number of years. Some agreements reduced work time by 27 hours per year, but left it to the parties at the company level or to individual employers and employees to decide whether this reduction should lead to a shorter workweek, longer holidays, or possibly even early retirement. Other agreements left it to local parties to choose between WTR and an increase in pay. In return for WTR, work-hour scheduling became somewhat more flexible.[110]

Sweden's Social Democratic party has favoured WTR as a way to improve the lives of workers, but it has preferred to leave the matter to collective bargaining. The Social Democrats, re-elected in September 1998, had to rely on parliamentary support from the Left Party and the Greens, both strong advocates of 35-hour legislation, resulting in a hot debate over the future of work-time policy.[111]

United Kingdom
Continental European workers once longed to catch up to England's ten-hour day. In 1883 Lafargue bemoaned the fact that the English had

proven the benefits of limiting work hours, "yet the French nation is not convinced."[112] The tables have since turned. Despite a few break-throughs, including a 37-hour week in the engineering industry, the United Kingdom has become one of Europe's work-time laggards, standing out for its minimal work-time regulation and earning the label of the continent's "long-hours capital." The EU's Working Time Directive of 1993, which included a maximum standard workweek of 48 hours, a minimum four weeks' paid vacation, and a maximum eight hours for night shifts, finally came into effect in 1998 under the Labour government of Tony Blair. Yet Britain was still the only EU country to allow even the minimal 48-hour regulation to be ignored if employees gave written consent to "opt-out." By 1998 an estimated 3.5 million British workers had jobs exceeding the 48-hour maximum standard, and a similar number were working night shifts longer than the EU's eight-hour limit.[113]

In response to the 1996 EU Parental Leave Directive, the Labour government planned to introduce unpaid parental-leave legislation. A coalition of trade unions and child-care organizations launched a campaign in November 1998 for the new parental leave to be paid so that workers could, in practice, afford to take it.[114] The lack of time parents have with their children has also contributed to another British problem: bad sex. According to the *British Medical Journal*, British teenagers have the worst sexual health in Europe, with extremely high rates of sexually transmitted diseases and teenage pregnancies. Reasons cited include Britain's poor record in education, high rate of poverty, and parents never being there for their children because they're too busy putting in the longest hours in Europe.[115]

Portugal, Spain, and Greece

WTR has not been limited to the more economically advanced nations of Northern Europe. In Portugal the workweek was reduced from 48 hours to 44 hours in 1991, followed by a legislated 40-hour standard in 1997. Portugal, the EU's poorest country, now has a stronger workweek standard than many Canadian provinces.[116] In neighbouring Spain, labour unions launched a concerted campaign in 1998 for French-style 35-hour legislation. The government and employers resisted the idea of WTR at the national level, but a flurry of initiatives took place at regional levels in 1998. Andalucia, the Community of Madrid, and Catalonia all announced subsidies for firms that created jobs by reducing work hours—in Catalonia, for example, through a 40 per cent reduction of employers' social security contributions for each new job created. Andalucia, Madrid, and Extremadura all committed to introducing a 35-hour week for their public employees.[117] Similarly, a 35-hour movement emerged in Greece, bearing fruit in September 1998 with the first company-level deal for a 35-hour week without loss in pay.[118]

ASSESSING THE EUROPEAN EXPERIENCE

In the 1990s, while European work-time standards were already relatively advanced compared to North America, a new European dynamic in favour of WTR appeared to be gaining steam. For many Europeans WTR stands out as a symbol of hope. For some it has become "the key to a social Europe" that would defeat unemployment and avoid a U.S.-style erosion of the social fabric. As in the case of ecological tax reform, Europe has the potential to become an important space for the evolution of another promising idea: WTR.

Despite commonalities, the debate on work time varies considerably from country to country. Different emphases are given to a shorter work-week, longer vacations, and leaves, or other possibilities, and different combinations of policy tools have been used to achieve them, resulting in a rich and varied range of work-time options. The two main historical motivations for WTR—creating jobs and establishing time away from the job—also play differing roles in the debate. France, Germany, and Italy have focused largely on creating jobs while Denmark and Sweden have emphasized the value of time away from work. Gender equity issues also play an important role in certain countries. The current push for WTR has come largely from left-of-centre political forces and the labour movement, with some exceptions, such as France's Robien Law, initiated by right-of-centre governments. In many cases employers have been able to see the benefits of WTR, often when it is linked to increased work-time flexibility and longer operating hours for capital.

Ecological motivations for WTR have played a role, although they have not been at the forefront of the discussion. Europe's Green parties have been persistent advocates of a 35-hour and even 30-hour week, but nowhere has there yet been a widespread embrace of a green vision of WTR in which growth of production is permanently downplayed in favour of the growth of free time. Governments led by "social-democratic productivists" in France, Italy, and elsewhere have favoured both WTR and more expansionary policies to promote growth. They appear to favour WTR not so much as a means of expanding growth—although some people make that case—but reason that growth alone is not enough to reduce unemployment. Even green advocates of WTR find it easier to focus on the employment, quality of life, and gender angles than to raise the more complex ecological issues. At the same time, the growth of post-materialist values in Denmark and the Netherlands is without doubt closely related to high support for WTR. These values were evident, for instance, in Denmark's 1998 strike, in which the nation was turned upside down over the demand, not for wages, but for more free time.

History shows that progress on WTR can occur in great, international leaps forward—as with the spread of the eight-hour day in 1917-19. It is too early to tell where the new wave of demands and initiatives for WTR in Europe will lead, but there are solid grounds for hope that we could well be experiencing another great historical moment of advance on this vital front.

JOSEPH HENZ

"I assume you don't approve of our new salary cuts, Ms. Smitt."

8 | With or without Loss in Pay? With or without the Revolution?

Capitalism has abolished everything in tradition, in the mode of life, in everyday civilization, that might serve as anchorage for a common norm of sufficiency; and has abolished at the same time the prospect that choosing to work and consume less might give access to a better, freer life. What has been abolished is not, however, impossible to re-establish.

André Gorz, "Political Ecology: Expertocracy versus Self-Limitation," 1993

The historic movement for WTR has seen two especially prominent issues: the question of payment—whether workers should be able to work fewer hours for the same pay—and, indeed, whether the full promise of WTR can be realized within capitalism.

The challenge on the question of wage compensation is to find a way to bridge the gap between employers and employees. Labour has traditionally sought WTR with no loss in pay and tends to resist any suggestion that workers make do with less income. Business resists changes that threaten to drive up hourly labour costs. As a result, we might expect business to be open to the idea of shorter hours only if the employees receive a proportionate cut in pay. Even then, business concerns about fixed benefit costs come to the fore.

There are a number of possible ways to bridge this gap. Business could be forced to cover the costs by cutting into profit shares. Productivity gains from a variety of sources could finance shorter hours without loss in pay. Governments could intervene, perhaps by rewarding businesses that reduce hours or by topping up the incomes of employees who work fewer hours. Or workers themselves could accept a loss in pay in return for working fewer hours.

Clearly, the dramatic reduction of work time within capitalism in the past two centuries illustrates that the system can adapt to WTR. Yet when WTR becomes part of a more comprehensive green challenge to productivism—a challenge that goes to the heart of the system's expansionary dynamics—the ability of capitalism to adapt becomes less clear. In a world in which social and ecological goals are constantly sidelined by the pursuit of short-term profit, does it still make sense to make WTR the focus of a political movement? Is the struggle not one of a higher order, requiring at a minimum the re-establishment of a "kinder, gentler" capital-labour compromise or perhaps going beyond capitalism altogether?

MAKING BUSINESS PAY

Worker mobilization and/or government legislation could make business pay the full cost of WTR by cutting into profit shares. In Europe, parties (like the French Communist Party and Italy's Rifondazione Comunista) and labour unions further to the left (like France's CGT) favour this option. Employers, not surprisingly, are not enthusiastic about this scenario, and their resistance to WTR more generally often appears to be based on fears of such an outcome. With wages in many countries, including Canada, lagging behind the growth of corporate profits, an argument can certainly be made that labour should get a larger share of those profits. But given the prevailing balance of economic power, this goal would not seem to be attainable in any more than a handful of workplaces—at best—in Canada. In the short term, at least, other options are more likely to play a role in resolving the question of how to pay for WTR.

THE "MAGIC" OF PRODUCTIVITY GAINS

Productivity increases can be the magic wand that eliminates the need for either capital or labour to make sacrifices, making it possible to reduce hours and protect incomes without undermining company profitability or competitiveness. Annual productivity increases based on improvements to work organization, improvements in workers' skills, and the introduction of labour-saving technologies have become a matter of course. Assuming that productivity grows at a moderate rate of 2 per cent per year, and that employers and employees share equitably in those gains, workers can get work-time reductions of 2 per cent per year with no loss in total remuneration and without increasing unit labour costs. (While a 2 per cent reduction of work time may not seem like much, it would equal an extra week's vacation for someone working 40 hours a week, 50 weeks a year.) Jeremy Rifkin has argued that much more rapid increases in labour productivity will come about as information technologies and automation work their way through the economy, although his predictions would seem to be exaggerated. Some analysts argue that, on the contrary, the increasing share in the economy of service employment, with its low productivity gains, will dampen overall productivity growth.[1]

Average annual productivity growth in 11 major industrialized nations fell from 4.6 per cent in the 1960s to 1.9 per cent in the 1990s. In Canada the corresponding figures showed a decline from an average of 2.6 per cent in 1961-69 to 0.9 per cent in 1990-96. In 1998 Canada experienced low labour productivity growth of 0.7 percent, although the rate was 2.9 percent in 1997. Considerable debate surrounds the question of whether these low rates are a sign of more to come, the result of statistics failing to capture productivity gains in the service sector, or simply a lull before new information technologies are harnessed to full effect.[2] In any case, even if we are not able, as yet, to determine future trends on productivity increases, we can consider these questions: how should productivity increases be shared between labour and capital, and how much of labour's share should go to higher wages versus shorter hours? Certainly, to avoid growing inequalities, labour should at least be getting its "fair share" of productivity gains. For example, 2 per cent productivity growth merits at least a 2 per cent pay increase or a 2 per cent reduction in work time with the same remuneration. And just as certainly, greens should be calling for all, or very close to all, productivity gains to be directed to shorter hours rather than higher wages.

The use of productivity increases to finance WTR rather than wage increases has been an essential element of recent European experience. In the Netherlands, the reduction of standard hours in the 1980s and 1990s did not reduce real wages over that period as a whole, but workers did accept the principle of wage moderation. In France and Italy it was expected that productivity gains over a few years would go largely to finance the introduction of a 35-hour week rather than salary hikes.

*Linking Work-Time Reduction with Flexibility and Work
Reorganization*

WTR can allow for a more efficient use of both labour and capital when it
is linked to greater work-time flexibility and longer operating hours. The
improvement in productivity can respond to business demands and make
WTR possible with little or no loss in pay—a crucial element in the
European experience of the 1980s and 1990s.[3] That trade-off may at first
be seductive, and may even be worthwhile in some cases, but if the goal is
to improve the quality of life and create employment in an ecologically
sound way the approach has potential pitfalls.

Greater work-time flexibility and work reorganization can in some
cases benefit both employers and employees. For example, part-time work
chosen by workers rather than imposed on them (and protected by strong
legislated standards) can give workers what they want while allowing
employers greater scheduling flexibility. Similarly, business can make positive and creative use of work-time schedules. A retail chain in France, for
instance, linked a four-day week, for most of the year, with new hiring,
which gave the firm more trained, permanent employees to work five-day
weeks during the pre-Christmas rush.[4]

Experience shows, though, that extreme flexibility on the employer's
terms can undermine the benefits of shorter work time for workers, leading to an increase in the number of "unsocial hours" worked on nights
and weekends as well as to increasingly variable hours. This reduces the
value of free time and makes it more difficult for families and friends to
synchronize desired or necessary activities.[5] Indeed, concerns over work-
time flexibility concessions have been a greater controversy in the first
phase of France's 35-hour implementation than wage levels. Fewer total
hours in compensation for more unsocial hours do not necessarily lead to
an improvement in welfare. When it comes to time, quality can be equally
or more important than quantity.

Concessions regarding flexibility can also reduce WTR's job-creation
effect. A prime objective of employers who seek work-time flexibility is to
reduce the need for labour by scheduling it more profitably.[6] Employers
want to pay for labour only at those times when they can make full use of
it, in order to produce a given output with as little total labour input as
possible. For example, the Dutch firm Niemeyer Tobacco introduced an
average 36-hour week in return for increased flexibility over the year and
longer weekly operating hours. In peak periods employees moved to 45
hours a week (five days of nine hours), but worked only 27 hours (three
days of nine hours) in slack periods.[7] Another benefit for employers is the

reduction of overtime costs that occurs when work-time calculations are averaged over periods longer than a week, resulting in long workweeks without overtime premiums because they are balanced off by shorter weeks at another time. The potential for employment creation through such measures is more indirect, based on lowering costs, enhancing competitiveness, and expanding output.[8] Although measures like these may give firms a competitive boost in international markets, they are not an adequate long-term solution. Competitors elsewhere eventually realize they must take the same action as well, and ultimately no one gains. We can end up in a situation in which everyone in the stadium has stood up, but no one has a better view. This is the logic of "workers of the world, compete."

The strategy of trading work-time flexibility and longer operating hours in return for WTR seems to have more in common with a productivist approach—by paying for WTR through more production—than a green vision. Although these kinds of attempts to achieve WTR with little or no loss in pay may appear to be an attractive option, they could undermine the achievement of goals with respect to jobs, the environment, and quality of life. With both employers and workers applying pressures for greater work-time flexibility, albeit on their own terms, we can't entirely avoid the issue, but we should at least be aware of the dangers.

FINANCIAL SUPPORT FROM THE STATE

Government financial support can also help bridge the employer-employee gap. The revenue could come from the savings to the public due to the jobs that WTR itself creates. Another source of revenue can be the taxation of overtime, which has the double benefit of creating a disincentive to long hours. Some interesting possibilities also exist for linking new forms of ecological taxation to the creation of incentives for WTR.

The provision of financial support for firms that reduce hours and create jobs is a major element in WTR debates and practice in Europe, particularly in France, Belgium, Italy, and Spain. The large number of firms (some 2,000) that went to a workweek of 35 hours or less in the two years following the introduction of France's Robien Law illustrates that incentives-based measures can help bridge the gap between business and labour, making WTR breakthroughs possible. That effect will be much greater now that such incentives have been combined with 35-hour legislation, an initiative that itself was made possible largely by the experience generated by the Robien incentives. In Canada, British Columbia and Quebec have also taken some first steps in introducing positive work-time incentives. These policies hold the promise of allowing workers to experience the benefits of WTR while bearing less, if any, of the cost, and without adding excessive cost burdens to firms.

Financial incentives have also been aimed at individual employees. Examples include the choice of a four-day week for roughly 90 per cent pay in Belgium's public sector and Finland's part-time income supplement. The right to partially paid sabbaticals in Denmark, Finland, and Belgium—and also under consideration in the Netherlands—is another variation on the theme.

Work-Time Reduction and the Welfare State

Enhancing social programs could also indirectly encourage the acceptance of WTR. A more comprehensive social welfare state would allow workers to work fewer hours without experiencing greater insecurity and a deterioration of living standards, and it could also help remove incentives for employers to prefer long hours over new hiring.

The comparison between the United States, with its weak welfare state and long work hours, and the European model, with its strong welfare states and relatively short hours of work, is revealing. Susan Christopherson argues that in the United States the priority given to earnings rather than shorter hours has financed a way of life in which individuals and families rather than the state have become primarily responsible for what many Europeans would consider to be social welfare services.[9] Health-care costs, for instance, are deemed to be an individual rather than a social responsibility. For many workers this is a source of great insecurity, creating a need for long hours to ensure they can pay for emergencies, such as debilitating illnesses. For employers, at least those who have to finance health benefit plans for lucky workers with "good jobs," the result is a strong preference for longer hours over new hiring and the associated benefit burdens. A shift to universal public health care in the United States would help relieve both problems.

In Canada the idea of a national prescription drug plan re-emerged in the late 1990s.[10] It could conceivably be financed solely through funds being spent on the inefficient existing patchwork of public and private benefit plans. Like a move to universal public health care in the United States, a national drug plan in Canada would make shorter work hours more attractive to many employees by improving economic security, while also reducing employer incentives for long hours over new hiring.

Similar arguments could be made for pensions and dental, eye-care, and other benefits. Whereas the decline of social spending creates new pressures for longer hours, the expansion of public services could support the move to shorter hours. However, the financing of these programs needs to be carefully thought out. Paying for universal social benefits could require payroll taxes, which, if badly designed, might create similar disincentives to new hiring. To avoid disincentives to shorter hours, payroll taxes and benefits need to be variable rather than fixed costs per employee. For example, the Employer Health Tax in Ontario, which is a flat percentage of a total payroll, is more favourable to shorter hours than Unemployment Insurance and Canada Pension Plan contributions, which are capped at a certain level of employee income, creating an incentive for employers to work existing employees longer to avoid the contributions they would have to make for additional workers.

The question of a guaranteed annual income (GAI) also comes into play here. Many proponents of WTR argue that the project must be accompanied by an income decoupled from participation in the labour market,[11] because, despite increasing Northern production, the labour market can no longer provide adequate access to employment and income. Although it goes against the emphasis on "self-reliance," that is, the dependence on income gained in the market, some form of guaranteed income could serve as an important complement to shorter hours.

The effect of a GAI largely depends on its level. A meagre sum that barely keeps people alive will do little to provide the security needed to support the free choice of working less. A GAI also does not necessarily serve progressive ends, as illustrated by Milton Friedman's proposed version of a "negative income tax," which would provide a basic income in return for eliminating other forms of social transfers and minimum wages. Even a more generous GAI, part of a more equitable sharing of wealth, needs to be linked to a sharing of available work. Otherwise it could simply be a tool to pacify the marginalized. Guy Aznar points out that a GAI could solidify the growing social divisions between a small hyperactive elite of core workers and others who have been shut out of the standard job market. It could thus serve to "legitimize social apartheid." He argues that the real priority project for a balanced society is not only to share income, but also to share work.[12] Given a society in which employment continues to play such a central role in granting status, identity, and opportunities for self-realization, a gradual reduction of work hours for all, with some form of income guarantee, is preferable to the relatively enlightened marginalization of a GAI without the sharing of work.

As a means of allowing all members of society to stay in touch with the world of work, Aznar advocates WTR with a "second cheque" to top up the incomes of all who work fewer hours. The second cheque is based on the idea that if, due to technological advances, wealth is no longer produced principally by labour, then income can no longer come exclusively from wages and salaries. It thus represents a mechanism to redistribute the wealth produced without labour. A "part-time salary" could be provided to anyone who voluntarily goes from full-time to half-time work, which would allow 70-75 per cent of the former income to be earned, but on the condition that another half-time worker was hired. A "technological salary" could also be provided to all workers to ensure no loss of pay as hours of work are reduced throughout society.[13] Unlike a GAI, the second cheque would be clearly linked to an opportunity for all citizens to participate in the work of society. Aznar sees policies of reducing payroll taxes to firms that reduce hours, who can then afford to pass on higher hourly pay to their workers, as one possible indirect form of a "second cheque." This approach is now in practice in France.[14]

Another ambitious and visionary scheme is Swedish economist Gösta Rehn's proposal to finance WTR over the human life cycle. Rehn calls for a single comprehensive system to finance all periods of withdrawal from the labour market, whether for retirement, parenting, continuing education, vacations, sabbaticals, voluntary work, or leisure. Individuals would be entitled to a certain amount of drawing rights throughout their lives, limited only by minimums that must remain for retirement and ceilings on the amount that can be overdrawn at specific ages. People could freely choose to draw on the insurance fund in response to their own life needs and desires.

By facilitating voluntary withdrawals from employment, the Rehn model would open up new opportunities for people excluded from the workforce. At the same time, it would maximize individual choice over when to withdraw from paid labour, allowing "self- management of time" over the life cycle. This would respond to the growing diversity of individual preferences regarding time and avoid the problem of uniform or standardized reductions in work time, which may impose leisure on people when they don't want it or would find it less beneficial. It represents a form of "time sovereignty," or work-time flexibility, from the perspective of employees, enhancing a person's control of time and capacities for life planning. It would also reduce bureaucratic supervision of how people use their time while receiving income through the state. In Rehn's words, it would promote the "security of wings," not just that of the "mussel shell." The model could reduce fluctuations in employment, because leaves could be synchronized with cyclical fluctuations in demand—for example, by making the level of benefits during leaves more or less generous depending on the phase of the business cycle. In addition, given that drawing rights would still be linked to contributions, the public would most likely see the program as being more legitimate than a guaranteed annual income. These advantages suggest that some version of the Rehn model could represent, over the long run, the most promising one for a progressive time politics.[15] The paid leaves policies in Scandinavia reflect this concept in an initial phase of practice.

These proposals, ranging from minor topping up of incomes to Rehn's comprehensive plan, will have to be financed. Some of the funds could come from existing amounts spent on unemployment, but limits exist on what these sums alone can achieve. This is true in all countries, but particularly so in Canada and the United States, where unemployment benefits are relatively miserly compared to most of Europe.

ETR + WTR

If there is to be a significant sharing of both wealth and work, there will be a need for new redistributive forms of taxation. The vast speculative profits of the financial sector are one obvious place to look for new revenues, and a Tobin tax on foreign currency transactions is one possibility. Another option is to tax the gains of sectors experiencing rapid labour-productivity growth. For example, Gorz calls for the loss of salary from shorter work hours to be compensated by funds raised from a tax on automated production, comparable to a Value Added Tax (VAT) or Goods and Services Tax (GST). The rate of taxation of products would rise as their production costs decreased due to automation. One of the points in favour of such a tax is that, like a VAT or GST, it would be deductible from export costs and added to imports, so that international competitiveness would not be undermined. Gorz adds that the less socially desirable or useful the production, the higher the tax would be.[16]

Similarly, some interesting possibilities exist for linking ecological tax reform (ETR) to the financing of WTR. Jacques Robin, for example, calls for an "eco-social VAT" on certain industrial products whose growing consumption is not in the interests of society or the environment. This tax would both finance a "second cheque" and orient production according to socio-cultural and ecological criteria.[17] This could be a dynamic combination for orienting society in a more ecologically sound direction. France's Greens, proponents of both ETR and WTR, proposed exactly such a linkage as part of the 35-hour-week initiative. In 1999 the government responded by announcing that new taxes on polluting sectors—chemicals, metals, energy—would help finance the reduction of payroll taxes on low-income workers, allowing firms to reduce hours with no loss in pay.[18]

In this case, too, however, green and productivist goals could conflict. One of the arguments in favour of an ETR is that by making energy and materials more expensive and labour less costly, it would promote the *employment of human labour* over the exploitation of natural resources. This approach appears to contradict the aspirations of those whose primary objective is a utopian leisure society, based on the *replacement of human labour* with machines. Aznar, for example, advocates ecotaxes as one way of taxing enterprises to pay for WTR. At the same time he seeks a world in which the "replacement of man by the machine would no longer be slowed down by fear of unemployment, but ardently activated to increase the production of wealth and liberation of time."[19] This tension between ecological and productivist aspirations also afflicts, to varying degrees, the approaches advocated by Gorz and Lipietz. If the goal is to promote environmentally sound solutions to unemployment, an ETR-WTR combination could be potent, but by promoting the use of human labour, ETR may well disappoint those whose priority is for machines to do more of the work.

As the French experience shows, state financial support for WTR can play an extremely important role in bridging the gap between employers and employees. Existing expenditures on the costs of unemployment could be redirected to this end, and new sources of tax revenue could be found. However, a world with both private ownership of capital and extreme levels of capital mobility puts significant limitations on the ability of states to fund WTR, which means we still need to consider additional ways of financing shorter hours.

WORKING LESS FOR LESS PAY

Any discovery which renders consumption less necessary to the pursuit of living is as much an economic gain as a discovery which improves our skills of production.

Kenneth Boulding, economist, 1945[20]

A willingness by workers, especially those at the higher end of the pay scale, to accept a reduction in income would facilitate WTR. It would also reduce the likelihood of concessions to productivism to finance WTR with no loss in pay. A reduction in income raises a number of complex questions, but it should not be ruled out as an option.

A key point in this discussion is to distinguish between collective reductions of hours and WTR based on individual choice. Many individual workers would voluntarily choose to reduce their work hours, even in return for a proportional loss of pay, if given the choice. With these individual options, the question of financing is usually clear and uncontroversial: the individual worker generally accepts a reduction of pay corresponding to the reduction of hours, though examples do exist in which the loss in pay is less than proportional due to income top-ups from the firm or the state.

More controversial is income reduction for collective hours reductions. However, some labour unions have been moving away from a rigid stance that in all cases calls for WTR for the same pay. Volkswagen's move to a 28.8-hour week is an important example of WTR with a loss in pay to save jobs. There has also been increasing consideration of a "solidaristic wage policy" in which employees, at least those at higher levels of income, accept a loss in pay in return for WTR and new hiring. Several European labour unions (the CFDT in France and IG Metall in Germany, for instance) have been open to that position, and so too has the Confederation of National Trade Unions (CSN) in Quebec. One French unionist argues, "To talk about a four-day week while refusing any loss in pay is to talk about extra vacations. In a country with four million unemployed, that's obscene."[21] The solidaristic wage position is a praiseworthy expression of unity among workers, has an affinity with ecological values of sufficiency, and can help bring about hours reductions. Still, income reductions should not be seen as an inevitable counterpart to work-time reduction.

Accepting lower incomes carries evident dangers. Aznar points out that employers may seize on the shorter hours solution with the goal of reducing salaries, in what amounts to social blackmail.[22] This also raises questions of the long-term political acceptability of shorter hours. How long will workers continue their support for the measure if they see that they are the only ones making financial sacrifices to create or preserve employment? This question of an equitable sharing of sacrifices is particularly pertinent to the situation of low-income workers. Many of them truly cannot afford any loss in income.

Macroeconomic balance is also a factor. Steffen Lehndorff points out that the bigger the reduction in income, the bigger the loss of purchasing power, which only threatens to aggravate economic difficulties. He adds that the problems with income reductions will not necessarily disappear even in cases in which WTR leads to new hiring. If shorter hours come with proportional wage cuts, even after more hiring there will still be a reduction in the total salary mass, because the productivity-boosting effect of shorter hours means that on average only half the hours vacated are available for new hiring. Thus a reduction in the salary mass and aggregate demand can only be prevented if at least partial wage compensation for hours no longer worked is guaranteed. Lehndorff concludes, "On the macro-economic level, the sharing of work does not work without one form or another of salary compensation."[23]

A superficial green response might be that lower incomes are inherently desirable because they lead to lower consumption. But lower consumption by whom? If labour as a whole gives up income to capital, through shorter hours with a proportionate cut in pay, this concession does not provide a solution to environmental problems. By exacerbating inequalities and possibly contributing to a deepening of the economic crisis, a proportional loss of income is also socially problematic. This could, in turn, generate negative ecological consequences as workers increasingly demand jobs regardless of the environmental costs and firms seek relaxation of environmental and other regulations to maintain profitability in a time of falling demand.[24]

These difficult but important issues are related to the larger problems inherent in bringing a high-flying consumer economy down to a soft landing. How do we begin reducing consumption without instigating severe social disruptions and worsening inequalities? Despite the difficulty of answering these questions and the understandable scepticism of some among labour and the left, ecological concerns make it essential to take seriously the green vision of living more satisfying lives with less income and less consumption.

WTR can in itself lead to a reduction in the amount of income required to maintain a given standard of living. One major saving for some is income tax, especially for those who move into a lower tax bracket. Working less can also lead to savings in costs directly related to work, such as transport, clothing, and meals away from home. For example, long hours of paid employment encourage the consumption of costly, pre-prepared, intensively packaged convenience foods, or what Wayne Roberts and Susan Brandum call "overtime foods." In contrast, the availability of more time can allow for an expanded provision of basic needs in the household economy. Roberts and Brandum argue that gardening and cooking at home save more than people make if they spend the same amount of time working for a boss. And if this can be linked to the development of community gardens, as has occurred in many cities, there is the additional benefit of improving the livability of neighbourhoods and strengthening community ties.[25] The key principle is that we could meet many of our needs at a lower cost than usual if we had more time. As Charles Handy argues, individuals who have made the trade-off between time and money often find that the freedom provided by their own capabilities is more lasting than the precarious freedom of money to buy what they need.[26] And, of course, many of the activities in the household economy, such as mending clothes and do-it-yourself repairs, are not only cheaper but also more environmentally sound than purchasing new items. The revitalization of the community economy through the construction of non-market alternatives, such as LETS, would also allow for economic needs to be fulfilled even with the reduction of market incomes. Studies in Germany have shown that people who participate in such non-market activities under their own self-determination experience significantly higher levels of satisfaction than people in traditional paid employment—a sign of the potential for increased well-being from greater wealth in time even with less income.[27]

Other measures that make it easier for people to afford to live on less could also help. As Barbara Brandt points out, the production of more long-lasting, more easily repairable goods would reduce the amount of income required to lead a decent life. Robin Murray suggests that governments could provide participants in work-sharing with a "time-off card" that would allow them, when they are off work, to use public facilities like swimming pools, museums, and galleries free of charge. Since public facilities are underused during regular work hours, this would provide a real benefit to shorter-hours workers at almost no environmental, social, or economic cost to society.[28] Roberts and Brandum suggest that private-sector and public-sector employers have access to relatively cheap credit that could be used to offer discounted mortgages to four-day workers. They also suggest providing tax receipts to four-day workers who donate time to community groups on their days off, just as donations of money are now rewarded.[29]

Although we may need to provide an incentive to individual people to work less, why limit these benefits to four-day workers? What about those in partial retirement or on parental or educational leave, or part-time workers, or people who are no longer counted as being part of the work-force for whatever reason? Rather than confining the benefits to a partic-ular class of shorter hours workers, why not provide such benefits to all citizens as part of a strategy to provide universal access to low-cost basic needs and a high quality of life?

The protection and reinforcement of the welfare state are central elements in a low-cost, universal basic needs strategy. Public guarantees of access to health care, education, transportation, food, housing, and income security at low or no cost are crucial in allowing people to mini-mize the number of hours they work in the market. Investment in low-cost public leisure would also help. For example, reducing the pollution in lakes near cities, or rivers that flow through them, would make a healthy day at the beach possible for all city-dwellers, who then wouldn't need an income high enough to buy cottages or pay for cars to make their escape. Often this is a matter of reducing the flow of sewage into the lakes or rivers, or of supporting organic agriculture and thus avoiding chemical run-off from farmlands into waterways.

Other forms of collective consumption, which can, despite the rhetoric of free-market right-wingers, be vastly more efficient than private consumption, merit exploration. For example, the economics of households that contain few people make little sense due to the high over-head costs of rent or mortgages, taxes, heating, and lighting.[30] In contrast, shared living arrangements or alternatives such as the Danish model of co-housing—which combines relatively small private living areas requir-ing less housework with access to common facilities such as laundry rooms and workshops, shared use of consumer durables, and the pooling of household tasks, such as child care for working parents—can help peo-ple enjoy a sense of community belonging and a high standard of living at lower economic and ecological costs. Labour unions would also do well to revive their historical efforts at pooling resources to provide mutual sup-port and reduce the cost of living for workers.[31]

Individual lifestyle changes can also help people live well on shorter hours and lower incomes, with some important reservations. Many people are in positions to make choices that both benefit the environment and reduce their income needs. They could, for instance, get rid of their cars or use them less, opt for moderate-sized accommodation, or avoid com-pulsive buying on credit and the subsequent drain of interest charges. But individualized approaches to living simply can also be twisted into allow-ing others to consume more. At its worst, this approach can degenerate into calls by an Ontario cabinet minister for welfare recipients to make do with lower benefits by buying dented cans of 69-cent tuna, while at the same time his government was planning a major tax cut for upper-income earners. Giving up income and consumption so that the wealthy can have more undermines social equality and does absolutely nothing for the environment. The individual adoption of less consumptive lifestyles, though needed, cannot be divorced from a larger political project to ensure an equitable sharing of wealth.

The opposite danger in individual lifestyle changes is the promotion of *sauve-qui-peut* solutions. The problem is evident in the innovative, but imperfect, model for a simpler lifestyle promoted by Joe Dominguez and Vicki Robin in their 1992 book *Your Money or Your Life?*[32] Their approach is based on helping individual people find out how much is enough for themselves and to reduce their needs for money. Subsequent steps involve getting out of debt, creating a nest egg, and eventually reaching a point of so-called "financial independence" at which paid employment is no longer needed. In other words, the goal is to reach a point at which individuals can live off their investment income. This is clearly something that not all members of a society will ever be able to do. We simply cannot all be rentiers, even simple-living rentiers. In effect, this approach amounts to finding a way to live off someone else's subjugation to paid employment.

The "Your Money or Your Life" approach is overly individualistic and of limited relevance to many people earning low incomes who have little hope of building up a sufficient nest egg no matter how "simply" they live. Is there any hope for a green politics committed to social justice to rescue anything from it? What is extremely valuable, and potentially even "revolutionary," is the first half of the approach: recognizing the extent to which many of us unnecessarily spend money, and the degree to which we could drastically reduce dependence on the sale of our labour by cutting out excess. The objective need not be to live off someone else's toil—the approach can help people to be able to live comfortably on fewer hours of their own labour. But there also has to be much greater attention given to addressing societal inequalities that prevent many from being able to work less.

In short, the idea that workers accept lower incomes in return for WTR raises complicated questions about equity and economic balance. Nevertheless, expecting workers, particularly those with above-average incomes, to give up income in return for more leisure and job creation for the unemployed is not unreasonable. Although labour and the left have traditionally been reluctant to accept any suggestion that workers make do with less income, concern for both social solidarity and ecological sustainability ought to make this a legitimate option. By going in that direction, the left could discover that there are ways to improve quality of life, promote social equity, reduce income needs, and decrease dependence on capital by "living better with less." At the same time, we have to be wary of how "doing more with less" can be used as a smokescreen for redistributing wealth upwards. Ultimately this comes down to a need for an equitable distribution of what is being produced, while shifting priorities away from production. Finding the appropriate balance between the left-labour emphasis on demanding a bigger share for workers and the green emphasis on "living better with less" is a difficult but important challenge. To work towards achieving it greens need to take a more systemic approach to analysing social inequalities and recognize the constraints and hardship experienced by many working people, and labour and the left need to more fully recognize the need for a political project that is compatible with ecological limits.

WORK-TIME REDUCTION IN GLOBALIZED CAPITALISM

According to Stanley Aronowitz and William DiFazio, "Reducing working hours without simultaneously addressing the issue of capital flight is unthinkable."[33] Examples of WTR today and in the past illustrate that they are not entirely correct; still, the extreme mobility of capital is a significant factor limiting the spread of shorter hours. Achievements in reducing work time will remain limited unless the global economic framework can be made less hostile to goals other than short-term profit. This is an age in which socially and ecologically needed measures are rarely possible unless they coincidentally bring greater profit and competitiveness. This creates enormous pressures to make questionable trade-offs to enhance profitability, such as granting increased operating hours and more work-time flexibility to firms, in order to achieve WTR. Those kinds of trade-offs can undermine the social and ecological desirability of shorter work time, threatening to pervert the original intentions.

The competitive pressures of globalization create other obstacles to WTR. The intense competition of global trade and the hypermobility of capital are generating downward pressure on wages, labour standards, and corporate tax rates. One result is a widening of inequalities. Whereas in the postwar "Golden Age" of capitalism, workers were able to gain an equitable share of productivity gains, the gains more recently have been concentrated in the hands of the economic elite. This is not only socially undesirable; the ecological vision of a new form of progress based on growth in free time rather than growth in production depends on the ability of workers to gain their fair share of productivity gains in one form or another. When capital pockets all the gains, WTR becomes politically unsustainable, leading to charges that the proposal is for "socialism in one class" or that it will "share the misery among the workers." Moreover, the economic insecurity generated by stagnant or declining wages, combined with cutbacks to social programs and the fear of impending job loss, is generating pressures on those with jobs to work more rather than less. Government intervention to provide financial support to those who reduce hours of work is limited by the ability of capital to move elsewhere in search of lower tax levels. All these factors make it much more difficult to achieve the sharing of wealth that must accompany the sharing of work if it is to flourish as an idea.

The competitive pressures of globalization also hinder the ability of WTR to bring full employment. According to economist Robert Heilbroner:

> As a self-contained matter, there is no great difficulty in designing policies that would effectively bring down unemployment . . . . Such policies would include reducing the size of would-be employees by lengthening the period of education, advancing the age of retirement, shortening the workweek or workday, expanding vacations and introducing training sabbaticals or encouraging employment-generating public projects. . . . Unfortunately, the pursuit of unemployment policies cannot be self-contained. The problem is the ability of any one country being able to cope with technological unemployment as it runs up against the constraints of globalization.[34]

Heilbroner notes that the more successful a country's anti-unemployment program, the more likely that same success will generate inflationary wage pressures as labour markets "firm up." In an age of extreme capital mobility, this would lead to the movement of capital to countries that tolerated unemployment and enjoyed lower inflation. With those concerns in mind, Will Hutton and Robert Kuttner, among others, argue that any successful national project for full employment will demand a wholly reformed international architecture designed to reign in international currency exchanges and to set boundaries to markets.[35]

The establishment of a more enlightened social compromise between labour and capital could increase the possibilities for fulfilling the promise of WTR. International environmental and labour standards, including standards for work hours, supported by eco-social tariffs against goods produced in violation of these standards, would help avoid a global race to the bottom. There is also a need for a greater tolerance of national and subnational social and environmental regulations than is seen under NAFTA and the GATT/WTO regime, which have struck down progressive measures as "impediments to free trade." To tame the power of financial markets to dictate their priorities at the expense of social, ecological, and employment objectives, we need limits on the movement of capital. The mobilization of domestic capital, through new public investment pools or worker-owned resources such as pension funds, can reduce vulnerability to the dictates of global finance.[36]

These types of measures could help ensure that workers gain a fair share of productivity gains. Also needed for this purpose are strong minimum-wage laws and labour legislation that protects union rights to organize and bargain collectively. A more progressive taxation system would be both helpful in itself and encourage WTR by reducing the need for those on low incomes to work long hours, while limiting the payoff from long hours of work to those at the upper end of the pay scale.[37]

Some may question whether it is possible to achieve the international measures required for a more enlightened capitalism. According to Heilbroner, "Certainly, an accord that dampens the capacity to move capital in order to encourage employment goes against the general imperative of an expansion-minded capitalist world order. . . . Yet, as with such threats as global warming, what is imaginable is likely to reflect the urgency of the crisis."[38] The global volatility due to the financial crises of 1997-99 suddenly brought many minds into focus around the need for global economic reform. If a deeper crisis were to ensue, we could well expect significant international reforms.

An Eco-Social Capitalism?

Perhaps a greater long-term concern is that a more socially progressive structure that promotes employment and economic growth will come at the expense of greater environmental degradation. Capitalism now faces two crises: "overproduction" in the economic sense of a growing gap between productive capacities and the purchasing power of the majority of the population; and "overconsumption" in the environmental sense of excessive demands being made on nature. Solving overproduction by creating the conditions for a new pro-growth regime for the world will almost certainly intensify the problem of overconsumption.

If unfettered global market forces are to be re-embedded in a framework designed to prioritize social goals over short-term profit, the great challenge will be to ensure that the new structure will not simply be another productivist tool for maximizing GDP growth irrespective of the ecological consequences. Here both an ecological tax reform and WTR are crucial. An ETR would ensure that we interact with nature as efficiently as possible to minimize the ecological impacts of economic activity. WTR would provide a way of sharing productivity gains with labour to maintain adequate purchasing power and economic balance, and at the same time it could represent an embrace of "sufficiency" in opposition to a vision of infinite growth of consumption. Indeed, if we channelled all future productivity gains in the North to WTR rather than into more production and consumption, this would in itself bring zero growth in GDP. (This assumes zero growth in the labour force, a reasonable assumption in most countries of the North, where population growth is minimal, or even negative.)[39] The capping of GDP growth would not be sufficient to achieve environmental sustainability, but it could in itself stop the increase in our demands on nature, allowing improved eco-efficiency to bring about the actual reductions in environmental impacts that are necessary. This scenario would be compatible with the idea of a steady-state economy, a concept that runs from John Stuart Mill in the 19th century to Herman Daly today.

Even if capitalism can adapt to this saner economic project—admittedly a big "if"—it is questionable whether it could sustain it over the long term. The postwar Golden Age, after all, lasted a mere 30 years and was closely followed by an erosion of its social achievements, such as they were. There are strong reasons to believe that the full promise of the project of working less, consuming less, and living more can only be truly achieved under a radically different socio-economic order. The reforms that make up any new eco-social compromise, then, should be seen as transitional measures, without abandoning the goal of going beyond capitalism at a later date.

At a fundamental level, capitalism's expansionary internal dynamics conflict with the notion of sufficiency. A widespread embrace of frugality in the North would cause turmoil in a system dependent on high levels of consumption. As Nash puts it, "frugality includes the reduction of wants" and "an appreciation of the free and ubiquitous goods of life."[40] In contrast, one retailing analyst pointed out about the postwar years: "Our enormously productive economy . . . demands that we make consumption our way of life, that we convert the buying and use of goods into rituals, that we seek our spiritual satisfaction, our ego satisfaction, in consumption. . . . We need things consumed, burned up, worn out, replaced, and discarded at an ever increasing rate."[41] Gorz outlined the conflict between an ecological rationality and capitalism's economic logic:

> Ecological rationality consists in satisfying material needs in the best way possible with as small a quantity of goods as possible with a high use-value and durability and thus doing so with a minimum of work, capital and natural resources. The quest for economic productivity, by contrast, consists in selling at as high a profit as possible the greatest possible quantity of goods produced with the maximum of efficiency, all of which demands a maximization of consumption and needs.[42]

WTR will only achieve its full ecological potential as a contributor to the reduction of consumption levels, while improving quality of life, if it is accompanied by measures that allow people to meet their basic needs with a minimum of market labour. Government strategies to provide low-cost access to basic needs such as education, health care, (public) transport, and income security, urban design that makes automobile use unnecessary and even burdensome, new forms of collective consumption from co-housing to car-sharing co-ops, and the production of durable and easily repairable goods, to name a few, are all examples of measures that allow people to live high-quality lives with low ecological impact and/or reduced needs for income. It is doubtful that capitalism is compatible with a much wider flourishing of such measures, which undermine many sources of private profit. Perhaps it might still be possible for capitalism to continue to expand into relatively non-material sectors, selling experiences and feelings, rather than ever more things you can drop on your foot. A "dreamworld capitalism," though, could easily degenerate into an expansion of trivial leisure (the 500-channel universe), or into making people pay for experiences that were once free, from human companionship (pay-per-call dating services) to access to nature (privatized parks and beaches). A dematerialized "virtual capitalism" would also face strong cultural contradictions by, on the one hand, having to keep material needs within bounds and, on the other, expanding desires for non-material products and services. Yet even these non-material, experience-based products are likely to bring with them demands for related material goods, from communications and computing hardware produced with toxic inputs to jet fuel for travel to the next "untouched," exotic locale.

A green vision of WTR also requires a relatively equal distribution of wealth, an issue that creates other difficulties for capitalism. The postwar Golden Age did show that under a socially enlightened capital-labour compromise with rapid economic growth, capitalism is capable of allowing labour to gain its share of productivity gains. However, it remains to be seen if the same is possible under the conditions of the low growth or no growth that appears necessary to respect ecological limits. Furthermore, the advance of new technologies raises more fundamental questions of ownership. A corporation such as Cineplex-Odeon, for instance, is able to use improved technology to threaten its projectionists with both a massive cut in work hours and a 50 per cent cut in hourly wages, turning decent jobs paying $30,000-40,000 annually into McJobs paying $6,000-8,000.[43] Similarly, CN Railways announced in 1998 that despite a record profit of $807 million, new technology had reduced the need for labour, and 3,000 jobs would have to go. CN's stock price boomed, netting CEO Paul Tellier $340,000 in increased stock option value the next day.[44] While the technological advances that eliminated the need for the labour of projectionists and railway workers are the fruit of centuries of human contributions, the benefits are concentrated in the hands of a small group. The situation would be quite different if ownership were more widely distributed. If machines are taking our jobs, to reap the dividends of higher productivity perhaps we need to own a piece of those machines. In a more rational economic order, technological improvements would be a benefit, not a threat. Likewise, meeting our needs in more ecologically sound ways requiring fewer commodities would be seen as progress, rather than as a threat to profits and jobs.

In response to the political challenge of full employment for capitalism, Michal Kalecki argued in 1943: "If capitalism can adjust itself to full employment a fundamental reform will have been incorporated into it. If not, it will show itself an outmoded system which must be scrapped."[45] The same can be said today about the challenge of adjusting to ecological limits in a way consistent with social equity and a high quality of life. It appears doubtful that capitalism can respond adequately to this challenge. If it can, some people will undoubtedly say that it is no longer truly capitalism. Ultimately, though, the label attached to the system is not what is important. What is essential is finding a way to begin the difficult project of pulling out of an overconsuming way of life and, in Gorz's words, subordinating economic rationality to eco-social rationality.[46]

To do that, we will need not only to dramatically improve eco-efficiency—reducing the amount of resource consumption and pollution for each unit of economic output—but also to embrace the idea of consumption sufficiency. WTR could be a visionary and pragmatic focus for beginning to address the concept of sufficiency in the North as part of an ecological restructuring of industrial societies. It can serve as a central element in a green response to unemployment, and a focus for an alternative vision of progress based on improved quality of life rather than growth in consumption. It can be a way to provide people time to think and act as participants in building a more ecologically sustainable and socially just society, and a measure that creates new opportunities for "simple living" and for challenging the dominant pattern of consumerism.

There remains the danger that WTR could be co-opted by the powerful forces of productivism. In navigating these waters, we need to be clear that the goals of WTR—if it is to serve ecological ends—should ultimately be to find an alternative to the growth of production and consumption rather than to stimulate it, to create leisure as an autonomous space outside of the market rather than as a new source of market opportunities, and to start subverting the machine of capitalist consumerism rather than to simply make that machine work more equitably and smoothly.

WTR is an issue that provides real opportunities for the green movement to address immediate economic priorities, such as unemployment, and to promote a new direction for Northern societies, one that has the potential of gaining widespread popular support by offering the promise of a more satisfying way of life. The issue could also serve as a

bridge for linking environmental, labour, feminist, and other social movements in pursuit of alternatives to neo-liberalism. As a focal point for
beginning the essential task of putting the question of sufficiency on the
agenda in the North, work-time reduction appears to be the best option
on the horizon. Getting there, however, will take a lot of work.

JOSEPH HENZ

Notes

1 INTRODUCTION

1. World Commission on Environment and Development (Brundtland Commission), *Our Common Future* (New York: Oxford University Press, 1987), p.8.
2. The term "North" as used here is synonymous with "developed" or "industrialized" nations or the "First World." A more nuanced understanding of the term includes the wealthy of the developing nations who consume at rates similar to the people of the developed nations; though we should also recognize that increasingly large numbers of people in the developed nations participate only marginally in overconsumption.
3. David T. Suzuki, "Saving the Earth," *Maclean's*, June 14, 1999, p.44.
4. "Global Warming Sinks Islands," *The Globe and Mail*, June 14, 1999.
5. Suzuki, "Saving the Earth," p.43.
6. Wolfgang Sachs, Reinhard Loske, Manfred Linz, et al., *Greening the North: A Post-Industrial Blueprint for Ecology and Equity* (London: Zed Books, 1998), p.xi.
7. Andrew Dobson, *Green Political Thought* (London: Routledge, 1995), p.11.
8. By "nature" I am referring to non-human nature, and more specifically to energy and material resources, the capacity of the non-human natural world to absorb human-generated pollutants, and the provision of "environmental services" such as the moderation of climate or the filtering of ultraviolet radiation by the ozone layer. By using this term in this way, I do not intend to imply that human beings themselves are not a part of nature.
9. Norm Ovenden, "Kyoto Targets a Long Shot," *Edmonton Journal*, May 21, 1999, p.A4.
10. "Environment in the European Union at the Turn of the Century," Environmental Assessment Report, no.2, European Environmental Agency, 1999, reported in Catherine Coroller, "Environnement européen: au secours!" *Libération* (Paris), June 25, 1999. See also European Environment Agency website: www.eea.eu.int/Document/3-yearly/eu98/en/index.html.
11. The 35 per cent and 90 per cent estimates are for Germany. Sachs, Loske, Linz, et al., *Greening the North*, p.30.
12. Coroller, "Environnement européen: au secours!"

13. Sachs, Loske, Linz, et al., *Greening the North*, p.x.
14. Organization for Economic Co-operation and Development, OECD *Employment Outlook: June 1998* (Paris: OECD, 1998), p.vii.
15. Ronald Colman, " 'More' May Not Be 'Better': Puncturing the Economic Growth Illusion," *The Daily News* (Halifax), June 18, 1999, p.15. See, for instance, the Index of Sustainable Economic Welfare in Herman Daly and John Cobb, *For the Common Good* (Boston: Beacon Press, 1989), p.420.
16. Merck Family Fund, "Yearning for Balance: Views of Americans on Consumption, Materialism and the Environment," July 1995, Fig. 9, p.16.
17. I use terms such as "work time" and "work hours" as shorthand for "hours of paid employment." Obviously, "work" does not consist only of paid employment outside the home. The distribution of unpaid household work hours and the gender division of labour are important related issues.
18. I use the term "progressive" here as it is commonly used in Canada today—to signify a commitment to social justice, equality, and other core values of the political left. I do so despite my disagreement with the prevailing conception of "progress" based on economic growth and increased consumption.
19. John Kettle, "Workers Toil Longer to Buy New Vehicles," *The Globe and Mail*, June 17, 1999.
20. In Ontario, the Canadian Auto Workers have fought for hemp to be reintroduced to both farms and industrial processes, and to replace mineral cutting-fluids with vegetable oils. John Cartwright, "The Greening of Canada: A Proposal," *Our Times*, January/February 1998, p.13.
21. David Pepper, *Eco-Socialism: From Deep Ecology to Social Justice* (London: Routledge, 1993), p.2. For other examples of efforts to bridge left and green, see Jesse Vorst, Ross Dobson, Ron Fletcher, eds., *Green on Red: Evolving Ecological Socialism* (Winnipeg: Society for Socialist Studies, 1993); special issue on "Red and Green: Eco-Socialism Comes of Age," *The New Internationalist*, November 1998; and the work of Alain Lipietz and André Gorz.
22. Dobson, *Green Political Thought*, p.1.
23. See, for instance, Carolyn Merchant, *Radical Ecology: The Search for a Livable World* (New York: Routledge, 1992).
24. Rudolf Bahro, "Theology Not Ecology," *New Perspectives Quarterly* 16,2 (Special Issue, 1999), p.52.

2 OVERCONSUMPTION, EFFICIENCY, AND SUFFICIENCY

1. World Commission on Environment and Development, *Our Common Future*, p.33.
2. Ernst U. von Weizsäcker, *Earth Politics* (London: Zed Books, 1994), p.8.
3. Matthias Wackernagel and William Rees, *Our Ecological Footprint* (Gabriola Island, B.C.: New Catalyst, 1996), p.89.
4. Edward Goldsmith et al., *Blueprint for Survival* (Boston: Houghton Mifflin, 1972), pp.8, 14, 16.
5. Jonathon Porritt, *Seeing Green* (Oxford: Blackwell, 1984), p.136; quoted in Dobson, *Green Political Thought*, p.17.
6. Ted Trainer, *Abandon Affluence!* (London: Zed Books, 1985); extracts in

Andrew Dobson, ed., *The Green Reader* (London: André Deutsch, 1991), p.84.

7. Bill McKibben, *Hope, Human and Wild: True Stories of Living Lightly on the Earth* (Toronto: Little, Brown and Company, 1995), pp.54-55.

8. Quotation from Goldsmith et al., *Blueprint for Survival*, p.157. See also Dobson, *Green Political Thought*, pp.17-18.

9. Kalle Lasn, "The New Activism," *Adbusters*, July-August 1999, p.37.

10. Donald Worster, "The Shaky Ground of Sustainability," in *Global Ecology: A New Arena of Conflict*, ed. Wolfgang Sachs (Halifax: Fernwood Publishing, 1993), p.132.

11. Ernst U. von Weizsäcker and Jochen Jesinghaus, *Ecological Tax Reform* (London: Zed Books, 1992), p.10.

12. William E. Rees, *The Ecological Meaning of Environment-Economy Integration* (Vancouver: University of British Columbia School of Community and Regional Planning, 1989), p.1.

13. World Commission on Environment and Development, *Our Common Future*, pp.28, 213. See also Worster, "Shaky Ground of Sustainability," p.133.

14. Wolfgang Sachs, quoted in Ray Rogers, "Political Economy and Natural Community: The Case of Canada's East Coast Fishery," in *Human Society and the Natural World: Perspectives on Sustainable Futures* (North York, Ont.: York University Faculty of Environmental Studies, 1994), p.79; Wolfgang Sachs, "Global Ecology and the Shadow of 'Development,'" in *Global Ecology*, ed. Sachs, p.xvi.

15. Robert Goodland, "The Case That the World Has Reached Limits: More Precisely That Current Throughput Growth in the Global Economy Cannot Be Sustained," in *Environmentally Sustainable Development: Building on Brundtland*, ed. Robert Goodland, Herman Daly, Salah El Serafy, and Bernd von Droste (Paris: UNESCO, 1991), p.23.

16. Statistics indicate that from 1950 to 1986 U.S. manufacturing output rose more than threefold, energy use nearly tripled, and the quantity of capital rose fourfold. Labour input, however, rose only by a third. Michael Renner, "Saving the Earth, Creating Jobs," *World Watch* 5,1 (1992), p.11.

17. Ernst von Weizsäcker, Amory B. Lovins, and L. Hunter Lovins, *Factor Four: Doubling Wealth—Halving Resource Use* (London: Earthscan, 1997), p.xviii; for reference to factor-ten, see pp.244-45. See also William Rees, "More Jobs, Less Damage: A Framework for Sustainability, Growth, and Employment," *Alternatives* 21,4 (1995), p.27.

18. Sachs, Loske, Linz, et al., *Greening the North*, pp.108-9, 129-30.

19. With "marketable depletion quotas," governments set the output or harvest of a resource at an ecologically sustainable level. These quotas are then sold on the market to the highest bidder. "Tradeable emission permits" make the release of pollution illegal without the purchase of a permit. The permit can also be sold on the market, creating profit opportunities for firms that reduce pollution and no longer need the permits. For a full range of financial incentives policies for environmental protection, see Michael Jacobs, *The Green Economy* (Vancouver: University of British Columbia Press, 1991), pp.138-46.

20. Von Weizsäcker and Jesinghaus, *Ecological Tax Reform*, pp.9, 19, 21; David Gee, "Economic Tax Reform in Europe: Opportunities and Obstacles," in

Ecotaxation, ed. Timothy O'Riordan (London: Earthscan, 1997), p.84.

21. Rees, "More Jobs, Less Damage," pp.26-27; see also his footnotes 15 and 16.

22. David Gee, "Making Pollution Pay," *New Statesman and Society*, April 14, 1995, p.30; David Gee, "Green Gravy Train," *New Statesman and Society*, May 21, 1993, p.27; "Money from Greenery," *The Economist*, Oct. 21, 1989, p.16; "Clean and Green, or Lean and Mean," *The Economist*, Dec. 12, 1992, p.73; Delors quoted in Gee, "Economic Tax Reform in Europe," p.81.

23. Von Weizsäcker and Jesinghaus, *Ecological Tax Reform*; von Weizsäcker, *Earth Politics*, ch. 11, "Ecological Tax Reform"; and Goldsmith et al., *Blueprint for Survival*, p.281.

24. Rees, "More Jobs, Less Damage," p.28.

25. In 1994 employers' social security contributions as a percentage of gross earnings were 46 per cent in France, 30.1 per cent in Sweden, 19.4 per cent in Germany, 7.7 per cent in the United States, 7.5 per cent in Japan, and 6.6 per cent in Canada. OECD, *Making Work Pay: Taxation, Benefits, Employment and Unemployment* (Paris: OECD, 1997), p.66.

26. Gee, "Making Pollution Pay," p.30.

27. Terry Barker, "Taxing Pollution Instead of Jobs: Towards More Employment without More Inflation through Fiscal Reform in the UK," in *Ecotaxation*, ed. O'Riordan, p.197.

28. William E. Rees, "Taxing Combustion and Rehabilitating Forests," *Alternatives* 21,4 (1995), p.34.

29. "Clean and Green," p.73.

30. Exemptions from CO_2 and energy taxes have been granted for competitiveness reasons in Sweden, Denmark, and Norway. Critics point out that this undermines the environmental effectiveness of the measure by exempting some of the main sources of consumption. Jean-Phillipe Barde, "Environmental Taxation: Experience in OECD Countries," in *Ecotaxation*, ed. O'Riordan, p.242; Gee, "Making Pollution Pay," p.30.

31. See, for example, von Weizsäcker, *Earth Politics*, pp.138-39.

32. Even though green taxes are in themselves regressive—the poor pay a higher proportion of their income than the rich—an ETR package could be made progressive simply by returning the revenues to people on an equal per person basis. Imagine, for instance, that a person earning $10,000 spends $500 on green taxes (5 per cent of income), while a person earning $100,000 spends $2,500 on green taxes (2.5 per cent of income). If the $3,000 raised from the two is given back on an equal basis—$1,500 each— $1,000 is transferred from the rich person to the poor person. The $1,500 could simply be returned to taxpayers in the form of a cheque, or alternatively as an increase in the "social wage"—say, for example, a new universal drug benefits plan.

33. Gee, "Economic Tax Reform," p.98; von Weizsäcker, Lovins, and Lovins, *Factor Four*, p.206; Barde, "Environmental Taxation," p.243.

34. Gee, "Green Gravy Train," p.27.

35. Von Weizsäcker, Lovins, and Lovins, *Factor Four*, pp.116-17.

36. Sachs, Loske, Linz, et al., *Greening the North*, p.62.

37. Jim MacNeill, Pieter Winsemius, and Taizo Yakushiji, *Beyond Interdependence* (Oxford: Oxford University Press, 1991), p.24.

38. Canadian Centre for Policy Alternatives, *Environmental Sustainability, Growth, and the Future of Jobs: A Debate between Cliff Stainsby and Andrew Jackson*, Ottawa, 1998, p.17.

39. Jesse H. Ausubel, "Can Technology Spare the Earth?" *American Scientist* 84 (March-April 1996), p.173.

40. Von Weizsäcker, Lovins, and Lovins, *Factor Four*, p.258.

41. Goldsmith et al., *Blueprint for Survival*, p.35, pointed out the same problem back in 1972.

42. Sachs, Loske, Linz, et al., *Greening the North*, p.199; Herman E. Daly, "Introduction to Essays toward a Steady-State Economy," in *Valuing the Earth: Economics, Ecology, Ethics*, ed. Herman E. Daly and Kenneth N. Townsend (Cambridge, Mass.: MIT Press, 1993), p.8.

43. Herman E. Daly, "Consumption: Value Added, Physical Transformation and Welfare," Proceedings of a Conference on "Consumption, Global Stewardship and the Good Life," Sept. 29-Oct. 2 1994, Institute for Philosophy and Public Policy, University of Maryland, p.2.

44. Statistics from *The Ecologist* 22,4 (July/August 1992), p.168; cited in Rees, "More Jobs, Less Damage," pp.29-30. Rees argues that this rebound effect can be minimized because ecological taxes allow governments to capture efficiency savings, preferably for investments in essential natural capital such as forest rehabilitation, and remove them from consumption-driven circulation.

45. World Resources Institute report, 1992, cited in Dobson, *Green Political Thought*, p.208.

46. "Environmental Taxes: Muck and Money," *The Economist*, Dec. 5, 1992, p.29.

47. Ausubel, "Can Technology Spare the Earth?" p.176.

48. It has been calculated that to avoid destabilizing climate change, each of the Earth's 5.8 billion citizens would have the right to discharge roughly 2.3 tonnes of carbon dioxide annually. In 1991 energy-linked CO_2 emissions were 19.5 tonnes per person in the United States. The figures in some other countries: Canada—15.2; Germany—12.1; Japan—8.8; China—2; Brazil and Egypt—1.5; India—O.8. See Sachs, Loske, Linz, et al., *Greening the North*, pp.3, 71.

49. Paul Ekins, "Making Development Sustainable," in *Global Ecology*, ed. Sachs, pp.92-93.

50. Ekins, "Making Development Sustainable," p.100.

51. Sachs, Loske, Linz, et al., *Greening the North*, p.45.

52. John S. Dryzek, "Foundations for Environmental Political Economy: The Search for Homo Ecologicus," *New Political Economy* 1,1 (1996), pp.36-38.

53. Sachs, "Global Ecology and the Shadow of 'Development,'" p.16.

54. Von Weizsäcker, Lovins, and Lovins, *Factor Four*, p.269.

55. Juliet B. Schor, "Can the North Stop Consumption Growth? Escaping the Cycle of Work and Spend," in *The North, the South and the Environment: Ecological Constraints and the Global Economy*, ed. V. Bhaskar and Andrew Glyn (London: Earthscan, 1995), p.71.

3 WORKING LESS, CONSUMING LESS, AND LIVING MORE: THE
ECOLOGICAL PROMISE OF WORK-TIME REDUCTION

1. Alain Lipietz, *Green Hopes* (Cambridge: Polity, 1995), p.47.
2. Will Hutton and Robert Kuttner, "Full Employment in a Free Society,"
   Fabian Review 106,3 (June 1994).
3. James Robertson, *Future Work: Jobs, Employment and Leisure after the
   Industrial Age* (Aldershot, Eng.: Gower, 1985), p.ix; Jeremy Rifkin, "Civil
   Society in the Information Age," *The Nation*, Feb. 26, 1996, p.11.
4. Sally Lerner, "The Future of Work in North America: Good Jobs, Bad
   Jobs, Beyond Jobs," *Futures*, March 1994, p.9.
5. Jeremy Rifkin has been the main exponent of this view, although he has
   rightly been criticized for overstating his point. For a more balanced statement of this perspective, see Robert Heilbroner, "The Ghosts of the ATM
   Machine," *New Perspectives Quarterly*, Spring 1996, pp.20-21. For a critique
   of the "end of work" thesis see Doug Henwood, "Work and Its Future,"
   Left Business Observer, April 3, 1996, p.7.
6. Advisory Group on Working Time and the Distribution of Work, *Report of
   the Advisory Group on Working Time and the Distribution of Work* (Ottawa:
   Human Resources Development Canada, 1994), p.5.
7. Stanley Aronowitz and William DiFazio, *The Jobless Future: Sci-Tech and the
   Dogma of Work* (Minneapolis: University of Minnesota Press, 1994), p.346.
8. See, for example, William Greider, "Global Warning: Curbing the Free-
   Trade Freefall," *The Nation*, Jan. 13/20, 1997, pp.11-17. A similar call for
   global expansionary measures comes from Ethan B. Kapstein, "Workers
   and the World Economy," *Foreign Affairs* 75,3 (May/June 1996), pp.16-37.
9. Alain Lipietz, "The Planet after Fordism," International Political Economy
   and Ecology Summer School, York University, Toronto, July 11, 1996. See
   also Alain Lipietz, *La société en sablier: Le Partage du travail contre la déchirure
   sociale* (Paris: Éditions La Découverte, 1996), p.145.
10. Les Verts, "Toyota, 35 heures et rapport Fuchs," press release, Paris, Dec.
    11, 1997. The numbers are based on a 10 per cent reduction of work time
    from the standard 39 to 35 hours, with an estimated 6 per cent increase in
    employment—a job-creation rate matched and exceeded in many recent
    French WTR examples.
11. Canadian Auto Workers' web site:
    www.caw.ca/caw/chrysler/chrysler/html. Steffen Lehndorff, "La redistribu-
    tion de l'emploi en Allemagne," *Futuribles*, February 1995, p.14.
12. In 1983 Dutch employees worked an average of 1,530 hours per year. This
    decreased to 1,397 hours by 1995. OECD, *OECD Employment Outlook: June
    1998*, pp.155, 207. One has to be cautious with international comparisons
    of work hours, because there is significant difference in how national statis-
    tics are calculated. Netherlands unemployment statistics for 1983 from
    Jean-Yves Boulin and Gilbert Cette, "Réduire la durée du travail: l'exemple
    des Pays-Bas," *Futuribles*, July-August 1997, p.13. Spring 1999 statistics
    from "Economic Indicators," *The Economist*, June 12, 1999, p.96.
13. Peter Cook, "No Dutch Miracle, After All," *The Globe and Mail Report on*

Business, Sept. 26, 1997.

14. Ruud Lubbers, "The Dutch Way," *New Perspectives Quarterly*, Fall 1997, p.15. It is worth noting that Lubbers is a Christian Democrat. Some social conservatives share with environmentalists and feminists a strong apprecia-tion for the value of what lies outside the market, creating at least some potential for unexpected political alliances.

15. Rifkin, "Civil Society in the Information Age," pp.14-15; Lipietz, *Green Hopes*, pp.54-55.

16. "Mme Aubry propose 22 métiers nouveaux pour lutter contre le chômage des jeunes," *Le Monde*, Aug. 21, 1997; Isabelle Mandraud, "Emploi-jeunes: dur de faire le plein," *Libération*, Oct. 17-18, 1998.

17. "Dutch Courage," *The Economist*, May 9, 1998, p.73. For a labour-initiated Canadian green jobs proposal, see John Cartwright, "The Greening of Canada: A Proposal," *Our Times*, January-February 1999, pp.13-14.

18. Stephen Cohen and John Zysman, *Manufacturing Matters: The Myth of the Post-Industrial Economy* (New York: Basic Books, 1987), p.3.

19. Economic Council of Canada, *Good Jobs, Bad Jobs: Employment in the Service Sector* (Ottawa: Ministry of Supply and Services, 1990), p.6.

20. See, for instance, "Jeeves Strikes It Rich," *The Economist*, Sept. 26, 1998.

21. Aaron Sachs, "Virtual Ecology: A Brief Environmental History of Silicon Valley," *World Watch*, January/February 1999, pp.12-21.

22. Paul Wachtel quoted in Donald G. Reid, *Work and Leisure in the 21st Century* (Toronto: Wall & Emerson, 1995), p.33.

23. "The Perils of Pork and Gravy: A Backlash Builds against Japan's Big Public Spending Plans," *The Economist*, June 12, 1999, p.38.

24. Colin Dodds and Ronald Colman, "The Cost of Crime in Nova Scotia," *GPI Atlantic*, Halifax, N.S., April 1999, pp.145-47; based on data from the U.S. Bureau of Justice Statistics, June 1998, showing 668 prisoners per 100,000 population in the United States (1.8 million total) in June 1998; as reported in *The Chronicle-Herald* (Halifax), March 15, 1999, p.A10.

25. Some studies suggest the net employment effects of an ecological restruc-turing would be positive. See, for example, Renner, "Saving the Earth, Creating Jobs."

26. Guy Aznar, "Revenu minimum garanti et deuxième cheque," *Futuribles*, April 1988, p.61.

27. Lipietz, *Green Hopes*, pp.47-48.

28. Stanley Aronowitz, "Overwork or the End of Work: Which Will It Be?" presentation at Our Time Famine Conference, Department of Sport, Health, Leisure, and Physical Studies, University of Iowa, Iowa City, March 9, 1996.

29. Bruce O'Hara, *Working Harder Isn't Working* (Vancouver: New Star Books, 1993), p.245.

30. Quoted in Alan Durning, *How Much Is Enough? The Consumer Society and the Future of the Earth* (London: Earthscan, 1992), p.113.

31. Lipietz, *Green Hopes*, p.48.

32. Durning, *How Much Is Enough?* p.116. The term "work and spend" cycle was coined by Schor. See Juliet B. Schor, *The Overworked American: The Unexpected Decline of Leisure* (New York: Basic Books, 1991).

33. Alain Lipietz, *Towards a New Economic Order: Postfordism, Ecology and Democracy* (Cambridge: Polity Press, 1992), p.91. I have "translated" the term "walking in Sicily" in the original as "hiking." For someone living in Lipietz's native France, walking in relatively nearby Sicily is not an ecologically extravagant form of holiday. For a North American it would require a transatlantic jet flight and would be comparable to a "Club Med" form of extravagance.

34. Statistics Canada survey, 1992, cited in *Advisory Group on Working Time and the Distribution of Work, Report*, pp.8, 23.

35. Barbara Moses, *Career Intelligence: Mastering the New Work and Personal Realities* (Toronto: Stoddart, 1997), p.79; "Workaholics Anonymous," *The Economist*, Oct. 22, 1994, p.20.

36. Betty Friedan, "A New Paradigm Beyond Social Politics," presentation at Our Time Famine Conference, Department of Sport, Health, Leisure, and Physical Studies, University of Iowa, Iowa City, March 9, 1996.

37. Durning, *How Much Is Enough?* p.116.

38. Carmen Sirianni, "The Self-Management of Time in Postindustrial Society," in *Working Time in Transition: The Political Economy of Working Hours in Industrial Nations*, ed. Karl Hinrichs, William Roche, and Carmen Sirianni (Philadelphia: Temple University Press, 1991), p.231.

39. Reid, *Work and Leisure in the 21st Century*, pp.62, 89, 91.

40. Ibid., p.2.

41. Schor, "Can the North Stop Consumption Growth?" p.70.

42. Michael Harrington, *Socialism: Past and Future* (New York: Arcade Publishing, 1989), p.213.

43. Sukomal Sen, *May Day and Eight Hours' Struggle in India: A Political History* (Calcutta: K P Bagchi & Company, 1988). pp.40-58, 65.

44. See Angela Howard Zophy, *Handbook of American Women's History* (New York: Garland Reference Library, 1990), p.287.

45. Sen, *May Day and the Eight Hours' Struggle in India*, p.12.

46. Bryan D. Palmer, *Working-Class Experience: Rethinking the History of Canadian Labour, 1800-1991* (Toronto: McClelland & Stewart, 1992), p.106.

47. Donald Sassoon, *One Hundred Years of Socialism: The West European Left in the Twentieth Century* (London: Fontana Press, 1997), p.55; Witold Rybczynski, *Waiting for the Weekend* (Toronto: Penguin, 1991), p.142.

48. Chris De Neubourg, "Where Have All the Hours Gone? Working-Time Reduction Policies in the Netherlands," in *Working Time in Transition*, ed. Hinrichs, Roche, and Sirianni, p.133. Canadian statistics from Advisory Group on Working Time and the Distribution of Work, *Report*, p.13.

49. Sen, *May Day and the Eight Hours' Struggle in India*, p.12; Gösta Langenfelt, *The Historic Origins of the Eight Hours Day* (Westport, Conn.: Greenwood Press, 1954), Preface.

50. Karl Marx, "Capital: Volume One," in *The Marx-Engels Reader*, ed. Robert C. Tucker (New York: W.W. Norton & Co., 1978), p.371.

51. Karl Marx, "Instructions for Delegates to the Geneva Congress," in *Karl Marx Political Writings*, vol. III, *The First International and After*, ed. David Fernbach (New York: Random House, 1974), p.87.

52. Marx, "Capital: Volume One," p.373.

53. David McLellan, *Marx's Grundrisse* (London: Macmillan Press, 1980), p.153; see also pp. 89, 147.

54. John Stuart Mill, *Principles of Political Economy*, vol. II (London: Longmans, Green, Reader and Dyer, 1871), pp.328-30.

55. Ibid., pp.330-32.

56. John Maynard Keynes, *The Collected Writings of John Maynard Keynes: Essays in Persuasion*, vol. IX (London: Macmillan Press, 1972), pp.325-26, 329, 331-32.

57. Bertrand Russell, *In Praise of Idleness and Other Essays* (London: Unwin, 1976), p.16.

58. Ibid., pp.16-17.

59. Benjamin Hunnicutt, "Kellogg's Six-Hour Day: A Capitalist Vision of Liberation through Managed Work Reduction," *Business History Review* 66 (Summer 1992), pp.486.

60. Benjamin Kline Hunnicutt, *Work without End: Abandoning Shorter Hours for the Right to Work* (Philadelphia: Temple University Press, 1988), ch.2, "The New Economic Gospel of Consumption," pp.37-66.

61. For an account of the attraction of mass consumption to ordinary working people during this period, see Gary Cross, *Time and Money: The Making of Consumer Culture* (London: Routledge, 1993).

62. Hunnicutt, *Work without End*, ch.6, "FDR Counters Shorter Hours," pp.159-90.

63. Canadian Auto Workers, *More Time: For Ourselves, Our Children, Our Community* (North York, Ont.: CAW Communications & Research, 1993); Aronowitz and DiFazio, *Jobless Future*, p.357.

64. Quoted in Benjamin Kline Hunnicutt, *Kellogg's Six-Hour Day* (Philadelphia: Temple University Press, 1996), p.148.

65. Aronowitz and DiFazio, *Jobless Future*, pp.6-7

66. Concepts of "welfare critique" and "environment critique" from Bob Sutcliffe, "Development after Ecology," in *The North, the South and the Environment*, ed. Bhaskar and Glyn, p.241.

67. For analysis of the sources of the work-and-spend cycle, see Schor, *Overworked American*, pp.126-32; capitalism's bias against leisure is out-lined, pp.59-72; for further discussion of the capitalist bias against leisure see the discussion of business opposition in chapter 5.

68. Juliet B. Schor, *The Overspent American: Upscaling, Downshifting and the New Consumer* (New York: Basic Books, 1998), p.107.

69. Daly, "Consumption," pp.17-18.

70. Daly, "Introduction," in *Valuing the Earth*, ed. Daly and Townsend, pp.26, 40.

71. Daly and Cobb, Jr., *For the Common Good*, p.420.

72. Daly, "Introduction," in *Valuing the Earth*, ed. Daly and Townsend, pp. 29, 36.

73. David Ransom, "Red and Green: Eco-socialism Comes of Age," *The New Internationalist*, November 1998, p.8.

74. Reid, *Work and Leisure in the 21st Century*, pp.14-15.

75. Michael Huberman and Robert Lacroix, "Worksharing in Historical Perspective: Implications for Current Policy," Canadian Employment Research Forum, Changes in Working Time in Canada and the United States Conference, Ottawa, June 13-15, 1996, p.23; Robert Lacroix quoted

in Rejean Bourdeau, "Travail partagé: 90% des employés sont contre," *Les Affaires*, March 2, 1996, p.14.

76. Hunnicutt, *Kellogg's Six-Hour Day*, p.65.

77. Alain Lipietz, "The Planet after Fordism," International Political Economy and Ecology Summer School, York University, North York, Ont., July 11, 1996.

78. Quoted in Studs Terkel, *Working* (New York: Pantheon, 1974), p.xxxiv.

79. Robin Murray, "History Pushing toward Four-day Working Week," *NOW* (Toronto), March 9-15, 1995. See also Debra Black, "Does Anyone Darn a Sock Any More?" *The Toronto Star*, April 24, 1993.

80. Robyn Eckersley, *Environmentalism and Political Theory: Toward an Ecocentric Approach* (Albany: State University of New York Press, 1992), p.143. Many green economists, like Robertson, have focused on the introduction of a guaranteed basic income to allow people to participate in the "informal economy." While Robertson is sceptical of how WTR fits into a green economic vision, others like Gorz see both a reduction of work hours and a guaranteed income as necessary if this sphere of civil society is to expand. Robertson, *Future Work*, p.1; André Gorz, *Ecology as Politics* (London: Pluto Press, 1983); extracts in Dobson, *Green Reader*, p.98.

81. Durning, *How Much Is Enough?* p.114.

82. Barbara Brandt, "Less Is More: A Call for Shorter Work Hours," *Utne Reader*, July-August 1991, p.84.

83. Canadian Auto Workers, *More Time*.

84. Ernest Mandel, cited in Aronowitz and DiFazio, *Jobless Future*, p.358.

85. Henry David Thoreau at Walden Pond, cited in Sachs, Loske, Linz, et al., *Greening the North*, p.126.

86. James Nash, *Frugality: A Just and Sustainable Alternative to Mass Consumption*, Proceedings of a Conference on "Consumption, Global Stewardship and the Good Life," Institute for Philosophy and Public Policy, University of Maryland, Sept. 29-Oct. 2, 1994, p.4.

87. Schor, "Can the North Stop Consumption Growth?" p.82; Marci McDonald, "Cashing Out," *Maclean's*, Oct. 28, 1996, pp.44-50; Walter Schwarz, "Volunteers for a Leisure America," *The Guardian Weekly*, Dec. 10, 1995, p.24.

88. Jerome Segal, "The Basics: Money and Our Economic Life," Our Time Famine Conference, Department of Sport, Health, Leisure and Physical Studies, University of Iowa, Iowa City, March 9, 1996.

89. Wolfgang Sachs, "Efficiency versus Sufficiency: On Conflicting Perspectives for Building Sustainable Economies," Towards an Ecological Economics, Schumacher College, Dartington, U.K., Jan. 19, 1996. See also Sachs, Loske, Linz, et al., *Greening the North*, pp.124-25.

90. André Gorz, *Capitalism, Socialism, Ecology* (London: Verso, 1994), p.42.

91. Max Weber, cited in André Gorz, "Political Ecology: Expertocracy versus Self-Limitation," *New Left Review*, November-December 1993, p.61. Gorz adds that one of the difficulties with this vision today is the lack of a collective norm of sufficiency by which to judge when further work is no longer desirable. This issue will be discussed further in chapter 6.

92. Interview with Diana de Wolff, political advisor to the Green Left, The

Hague, June 24, 1998. "New initiatives to grant employees the right to work part time," *EIROnline*, March 1998: www.eiro.eurofound.ie/servlet/ptconvert?NL9803164F. In Canada University of Toronto economist Frank Reid has proposed a similar measure for its potential benefits in reducing unemployment.

93. Nash, *Frugality*, pp.16-17.
94. Ibid., pp.17-18.

4 PERVERTED BY PRODUCTIVISM? WORK-TIME REDUCTION AND AN EXPANSIONARY VISION

1. Lipietz, *La société en sablier*, pp.154-55; "The 12% Shame," *The Economist*, April 1, 1995.
2. Arthur Kelly, "The Great Society," *Biz*, Winter 1996, p.37.
3. Cross, *Time and Money*, pp.99, 103.
4. Pierre Larrouturou, *35 Heures: Le Double Piège* (Paris: Belfond, 1998), pp.30, 32.
5. Paul Morin, "La création d'emplois par la réduction du temps de travail: Partie 1—Proposition de mesure fiscales incitatives," *Canadian Tax Journal* 41,1 (1993), p.44. See also Advisory Group on Working Time and the Distribution of Work, *Report*, p.4; Tibor Scitovsky, "More Workers and Fewer Hours = Higher Productivity, *New Perspectives Quarterly*, Spring 1996, pp.38-40.
6. Overwork is widely recognized as a cause of deteriorating physical and mental health; meanwhile the National Forum on Health Policy concluded that unemployment was the main determinant of health problems in Canada. David Vinneau, "Joblessness Called Our Number One Health Threat," *The Toronto Star*, Feb. 2, 1997, p.A3.
7. Greider, "Global Warning." See also Kapstein, "Workers and the World Economy," pp.31-32.
8. Canadian Centre for Policy Alternatives and Cho!ces: A Coalition for Social Justice, *The 1997 Alternative Federal Budget Framework Document* (Ottawa-Winnipeg, 1997), pp.10-11, 13-14, 17-18, 80.
9. WTR is proposed, for instance, by Hutton and Kuttner, "Full Employment," and by Heilbroner, "Ghosts of the ATM Machine," p.21. In contrast, neither Greider, "Global Warning," nor Kapstein, "Workers and the World Economy," for instance, mention WTR in their calls for global expansionary measures.
10. Alessandro Motter, "The Struggle for Work Time Reductions: Labour's Last Frontier," unpublished manuscript, York University, Toronto, January 1995, pp.1-2.
11. One Swedish official commented at an October 1998 summit of the EU's predominantly social-democratic leaders, "tongue not altogether in cheek," that "We're all Keynesians now." Martin Walker, "Centre-Left Leaders Whistle New Tune," *The Guardian Weekly*, Nov. 1, 1998, p.6.
12. Jean-Pierre Jallade, "Working Time Policies in France," in *Working Time in Transition*, ed. Hinrichs, Roche, and Sirianni, p.79.

13. Aznar, "La semaine de quatre jours," p.68. See also Aznar, "Revenu mini-mum garanti et deuxième chèque," p.66.

14. Gorz, "Political Ecology," p.64.

15. Rybczynski, *Waiting for the Weekend*, p.142.

16. Lipietz, "Planet after Fordism."

17. Jamie Swift, "The Brave New World of Work," *Ideas*, CBC Radio, June 29, 1994.

18. Theo Beckers, "The Hidden Agenda: On the Expropriation of Time in Europe," Our Time Famine Conference, Department of Sport, Health, Leisure and Physical Studies, University of Iowa, Iowa City, March 9, 1996.

19. Reid, *Work and Leisure in the 21st Century*, p.88.

20. Durning, *How Much Is Enough?* p.47.

21. Sachs, Loske, Linz, et al., *Greening the North*, pp.54-55, 58-59.

22. Karl Hinrichs, "Working-Time Development in West Germany: Departure to a New Stage," in *Working Time in Transition*, ed. Hinrichs, Roche, and Sirianni, p.30.

23. Reid, *Work and Leisure in the 21st Century*, p.79. This training argument appears, for example, in Advisory Group on Working Time and the Distribution of Work, *Report*, p.61. It is also made by the Canadian Auto Workers in *More Time*, although the CAW vision of training pushes the boundaries of the dominant discourse back by also including time to study labour history, political economy, and union organizing, among other things.

24. Dobson, *Green Political Thought*, p.105.

25. Porritt, quoted in Dobson, *Green Political Thought*, p.105; Bob Black, "The Abolition of Work," *Resurgence* 166 (September-October 1994), p.25. For advocacy of "Athens without Slaves," see Kimon Valaskakis, "Does Human Work Have a Future?" *Vice Versa* 39 (October-November 1992), p.20.

26. Lipietz, *Towards a New Economic Order*, pp.86-87.

27. Gorz, cited in Eckersley, *Environmentalism and Political Theory*, p.134.

28. Lipietz, *Green Hopes*, pp.36-38, 45.

29. Elmar Altvater, "The Challenge of Ecology for Democracy," lecture, Faculty of Environmental Studies, York University, North York, Ont., March 4, 1997.

30. Robertson, *Future Work*, p.1.

31. Wayne Roberts and Susan Brandum, *Get A Life!* (Toronto: Get A Life Publishing, 1995), p.81.

32. Lehndorff argues that this has been the case in Germany with the ground-breaking accord at Volkswagen in 1993, which reduced regular weekly hours from 36 to 28.8 to save 30,000 jobs. Lehndorff, "La redistribution de l'emploi en Allemagne," p.10.

33. Advisory Group on Working Time and the Distribution of Work, *Report*, p.41.

34. Roberts and Brandum, *Get a Life!* p.81.

35. Durning, *How Much Is Enough?* p.146.

36. See, for instance, Cartwright, "Greening of Canada."

37. Canadian Centre for Policy Alternatives, *Environmental Sustainability, Growth, and the Future of Jobs.*

38. One example is the "Genuine Progress Indicator." See www.gpiatlantic.org.

5 WHY IT'S SO HARD TO WORK LESS

1. Scitovsky, "More Workers and Fewer Hours = Higher Productivity," pp.38-40; Advisory Group on Working Time and the Distribution of Work, *Report*, p.4; Morin, "La création d'emplois par la réduction du temps de travail," p.44.

2. This, of course, assumes that workers do actually receive their share of productivity gains. Such an assumption was a relatively safe one to make in the postwar Fordist "Golden Age of Capitalism" (roughly 1945-73), but in today's Post-Fordist world this can no longer be taken for granted.

3. Schor, "Can the North Stop Consumption Growth?" pp.72-73.

4. Hinrichs, "Working-Time Development in West Germany," p.36.

5. William K. Roche, Brian Fynes, and Terri Morrissey, "Working Time and Employment: A Review of International Evidence," *International Labour Review* 135,2 (1996), p.140.

6. De Neubourg, "Where Have All the Hours Gone?" p.139.

7. Larrouturou, *La Double Piège*, pp.75-76.

8. Huberman and Lacroix, "Worksharing in Historical Perspective," pp.20, 25.

9. "Focus On Working Time," *European Industrial Relations Review* 273 (October 1996), p.14; "La loi Aubry: une méthode et des outils," *CFDT en direct*, February 1998, pp.2-3.

10. Hinrichs, "Working-Time Development in West Germany," p.40.

11. Karl Hinrichs, William Roche, and Carmen Sirianni, "From Standardization to Flexibility: Changes in the Political Economy of Working Time," in *Working Time in Transition*, ed. Hinrichs, Roche, and Sirianni, p.24.

12. W.J. Shaxby, *An Eight-Hours Day: The Case against Trade-Union and Legislative Interference* (London: The Liberty Review Publishing Co., 1898), p.2.

13. "The Grand Illusion: A Survey of France," *The Economist*, June 5, 1999, p.5; *35 Heures La dépêche du ministère de l'Emploi et de la Solidarité* 36, May 11-17, 1999; Nikhil Deogun and Amy Barrett, "France Won't Let Coke Buy Orangina," *The Globe and Mail Report on Business*, Sept. 18, 1998.

14. Quoted in Moses, *Career Intelligence*, pp.82-83.

15. Studies in the early 1990s by the American Management Association and the Wyatt Companies found that companies that repeated downsizings produced "lower profits and declining worker productivity." Less than half the companies achieved the savings they had planned, fewer than one-third increased profitability, and less than a quarter increased their productivity. Desmond Christy, "Downsizing to Disaster," *The Guardian Weekly*, Nov. 15, 1998. See also Fred R. Bleakley, "Guru of Downsizing Changes His Mind," *The Globe and Mail*, May 20, 1996.

16. Marilyn Gardner, "Wanted: Employees to Work 30-Hour Weeks for 40 Hours' Pay," *Christian Science Monitor*, March 20, 1997; Wayne Roberts, "Same Pay for Shorter Hours Adds up to Profits," *NOW*, Sept. 18, 1997, pp.29, 31.

17. Roche, Fynes, and Morrissey, "Working Time and Employment," p.143; "Job-sharing: Box and Cox," *The Economist*, Aug. 6, 1994, p.56.

18. Quoted in Stanley K. Sheinbaum, "Educate the Leaders, Not Just the Workers," *New Perspectives Quarterly*, Spring 1996, p.64.
19. Greider, "Global Warming"; Kapstein, "Workers and the World Economy," pp.31, 35-37.
20. Margot Gibb-Clark, "Workers Lose Taste for Shorter Hours: Statscan," *The Globe and Mail*, March 17, 1997; Pierre O'Neill, "Solidaire des jeunes," *Le Devoir*, March 27, 1998.
21. Jamie Swift, quoted in Murray MacAdam, "Time of Our Lives: Sharing the Work Through Shorter Hours," *Our Times*, May/June 1996, p.38.
22. Response of a caller to radio phone-in show in which the author tried to make the case for shorter hours, CFRB Radio, Toronto, Sept. 11, 1996.
23. MacAdam, "Time of Our Lives," p.38.
24. Swift, "Brave New World of Work."
25. Workers' Information and Action Centre of Toronto, "Women's Time, Women's Work: Or Is the 4-Day Week the Answer?" Toronto, 1994, pp.3, 6.
26. Ibid., p.6.
27. Sam Gindin, Address, 32 HOURS: Action for Full Employment, Time for Change: A Conference on Reduced Work Time, Toronto, April 20, 1996.
28. Segal, "The Basics."
29. Gindin, Address.
30. Marc Breslow, "How People Spend Their Money: Socially Determined Needs in America," *Dollars and Sense*, January-February 1998, p.14.
31. David Noble, interviewed by Swift, "Brave New World of Work."
32. Segal, "The Basics."
33. Gerard Grannec, technician at electronics plant in a Paris suburb, quoted in Roger Cohen, "Europeans Considering Shortening Workweek to Relieve Joblessness," *The New York Times*, Nov. 23, 1993, p.A1.
34. Presumably one could argue that this failure of the imagination is itself a reflection of capitalism's generation of "worker-drones." Acceptance of such an argument, although tempting, means embracing the debilitating belief that the system is so strong that ordinary people have no power of agency.
35. Schor, "Can the North Stop Consumption Growth?" p.73.
36. Frank Reid, "Combatting Unemployment through Work Time Reductions," *Canadian Public Policy* XII,2 (1986), pp.280-81.
37. Paul Wachtel, cited in Reid, *Work and Leisure in the 21st Century*, p.84.
38. Sirianni, "Self-Management of Time," p.247.
39. Hinrichs, Roche, and Sirianni, "From Standardization to Flexibility," p.17; Hinrichs, "Working-Time Development in West Germany," pp.45-46.
40. Kevin Wilson, "Hooked on Killer Overtime," *NOW*, June 11-17, 1998, p.19.
41. Hinrichs, "Working-Time Development in West Germany," p.46.
42. Ibid.
43. Further details of this case cannot be revealed due to controversy about the legality of a union-led overtime boycott—an issue illustrating yet another obstacle to labour action on this issue.
44. Reid, "Combatting Unemployment through Work Time Reductions," p.278.
45. Hinrichs, Roche, and Sirianni, "From Standardization to Flexibility," p.13.

46. Hinrichs, "Working-Time Development in West Germany," p.41.

47. Hinrichs, Roche, and Sirianni, "From Standardization to Flexibility," p.16.

48. Sirianni, "Self-Management of Time," p.263.

49. André Gorz, *Critique of Economic Reason* (London: Verso, 1989), p.233.

50. Canadian Auto Workers, *More Time*; Canadian Auto Workers, "Turnaround Tools," *Our Times*, May/June 1998, p.23; Communications, Energy and Paperworkers (CEP), *More Jobs, More Fun: Shorter Hours of Work in the CEP* (Ottawa, 1997); Canadian Centre for Policy Alternatives and Cholces, *The 1997 Alternative Federal Budget Framework Document.*

51. Hinrichs, Roche, and Sirianni, "From Standardization to Flexibility," p.22.

52. Theresa Boyle, "GM Blasted on Overtime Request," *The Toronto Star*, Oct. 14, 1995, p.A26; Kelly Toughill, "Rights System a 'Barrier to Jobs,'" *The Toronto Star*, Jan. 23, 1997, p.A2. See also Ontario Red Tape Commission, "Cutting the Red Tape Barriers to Jobs and Better Government: Final Report," Province of Ontario, Toronto, January 1997.

53. Klaus Friedrich, chief economist at Dresden Bank, quoted in Cohen, "Europeans Considering Shortening Workweek to Relieve Joblessness." See also "Job-sharing: Box and Cox."

54. Guy Aznar, "Réduction du temps de travail: la loi Robien," *Futuribles*, February 1997, pp.15-28; Olivier Costemalle and Isabelle Mandraud, "L'Assemblée adopte les 35 h en première lecture," *Libération*, Feb. 11, 1998; Confédération des Syndicats Nationaux (CSN), *Les politiques gouvernementales en matière de la réduction du temps de travail au Québec* (Montreal, 1998), pp.7-9, 19-25; Craig McInnes, "B.C. to Make 40,000 Jobs out of Timber, Clark Says," *The Globe and Mail*, June 20, 1997, p.A10.

55. Michael Millett, "Less Work and More Jobs in Labor's Vision," *Sydney Morning Herald*, Nov. 13, 1997, p.5; "Labor Backs Campaign for Shorter Working Hours to Cut Jobless," *The Australian*, Jan. 6, 1997, p.2.

56. OECD, *OECD Employment Outlook: June 1998*, p.183.

57. Letter from Finance Minister Paul Martin to Rivka Philips, a member of 32 HOURS: Action for Full Employment, Nov. 28, 1996.

58. John Crispo, "Less Hours Equals More Jobs? Absurd," *The Toronto Star*, May 27, 1996.

59. Advisory Group on Working Time and the Distribution of Work, *Report*, p.52.

60. This is the response provided by one proponent of shorter work time, Judy Rebick, in an exchange on *Morningside*, CBC Radio, Jan. 3, 1997.

61. Sachs, Loske, Linz, et al., *Greening the North*, pp.117-18, 120.

62. Schor, *Overspent American*, pp.4-5, 37-38, 84-88.

63. Durning, *How Much Is Enough?* p.40.

64. Jonathan Kaufman, "Striking It Richer: U.S. Haves Envy the Have-Mores," *The Globe and Mail Report on Business*, Aug. 4, 1998.

65. Marc Cooper, "Twenty-Five Years after Allende: An Anti-Memoir," *The Nation*, March 23, 1998, p.12.

66. Schor, "Can the North Stop Consumption Growth?" p.75. See also Gorz, "Political Ecology," p.64.

67. Hunnicutt, *Kellogg's Six-Hour Day*, pp.139-42. In the original of the last quotation the worker himself underlined the word learning in the survey.

68. Oscar Wilde, quoted in "Workaholics Anonymous," p.20.

69. Quoted in Hunnicutt, *Kellogg's Six-Hour Day*, p.62.

70. Brandt, "Less Is More," p.83; Klaus Friedrich of Dresden Bank, quoted in Cohen, "Europeans Considering Shortening Workweek to Relieve Joblessness."

71. D. Benjamin, "Germany Is Troubled by How Little Work Its Workers Are Doing," *The Wall Street Journal*, May 6, 1993.

72. Reid, *Work and Leisure in the 21st Century*, p.65.

73. Harrington, *Socialism*, p.215; Aronowitz and DiFazio, *Jobless Future*, pp.328-29; Reid, *Work and Leisure in the 21st Century*, p.6.

74. Betty Friedan, "A New Paradigm beyond Social Politics," *Shift* (Iowa City) 1,1 (Fall 1996), p.4; Durning, *How Much Is Enough?* pp.115-16.

75. O'Hara, interviewed by Swift, "Brave New World of Work."

76. Bertrand Russell, quoted in The New Internationalist, *Sound Bites* (Oxford: New Internationalist Publications, 1997), p.98.

77. Alanna Mitchell, "Kids Face a Summer of All Work and No Play," *The Globe and Mail*, July 21, 1998, p.A1.

78. Lafargue, *Right to Be Lazy*, p.59.

79. Reid, *Work and Leisure in the 21st Century*, pp.77, 114.

80. Charles Handy, *The Future of Work* (London: Basil Blackwell, 1985), pp.11-12; quotation from Keynes, "Economic Possibilities for Our Grandchildren," p.328.

81. Reid, *Work and Leisure in the 21st Century*, p.92.

82. Keynes, "Economic Possibilities for Our Grandchildren," p.329.

83. Reid, *Work and Leisure in the 21st Century*, p.111.

84. Hunnicutt, interviewed by Swift, "Brave New World of Work"; Hunnicutt, *Kellogg's Six-Hour Day*, pp.10, 169-76.

85. John Clarke and Charles Critcher, quoted in Reid, *Work and Leisure in the 21st Century*, p.91.

86. The term serious leisure was coined by Robert A. Stebbins, cited in Reid, *Work and Leisure in the 21st Century*, p.62. See also p.111.

87. Brandt, "Less Is More," p.83.

88. De Neubourg, "Where Have All the Hours Gone?" p.132; Advisory Group on Working Time and the Distribution of Work, *Report*, p.13.

89. Schor, *Overworked American*, p.45. Work hours for the Dobe section of !Kung Bushmen from Marshall Sahlins, *Stone-Age Economics* (Chicago: Aldine Atherton, 1972), p.21.

6 WORK-TIME POLICY AND PRACTICE

1. This is the primary reason why the Toronto-based group "32 HOURS: Action for Full Employment" chose the name it did, despite recognizing the dangers of a name implying a narrow focus on the workweek. See also Handy, *Future of Work*, p.57.

2. Gorz, "Political Ecology," p.64.

3. Michel Rocard, "Editorial," *La Lettre du Député Européen Michel Rocard*, November 1996.

4. Morin, "La création d'emplois par la réduction du temps de travail," p.38.
5. Madelaine Drohan, "Jospin Faces Delicate Talks on Workweek," *The Globe and Mail Report on Business*, Oct. 10, 1997, p.B10.
6. Lubbers, "Dutch Way"; "Tripartite Agreement Establishes National 'Alliance for Jobs,'" EIROnline, December 1998: www.eiro.eurofound.ie/servlet/ptconvert?de9812286N; Confédération des Syndicats Nationaux (CSN), *Les politiques gouvernementales en matière de la réduction du temps de travail au Québec* (Montreal, 1998).
7. Jallade, "Working Time Policies in France," p.77. See also Hinrichs, Roche, and Sirianni, "From Standardization to Flexibility," p.23.
8. Hinrichs, "Working-Time Development in West Germany," p.43.
9. Reid points out that enforceability is generally not a problem if WTR is achieved through collective bargaining, because one or both parties has an interest in enforcing agreement. Reid, "Combatting Unemployment through Work Time Reductions," p.278.
10. Sirianni, "Self-Management of Time in Postindustrial Society," pp.250-51; Hinrichs, "Working-Time Development in West Germany," pp.53-54.
11. Jallade, "Working Time Policies in France," p.77; "Sharing the Burden," *The Economist*, Nov. 13, 1993, p.18. See also Hinrichs, "Working-Time Development in West Germany," p.54.
12. Lipietz, *Green Hopes*, p.50.
13. Reid, "Combatting Unemployment through Work Time Reductions," pp.278-79; Pierre Larrouturou and Michel Rocard, "Un nouvel enthousiasme," *Le Monde*, May 21, 1998. For a detailed argument of why 32 hours rather than 35 is needed, see Larrouturou, *35 Heures: Le Double Piège*. O'Hara also calls for a major one-time reduction in work time, arguing for a jump to a 32-hour workweek; see O'Hara, "Case for Shorter Working Time," p.23. Others point to the dangers of going too far, too fast. Some argue that the risk of income loss for workers is greater the bigger the reduction, raising fears about reductions of aggregate demand. Lehndorff, "La redistribution de l'emploi en Allemagne," p.17. Others fear the opposite, that reducing work time on a large scale will increase the risks that wage costs will get out of control. See Jallade, "Working Time Policies in France," p.72. These concerns highlight the challenge of finding the appropriate balance in sharing the costs of WTR, a balance that becomes ever more important to find the larger the size of the reduction.
14. Gorz, "Political Ecology," pp.64-65.
15. Reid, *Work and Leisure in the 21st Century*, p.111.
16. Jallade, "Working Time Policies in France," p.69.
17. Ulla Weigelt, "On the Road to a Society of Free Choice: The Politics of Working Time in Sweden," in *Working Time in Transition*, ed. Hinrichs, Roche, and Sirianni, pp.218-19.
18. Families and Work Institute, *Women: The New Providers* (Benton Harbor, Mich.: Whirlpool Foundation, 1995), pp.56-57; Gibb-Clark, "Workers Lose Taste for Shorter Hours"; Advisory Group on Working Time and the Distribution of Work, *Report*, p.87; Weigelt, "On the Road to a Society of Free Choice," p.222. See also Hunnicutt, "Kellogg's Six-Hour Day," p.154.
19. Workers' Information Action Centre, "Women's Time, Women's Work," p.5.

20. Theobald, "Rethinking Jobs, Work and Income," p.8.
21. Jean-Yves Boulin and Gilbert Cette, "Réduire la durée du travail: l'exemple des Pays-Bas," *Futuribles*, July-August 1997, pp.13-21; Lubbers, "Dutch Way"; Marie Wierink, "Temps de travail aux Pays-Bas: la voix des femmes," *Futuribles*, November 1998.
22. Jan Peter Van den Toren, "A 'Tripartite Consensus Economy': The Dutch Variant of a Social Pact," in *Social Pacts in Europe*, ed. Giuseppe Fajertag and Philippe Pochet (Brussels: European Trade Union Institute, 1997), p.188; OECD, *OECD Employment Outlook: June 1998*, p.161; Jean-Yves Boulin and Gilbert Cette, "La réduction du temps de travail aux des Pays-Bas," *Futuribles*, December 1997, p.63. See also "The Dutch Model's Vital Statistics," *The Economist*, May 2, 1998, p.49.
23. Meeting with Diana de Wolff, political advisor to the Green Left, The Hague, June 24, 1998.
24. Sirianni, "Self-Management of Time in Postindustrial Society," p.264.
25. Ontario Task Force on Hours of Work and Overtime, *Working Times: The Report of the Ontario Task Force on Hours of Work and Overtime*, Toronto, May 1987, pp.114-16; *Collective Reflection on the Changing Workplace: Report of the Advisory Committee on the Changing Workplace* (Ottawa: Ministry of Labour, 1997), pp.xvi, 155-58.
26. Statistics Canada study reported in Bruce Little, "Canadians Work Overtime—for Free," *The Globe and Mail*, July 15, 1997, p.B1.
27. Statistics for the United States show only about 4 per cent of men in very short-hours work, but this may be misleadingly low because only those with less than 15 hours are counted. OECD, *OECD Employment Outlook: June 1998*, p.158; Armine Yalnizyan, *The Growing Gap: A Report on Growing Inequality between the Rich and Poor in Canada* (Toronto: Centre for Social Justice, October 1998), pp.26-27.
28. Advisory Group on Working Time and the Distribution of Work, *Report*, pp.42, 79-81.
29. McInnes, "B.C. to Make 40,000 Jobs out of Timber," p.A10. See also B.C. government website: www.for.gov.bc.ca/PAB/JOBS/accord.accord.htm.
30. John Willis, "This Week Has 32 Hours," *This Magazine*, March 1998.
31. Julie White, "A Matter of Time," letter, *This Magazine*, July/August 1998, p.2; and personal communication with White.
32. Advisory Group on Working Time and the Distribution of Work, *Report*, p.41.
33. Canadian Union of Public Employees, *Policy Statement on Work Time*, Ottawa, 1995, p.6.
34. Dagmar S. Boettcher, "Off the Treadmill," Occasional Paper Series 4,2, Faculty of Environmental Studies, York University, North York, Ont., September 1998, p.23.
35. Enforcement of employment standards has been weakened through cutbacks to Ministry of Labour staffing and the provisions of the Orwellian-named "Bill 49: Employment Standards Improvement Act." The same bill originally included the "flexible standards" provision, which was dropped temporarily with the promise/threat of later resurrection. Toughill, "Rights System a 'Barrier to Jobs,'" p.A2. See also Ontario Red Tape Commission,

"Cutting the Red Tape Barriers to Jobs and Better Government: Final Report," Province of Ontario, Toronto, January 1997.

36. Confédération des Syndicats Nationaux (CSN), *Les politiques gouvernementales en matière de la réduction du temps de travail au Québec* (Montreal, 1998), pp.7-9, 19-25.

37. City of Vancouver Clerk's Office, Memorandum to Vancouver City Council, Compressed Work Week, June 25, 1998; Ian Mulgrew, "Ending Compressed Civic Work Week Makes No Sense," *The Vancouver Sun*, June 3, 1999, p.B1; Tom Walker, "'Five Days Costs More' Say Vancouver Workers," *Better Times* (The Newsletter of 32 HOURS: Action for Full Employment and the Shorter Work Time Network of Canada), June 1998, p.4.

38. Personal communication with Jim Stanford, economist with the Canadian Auto Workers. See also Canadian Auto Workers' web site: www.caw.ca/caw/chrysler/chrysler/html.

39. Advisory Group on Working Time and the Distribution of Work, *Report*, p.41; personal communication with Jim Stanford, economist with the Canadian Auto Workers.

40. Kevin Wilson, "Hooked On Killer Overtime," *NOW*, June 11-17, 1998, p.19; "Autoworker Urges 6-Hour Day, Says Overtime a Drug," *Better Times*, October 1998, p.3.

41. Communications, Energy and Paperworkers, "More Jobs, More Fun," pp.6-7.

42. Julie White, quoted in "Are Canadians Working Too Many Hours? How to Reduce Work Time for Canadians," *Atkinson Letter* (Toronto: Atkinson Charitable Foundation, forthcoming 1999).

43. Advisory Group on Working Time and the Distribution of Work, *Report*, p.40.

44. Julie White and Diane Goulet, "Contemplating the Four-Day Week: Lessons from Bell Canada," *Policy Options*, April 1998, pp.30-32.

45. Vanessa Lu, "Retirement Plan Aids Workers of All Ages," *The Toronto Star*, Dec. 7, 1998, p.B1.

46. Work/Family Directions Canada: www.wfdcanada.com/nws_flex.htm; Royal Bank: www.royalbank.com/hr/world/workfamily.html.

47. Canadian Labour Market Productivity Centre, *Case Studies of Alternative Working Arrangements and Changes in Working Time* (Ottawa, April 1997), pp.3-7.

48. Duncan Green, *Fashion Victims: The Asian Garment Industry and Globalisation* (London: CAFOD, 1998), pp.14-15.

49. *The U.S. in Haiti: How to Get Rich on 11¢ an Hour* (New York: National Labour Committee Education Fund, January 1996), pp.1, 7, 19.

50. *Conditions of Workers in the Garment Industry in China* (Asia Monitor Resource Centre [Hong Kong] and Sudwind Institute of Economics & Ecumenism [Germany], March 1997), p.1; *Labour Rights Report on Hong Kong Invested Toy Factories in China*, 2 (Asia Monitor Resource Centre and the Coalition for the Charter on the Safe Production of Toys, April 1997), p.3, Appendix I; Charles Kernaghan, *Behind the Label: Made in China* (New York: National Labor Committee, March 1998), p.71. Information provided by Labour Behind the Label Coalition / Maquila Solidarity Network, Toronto (www.web.net/~msn).

51. "Nike: Doing It Just?" *LBLC* (Newsletter of the Labour Behind the Label Coalition, Toronto), September 1997.
52. Mark Anner, quoted in Lynda Yanz, Bob Jeffcott, et al., *Policy Options to Improve Standards for Garment Workers in Canada and Internationally* (Ottawa: Status of Women Canada, January 1999), p.53.
53. "Unions, Who Needs Them?" *The Economist*, May 13, 1995.
54. "A Survey of South Korea: The House That Park Built," *The Economist*, June 3, 1995.
55. "A Survey of South Korea"; OECD, *OECD Employment Outlook: June 1998*, p.207.
56. "Korean Glums," *The Economist*, Jan. 10, 1998; "South Korea: More Troubles," *The Economist*, May 16, 1998; "South Korea: Making a Comeback," *The Economist*, Feb. 20, 1999; "South Korea's Workers Return to the Street," *The Economist*, May 1, 1999.
57. "Brazil: The Campaign Kicks Off," *The Economist*, July 11, 1998; Partido dos Trabalhadores, *Resoluções do 1° Congresso*, November-December 1991, pp.14, 16; author's translation.
58. Hein Marais, "Business Discontent with ANC Growing," *The Globe and Mail*, Nov. 22, 1997, p.A16; Zwelinzima Vami, COSATU press statement to mark the launch of the Basic Conditions of Employment Act, Dec. 2, 1998.
59. David Aquila Lawrence, "Colombian Prisoners to Get Vacations," *The Globe and Mail*, Dec. 20, 1997, p.A20.

7 EUROPE'S NEW MOVEMENT FOR WORK-TIME REDUCTION

1. Interview with Pierre Larrouturou, President, 4 Jours-Nouvel Equilibre, Paris, June 9, 1998.
2. Marcus Rubin and Ray Richardson, *The Microeconomics of the Shorter Working Week* (Aldershot, U.K.: Avebury, 1997), p.143.
3. An important intervention in this debate came from Pierre Larrouturou, who, as an Arthur Andersen consultant, was able to depoliticize the discussion and convince moderate members of the right-wing government of the economic merits of WTR. Interview with Larrouturou. See also Pierre Larrouturou, "Pour la semaine de quatre jours," *Le Monde*, Sept. 26, 1993.
4. Aznar, "Réduction du temps de travail," pp.15-28.
5. "RTT: Négocier à grande échelle," *Syndicalisme Hebdo (CFDT-France)*, May 22, 1998, p.4.
6. Confédération Française Démocratique du Travail, "Réduction du Temps de Travail: C'est maintenant qu'il faut négocier l'emploi gagnant," press release, Jan. 26, 1998.
7. Quoted in Aznar, "Réduction du temps de travail."
8. Interview with Larrouturou; Confédération Française Démocratique du Travail, "Réduction du Temps de Travail."
9. "Les principales dispositions du projet du loi," *Libération*, May 19, 1998. French government 35-hour website: www.35h.travail.gouv.fr; OECD, *OECD Employment Outlook: June 1998*, p.169; "35-Hour Working Week Law Adopted," *EIROnline*, June 1998: www.eiro.eurofound.ie/servlet/ptconvert/fr9806113f.sgm.

10. Isabelle Mandraud, "Chez Gandois, 34 h sans perte de salaire," *Libération*, Sept. 29, 1997.

11. Olivier Costemalle et al., "Sellière prie Aubry de respecter le terrain,'"*Libération*, Sept. 7, 1998.

12. "35-Hour Working Week Law Adopted"; Confédération Française Démocratique du Travail, "Réduction du Temps de Travail"; "La loi Aubry: une méthode et des outils," *CFDT en direct*, February 1998, pp.2-3.

13. "35-hour Working Week Law Adopted"; Christophe Forcari, "35 heures: 2 000 emplois créés," *Libération*, Sept. 7, 1998; UGICT-CGT Paris, *La Réduction du Temps de Travail*, 1998.

14. Christophe Forcari and Hervé Nathan, "Louis Viannet: ce qui a fait changer la CGT," *Libération*, Nov. 6, 1998; "CFDT and CGT Hold Congresses and Move Closer Together," *EIROnline*, February 1999: www.eiro.eurofound.ie/servlet/ptconvert?FR9902154F.

15. "35-Hour Working Week Law Adopted"; "Agreement in Metalworking: For or against the 35-Hour Working Week?" *EIROnline*, August 1998: www.eiro.eurofound.ie/servlet/ptconvert/fr9808129f.sgm.

16. Ministère de l'emploi et de la solidarité, "35h: Première étape," May 1999: www.35h.travail.gouv.fr; Antoine Guiral, "Le PS prépare le front des 35 heures," *Libération*, Sept. 1, 1999.

17. Hervé Nathan, "Ce que les 35 heures ont déja changé," *Libération*, May 20, 1999; "Implementing the 35-Hour Week Legislation: The First Six Months," *EIROnline*, January 1999: www.eiro.eurofound.ie/servlet/ptconvert?FR9901151F. Of the first 3,291 accords, 1,501 were in firms with fewer than 20 employees and another 724 were in firms with between 20 and 50 employees. Ministry of Employment and Solidarity, "Réduire la durée du travail pour l'emploi," press release, April 7, 1999: www.35h.travail.gouv.fr/actualite/presse/bilan070499.htm.

18. Hervé Nathan, "Les 35 heures accélèrent le tempo," *Libération*, Feb. 13-14, 1999; Hervé Nathan, "35 heures: les députés PS optimistes pour l'emploi," *Libération*, March 11, 1999; Hervé Nathan and François Wenz-Dumas, "Martine Aubry: '57 000 emplois, ce n'est pas rien," *Libération*, May 20, 1999; Hervé Nathan, "350 000 emplois créés en 1998, un record de trente ans," *Libération*, March 13-14, 1999.

19. "Agreement in Metalworking"; Christophe Forcari and Isabelle Mandraud, "Métallurgie: l'accord attendra l'an 2000," *Libération*, July 30, 1998; Laurent Joffrin, "L'emploi? On s'en fiche," *Libération*, July 29, 1998; Christophe Forcari and Stanislas Noyer, "35 heures: L'accord qui fait réver les patrons," *Libération*, Aug. 10, 1998; Hervé Nathan, "Deux recettes pour les 35 heures," *Libération*, Oct. 20, 1998.

20. Herve Nathan, "Peugeot-Citroën bute sur les 35 heures," *Libération*, Jan. 30-31, 1999; "Peugeout aux 35 heures (hors pause-pipi)," *Libération*, Jan. 23-24, 1999; Cécile Daumas, Marie-Joelle Gros, and Hervé Nathan, "Le week-end commencera le dimanche," *Libération*, Feb. 28-29, 1999.

21. Hervé Nathan, "Le 1er mai dit merci aux 35 heures," *Libération*, April 30-May 2, 1999; "35h: Première étape." A separate CFDT survey of 6,000 workers who moved to 35 hours found that 61 per cent were satisfied to have contributed to job creation. Ministry of Employment and Solidarity, *35*

Heures: La dépêche du ministère de l'Emploi et de la Solidarité 30 (March 2-8, 1999).

22. "35 heures cousues main pour Aubry"; "Deux recettes pour les 35 heures"; Stanislas Noyer, "35 heures dans le textile: la CGT se fait désirer," *Libération*, Oct. 28, 1999.

23. Nadya Charvet and Cécile Daumas, "35 h: pressés par la loi les patrons s'activent," *Libération*, Sept. 14, 1998; French government website: www.35h.travail.gouv.fr/guide/entreprise/index.htm

24. "Eurocopter Lands on a 35-Hour Week," *EIROnline*, June 1998: www.eiro.eurofound.ie/servlet/ptconvert/fr9806115f.sgm; "Eurocopter: L'Emploi Décolle," CFDT *Magazine*, May 1998, p.13.

25. Nicole Gauthier, "Strasbourg se met aux 35 heures," *Libération*, Aug. 18, 1998.

26. "Accord parfait," *Libération*, Jan. 13, 1999; "Flagship Agreement on Working Time Cuts at EDF-GDF," *EIROnline*, February 1999: www.eiro.eurofound.ie/servlet/ptconvert?FR9902155N.

27. Pascal Riché, "Les 35 heures sonnent pour les cadres," *Libération*, June 22, 1999; M.-J.G. and Hervé Nathan, "Délit de travail dissimulé chez Thomson-RCM," *Libération*, June 22, 1999; Frederic Filloux, "Paradoxe," *Libération*, May 20, 1999; author's translation of quotation.

28. Nathalie Raulin and François Wenz-Dumas, "Surprises de dernière heure pour les 35 heures," *Libération*, June 26-27, 1999; Isabelle Mandraud and Laurent Mauduit, "Ce que prévoit l'avant-projet de loi de Mme Aubry sur les 35 heures," *Le Monde*, June 25, 1999; Jean Michel-Bezat, Isabelle Mandraud, and Laurent Mauduit, "35 heures: Martine Aubry dévoile au Monde sa seconde loi," *Le Monde*, June 21, 1999.

29. Caroline Monnot, "35 heures: les projets de Mme Aubry critiqués de toutes parts," *Le Monde*, June 24, 1999; Jean-Michel Bezat and Isabelle Mandraud, "35 heures: M. Jospin exclut une 'loi de proclamation radicale,'" *Le Monde*, June 23, 1999; Hervé Nathan and François Wenz-Dumas, "Sans période de transition, le bug des 35 heures était garanti," *Libération*, June 28, 1999; Judith Perrignon, "On s'achemine vers le renoncement," *Libération*, June 22, 1999.

30. Interview with Larrouturou; Larrouturou, *35 heures*.

31. Interview with Larrouturou; interview with Michel Rocard, Member of European Parliament, Paris, June 29, 1998; Pierre Larrouturou and Michel Rocard, "Un nouvel enthousiasme," *Le Monde*, May 21, 1998.

32. Lipietz, *La Société en Sablier*, p.150.

33. Institute for Economics and Social Science (WSI), *Industrial Relations in Germany 1997: WSI-Contributions to the European Industrial Relations Observatory* (Dusseldorf: Institute for Economics and Social Science [WSI], 1997), pp.23-24; "Provisions on 'Working Time Accounts' in Collective Agreements," *EIROnline*, March 1998: www.eiro.eurofound.ie/servlet/ptconvert?de9803255f.

34. Interview with Reinhard Bispinck, Collective Bargaining Researcher, Institute for Economics and Social Science (WSI), Dusseldorf, June 17, 1998; Jonathan Steele, "The Beetle's Punctured Pride," *The Guardian Weekly*, Oct. 1, 1995, p.13. See also Scitovsky, "More Workers and Fewer

Hours = Higher Productivity," p.40.

35. Interview with Bispinck; interview with Manfred Muster, Chair, IG Metall—District Bremen, Hamburg, June 18, 1998.

36. "New IG Metall Initiative Demands Further Reduction in Working Time," *EIROnline*, May 1998: www.eiro.eurofound.ie/servlet/ptconvert/de9805262f.sgm.

37. "ÖTV Leader Sets 30-Hour Week as Long-term Goal," *EIROnline*, February 1998: www.eiro.eurofound.ie/ptconvert/de9802252n.sgm; "Debate on Working Time: What Workers Want," *EIROnline*, September 1997: www.eiro.eurofound.ie/servlet/ptconvert/de9709127f.sgm.

38. Interview with Bispinck; WSI, *Industrial Relations in Germany 1997*, p.22.

39. "ÖTV Leader Sets 30-Hour Week as Long-term Goal."

40. Interview with Muster.

41. WSI, *Industrial Relations in Germany 1997*, p.24; interview with Bispinck.

42. Interview with Muster.

43. Interview with Willi Hilger, Labour Market Policy Advisor, Social Democratic Party, Bonn, June 17, 1998; "DGB Quits Employment Alliance for Eastern Germany," *EIROnline*, June 1998: www.eiro.eurofound.ie/servlet/ptconvert?de9806166f; "Unions Demand Creation of New Jobs through Reduction of Overtime," *EIROnline*, January 1999: www.eiro.eurofound.ie/servlet/ptconvert?de9901289n; "Tripartite Agreement Establishes National 'Alliance for Jobs,'" *EIROnline*, December 1998: www.eiro.eurofound.ie/servlet/ptconvert?de9812286N; Andrea Tarquini, "Pensione a 60 anni, è scontro," *La Repubblica* (Rome), Nov. 9, 1998, p.4.

44. Rubin and Richardson, *Microeconomics of the Shorter Working Week*, p.144; WSI, *Industrial Relations in Germany 1997*, p.24.

45. Interview with Bispinck; Rubin and Richardson, *Microeconomics of the Shorter Working Week*, p.145.

46. "New IG Metall initiative."

47. Steffen Lehndorff, "La redistribution de l'emploi en Allemagne," *Futuribles*, February 1995, p.14.

48. Rubin and Richardson, *Microeconomics of the Shorter Working Week*, p.145; interview with Bispinck.

49. Interview with Muster; interview with Hilger. Hourly productivity in German metalworking grew by between 5 and 6 per cent in 1998: Lorraine Millot, "Salaires: les métallos allemands arrachent 4%," *Libération*, Feb. 19, 1999.

50. OECD, *OECD Employment Outlook: June 1998*, p.156; interview with Bispinck. Unemployment statistics from "Economic Indicators," *The Economist*, June 12, 1999.

51. Nadya Charvet, "La Basse-Saxe explore l'après-35 heures," *Libération*, Sept. 26, 1998; "Innovative Package Deal in Lower-Saxony Metalworking," *EIROnline*, August 1998: www.eiro.eurofound.ie/servlet/ptconvert?de9808175n; "Municipal Pact for Jobs in Wuppertal Local Administration," *EIROnline*, December 1999: www.eiro.eurofound.ie/servlet/ptconvert?DE9812284N.

52. Interview with Eckart Hildebrandt, Professor, WZB, Berlin, June 20, 1998.

53. "Jobless Demand More Leisure," *The Globe and Mail*, Aug. 4, 1998.

54. "New IG Metall initiative."

55. OECD, *OECD Employment Outlook: June 1998*, p.166.

56. Interview with Christoph Scherrer, Professor of Political Science, Kennedy Institut—Freie Universität Berlin, Berlin, June 19, 1998; Helmut Kohl, quoted in D. Benjamin, "Germany Is Troubled by How Little Work Its Workers Are Doing," *The Wall Street Journal*, May 6, 1993.

57. Unemployment rate from "Economic Indicators," *The Economist*, June 12, 1999.

58. Swedish sociologist Göran Therborn, *Why Some People Are More Unemployed than Others* (1986), cited in Jelle Visser, "Two Cheers for Corporatism, One for the Market: Industrial Relations, Wage Moderation and Job Growth in the Netherlands," *British Journal of Industrial Relations* 36,2 (June 1998), p.269.

59. OECD, *OECD Employment Outlook: June 1998*, pp.155, 207. One has to be cautious with international comparisons of hours, because there is significant difference in how national statistics are calculated. See also Jean-Yves Boulin and Gilbert Cette, "Réduire la durée du travail: l'exemple des Pays-Bas," *Futuribles*, July-August 1997, pp.13-21; Jean-Yves Boulin and Gilbert Cette, "La réduction du temps de travail aux des Pays-Bas," *Futuribles*, December 1997, pp.61-65.

60. Visser, "Two Cheers for Corporatism," pp.269-70, 274; Jelle Visser and Anton Hemerijck, *A Dutch Miracle: Job Growth, Welfare Reform and Corporatism in the Netherlands* (Amsterdam: Amsterdam University Press, 1997), p.137; Ministry of Economic Affairs, "The Development of the Dutch Economy: An International Perspective," The Hague, May 1997.

61. Visser, "Two Cheers for Corporatism," pp.279-80; Joop Hartog and Jules Theeuwes, "Explaining the Dutch Economic Miracle," *Policy Options*, October 1997, p.39; René A.C. Blijlevens, VNO-NCW (Confederation of Netherlands Industry and Employers), Address, 1998 European Employee Relations Conference, Brussels, June 23, 1998; Jan Peter Van den Toren, "A 'Tripartite Consensus Economy': The Dutch Variant of a Social Pact," in *Social Pacts in Europe*, ed. Giuseppe Fajertag and Philippe Pochet (Brussels: European Trade Union Institute, 1997), p.185.

62. Interview with Jan Peter Van den Toren, Christian Trade Union Federation (CNV), Utrecht, June 23, 1998; Van den Toren, " 'Tripartite Consensus Economy,'" p.188; Blijlevens, Address.

63. Boulin and Cette, "Réduire la durée du travail: l'exemple des Pays-Bas," p.20; De Neubourg, "Where Have All the Hours Gone?" p.138.

64. OECD, *OECD Employment Outlook: June 1998*, p.161; Blijlevens, Address; "Employers Oppose 'Work and Care' Framework Bill," *EIROnline*, March 1999: www.eiro.eurofound.ie/servlet/ptconvert?NL9903128F.

65. OECD, *OECD Employment Outlook: June 1998*, p.176; Roche, Fynes, and Morrissey, "Working Time and Employment," p.145.

66. Van den Toren, " 'Tripartite Consensus Economy,'" p.188.

67. Eurostat study, 1996, cited in Boulin and Cette, "Réduction du temps de travail aux des Pays-Bas," p.63. A 1993 study found that only 15 per cent of Dutch part-timers would have preferred but could not find a full-time job. A similar proportion of full-timers said they wanted to go to part-time in the

form of a four-day week. Cited in Visser, "Two Cheers for Corporatism," p.273. See also "The Dutch Model's Vital Statistics," *The Economist*, May 2, 1998, p.49.

68. Blijlevens, Address.
69. Schor, *Beyond an Economy of Work and Spend*, p.7; "Agreement between AKZO-Nobel and the Trade Unions," *EIROnline*, April 1997: www.eiro.eurofound.ie/servlet/ptconvert?nl9704111n; Blijlevens, Address.
70. Interview with Van Den Toren; "Agreement between AKZO-Nobel and the Trade Unions."
71. OECD, *OECD Employment Outlook: June 1998*, p.177; "New Career Breaks Bill Promotes Care and Study Leave," *EIROnline*, May 1997: www.eiro.eurofound.ie/servlet/ptconvert?NL9705115N.
72. Interview with Diana de Wolff, political advisor to the Green Left, The Hague, June 24, 1998; "New Initiatives to Grant Employees the Right to Work Part Time," *EIROnline*, March 1998: www.eiro.eurofound.ie/servlet/ptconvert?NL9803164F; Marie Wierink, "Temps de travail aux Pays-Bas: la voix des femmes," *Futuribles*, November 1998, p.63; "Employers Oppose 'Work and Care' Framework Bill."
73. Interview with de Wolff.
74. "Employers Oppose 'Work and Care' Framework Bill"; Wierink, "Temps de travail aux Pays-Bas," pp.58-60.
75. Sophie Perrier, "Quand l'homme apprend le temps partiel," *Libération*, May 3, 1999.
76. Schor, *Overspent American*, p.171; OECD, *OECD Employment Outlook: June 1998*, pp.166-67.
77. Meeting with Stephan Schrover, Church Campaign Against the 24-Hour Economy, Utrecht, June 25, 1998; "Churches Rally against the 24-Hour Economy," *EIROnline*, July 1998: www.eiro.eurofound.ie/servlet/ptconvert?nl9807189f.
78. For a critique from the right, see Peter Cook, "No Dutch Miracle after All," *The Globe and Mail Report on Business*, Sept. 26, 1997. For a rather unbalanced critique from the left, see Dietmar Henning and Wolfgang Weber, "The Dutch Model," *Canadian Dimension*, September-October 1998, pp.32-35. See also "Occupational Disability: A Dutch Disease?" *EIROnline*, February 1999: www.eiro.eurofound.ie/servlet/ptconvert?NL9902124F.
79. Visser, "Two Cheers for Corporatism," pp.270-71.
80. In the 1980s worker compensation relative to GDP fell by 1.3 per cent annually in the Netherlands, compared to an average annual fall of 0.5 per cent in 11 major industrialized countries. In 1990-96 there was a further 0.4 per cent annual decline in the Netherlands, versus an average 0.5 per cent. OECD, *OECD Employment Outlook: June 1998*, p.165. Labour's share of national income fell from 93 per cent in 1983 to 83 per cent in 1997, although there are signs that the trend has since levelled off. Ministry of Economic Affairs, "Development of the Dutch Economy." See also Visser, "Two Cheers for Corporatism," pp.280, 284; Hartog and Theeuwes, "Explaining the Dutch Economic Miracle," p.38. For labour's new coordination of bargaining demands, see "Unions in Benelux and Germany

Favour Close Transnational Coordination of Bargaining Policy,"
EIROnline, October 1998:
www.eiro.eurofound.ie/servlet/ptconvert?DE9810278F.

81. OECD, *OECD Employment Outlook: June 1998*, p.168; "Economic Indicators,"
The Economist, June 5, 1999, p.98; "LO Evaluates the 1998 Collective
Bargaining Round," *EIROnline*, July 1998:
www.eiro.eurofound.ie/servlet/ptconvert?dk9807178f.

82. OECD, *OECD Employment Outlook: June 1998*, pp.173, 176; Paul Knox, "The
Danes Give Themselves a Chance to Think," *The Globe and Mail*, April 1,
1995, p.D4; Olivier Truc, "La rançon de la gloire," *Libération*, March 15,
1999.

83. Hilary Barnes, "Danish Action to Settle Strikes Raises Doubts," *The
Financial Times*, May 8, 1998; "Parliament Intervenes to End Major
Conflict," *EIROnline*, May 1998:
www.eiro.eurofound.ie/servlet/ptconvert?dk9805168f; "Trade Union
Demands Sixth Week of Paid Holiday," *EIROnline*, September 1998:
www.eiro.eurofound.ie/servlet/ptconvert?dk9809184n.

84. Olivier Truc, "Ces Danoises qui préfèrent le temps à l'argent," *Libération*,
May 8, 1998.

85. Ibid.

86. "Improved Conditions for Families with Small Children Top the Agenda,"
EIROnline, June 1998: www.eiro.eurofound.ie/servlet/ptconvert?dk9806172f;
Truc, "Ces Danoises."

87. "Improved Conditions for Families with Small Children Top the Agenda."

88. "Trade Union Proposes Flexible Legislation on Leave," *EIROnline*,
February 1998: www.eiro.eurofound.ie/servlet/ptconvert?dk9802156n.

89. "Danemark, l'Europe sans enthousiasme," *CFDT Magazine* (France), May
1998, p.30.

90. Schor, *Overspent American*, p.171.

91. Bénédicte Vaes, "La Belgique Lance la Semaine de Quatre Jours," *Alternatives
Economiques*, April 1995, pp.22-23; OECD, *OECD Employment Outlook: June
1998*, p.175.

92. Rubin and Richardson, *Microeconomics of the Shorter Working Week*, p.140;
Roche, Fynes, and Morrisey, "Working Time and Employment," pp.145, 147.

93. "New Sectoral Collective Agreements Cover 1.4 Million Workers,"
EIROnline June 1997: www.eiro.eurofound.ie/servlet/ptconvert?be9706205f;
OECD, *OECD Employment Outlook: June 1998*, pp.174-75.

94. OECD, *OECD Employment Outlook: June 1998*, pp.174, 176.

95. "Debate on Overall Reduction of Working Time in Belgium"; "Belgian
Government Launches New Plan for Jobs," *EIROnline*, July 1997:
www.eiro.eurofound.ie/servlet/ptconvert?be97072313f; "Experimental
Reduction of Working Time at Interbrew," *EIROnline*, May 1997:
www.eiro.eurofound.ie/servlet/ptconvert?be9705106n.

96. "Pioneering Sectoral Agreement at Electrabel: 35-Hour Week and Job
Creation," *EIROnline*, January 1998:
www.eiro.eurofound.ie/ servlet/ ptconvert?be9801130n.

97. "Agreement to Reduce Working Time at Volkswagen Belgium,"
EIROnline, September 1997:

www.eiro.eurofound.ie/servlet/ptconvert?BE9709116N; "Five-shift System Could Create Jobs in Antwerp's Chemicals Sector," *EIROnline*, April 1999: www.eiro.eurofound.ie/servlet/ptconvert?BE9904270N.

98. "Building Public Opinion behind the 35-Hour Week Campaign," *EIROnline*, November 1997: www.eiro.eurofound.ie/servlet/ptconvert?be9711124n; "A 32-Hour Working Week—The Key to Employment in Belgium?" *EIROnline*, October 1997: www.eiro.eurofound.ie/servlet/ptconvert?be9710221n; "Debate on Overall Reduction of Working Time in Belgium," *EIROnline*, November 1997: www.eiro.eurofound.ie/servlet/ptconvert?be9711123f.

99. "TT and STTK Disagree Sharply on Working Time," *EIROnline*, July 1998: www.eiro.eurofound.ie/servlet/ptconvert?fi9807169n; "SAK and STTK Propose Hours Cuts as Part of Next Government's Programme," *EIROnline*, August 1998: www.eiro.eurofound.ie/servlet/ptconvert?FI98081714N; "Working Time Experiments Introduced in 20 Municipalities," *EIROnline*, March 1997: www.eiro.eurofound.ie/servlet/ptconvert?fi9703108n.

100. OECD, *OECD Employment Outlook: June 1998*, p.177; "Sabbatical Leave Scheme Gains in Popularity," *EIROnline*, April 1997: www.eiro.eurofound.ie/servlet/ptconvert?FI9704110F; "Sabbatical Leave Scheme to Be Continued," *EIROnline*, September 1997: www.eiro.eurofound.ie/servlet/ptconvert?fi9709131n; Antoine Jacob, "Finnish PM Is Parental Role Model," *The Guardian Weekly*, Sept. 13, 1998.

101. "Avanti con le 35 ore, Fossa non ci sta," *Corriere della Sera* (Milan), March 25, 1998, p.3; "Government Approves Bill on the 35-Hour Week," *EIROnline*, March 1998: www.eiro.eurofound.ie/servlet/ptconvert?it9803159n.

102. "Parliament Approves Law on Overtime," *EIROnline*, December 1999: www.eiro.eurofound.ie/servlet/ptconvert?IT9812192N; "Working Hours Still a Controversial Issue in Italy," *EIROnline*, November 1998: www.eiro.eurofound.ie/servlet/ptconvert?IT9811238F; "Tetto agli straordinari, multa per chi 'sfora,'" *La Repubblica*, Nov. 10, 1998; "'Relay Part-time' Scheme to Be Implemented," *EIROnline*, April 1999: www.eiro.eurofound.ie/servlet/ptconvert?IT9904245F.

103. "Avanti con le 35 ore, Fossa non ci sta," *Corriere della Sera*, March 25, 1998, p.3; "L'Italie tergiverse," *Libération*, May 19, 1998; "Employers React to the Government's Commitment to the 35-Hour Week," *EIROnline*, November 1997: www.eiro.eurofound.ie/servlet/ptconvert?IT9711216F; interview with Vittorio Milano, Confederazione Italiana Sindicati Lavorativi (CISL), Milan, June 12, 1998; interview with Antonio Panzeri, Confederazione Generale Italiana di Lavoro (CGIL), Milan, June 12, 1998; "Sì a una legge che sostenga la contrattazione," *Milano Sindicale (CISL)*, March 1998, p.2.

104. "National Agreement Signed for the Chemicals Industry," *EIROnline*, June 1998: www.eiro.eurofound.ie servlet/ptconvert?it9806325f.

105. "Agreements Renewed for Ministries and State Controlled Bodies," *EIROnline*, August 1998: www.eiro.eurofound.ie/servlet/ptconvert?it9808329f; "Gli statali vanno a 35 ore," *La Repubblica*, July 27, 1998.

106. *EIRO 1997 Annual Review—Sweden*: www.eiro.eurofound.ie/1997/review/eiroar22.htm.

107. Weigelt, "On the Road to a Society of Free Choice," pp.215-16; "Government Proposes Law on Leave for Urgent Family Reasons," *EIROnline*, March 1998: www.eiro.eurofound.ie/servlet/ptconvert?se9803176n.
108. Weigelt, "On the Road to a Society of Free Choice," pp.215-16; "Personal Educational Accounts May Complement Collectively Agreed Measures," *EIROnline*, August 1997: www.eiro.eurofound.ie/servlet/ptconvert?se9708132f.
109. OECD, *OECD Employment Outlook: June 1998*, pp.156, 207.
110. "Engineering Agreements Provide for Reduction in Working Time," *EIROnline*, March 1998: www.eiro.eurofound.ie/servlet/ptconvert?SE9803177N; "1998 Bargaining Brings Moderate Pay Increases, Flexible Working Time Rules and Declarations on Skill Development," *EIROnline*, June 1998: www.eiro.eurofound.ie/servlet/ptconvert?se9806190f.
111. "Government Forced to Cooperate after Election Setback," *EIROnline*, October 1998: www.eiro.eurofound.ie/servlet/ptconvert?se98110116neiro; "Swedish Employers Urged to Negotiate on the Reduction of Working Time," *EIROnline*, May 1997: www.eiro.eurofound.ie/servlet/ptconvert?se9705119f; *EIRO 1997 Annual Review—Sweden*.
112. Lafargue, *Right to Be Lazy*, p.58.
113. Roche, Fynes, and Morrissey, "Working Time and Employment," p.134; OECD, *OECD Employment Outlook: June 1998*, p.180; "New Working Time Regulations Take Effect," *EIROnline*, October 1998: www.eiro.eurofound.ie/servlet/ptconvert?uk9810154f; "Working Time Moves to the Top of the Agenda," *EIROnline*, February 1997: www.eiro.eurofound.ie/servlet/ptconvert?uk9702103f.
114. "Campaign for Paid Parental Leave Launched," *EIROnline*, November 1998: www.eiro.eurofound.ie/servlet/ptconvert?UK9811160N.
115. Sarah Boseley, "British Teenagers Have Worst Sexual Health in Europe," *The Guardian Weekly*, May 23, 1999, p.11.
116. "The 40-Hour Working Week Finally in Force in Portugal," *EIROnline*, December 1997: www.eirofound.ie/servlet/ptconvert?pt9712154f.
117. "Subsidies Proposed for Companies That Introduce 35-Hour Week," *EIROnline*, September 1998: www.eiro.eurofound.ie/servlet/ptconvert?es9809282n; "La Junta andaluza implantará en breve la jornada de 35 horas," *El Pais* (Madrid), Aug. 31, 1998; "La Comunidad de Madrid implantará las 35 horas semanales a 30.000 funcionarios," *El Pais*, July 21, 1998; "La Comunidad de Madrid urge la reducción de jornada," *El Pais*, July 10, 1998; "Working Time and Employment: The Balance Sheet So Far," *EIROnline*, July 1998: www.eiro.eurofound.ie/servlet/ptconvert?es9807178f; "Pact for Employment Agreed in Catalonia (1998-2000)," *EIROnline*, May 1998: www.eiro.eurofound.ie/servlet/ptconvert?es9805154f; "Arenas critica los incentivos a la reducción de jornada propuestos por Pujol y Ruiz-Gallardón," *El Pais*, July 8, 1998; "Incentives to Reduce Working Time and Create Employment in Catalonia," *EIROnline-Spain*, October 1998: www.eiro.eurofound.ie/servlet/ptconvert?es9810186n; "La Junta de Extremadura aprueba la jornada de 35 horas para sus trabajadores," *El Pais*, Dec. 4, 1998.

118. "First Agreement on the 35-Hour Week," *EIROnline*, October 1998: www.eiro.eurofound.ie/servlet/ptconvert?GR9810197N.

8 WITH OR WITHOUT LOSS IN PAY? WITH OR WITHOUT THE REVOLUTION?

1. For a critique of Rifkin, see Henwood, "Work and Its Future." For the case that productivity growth will remain slow, see Andrew Glyn, "Northern Growth and Environmental Constraints," in *The North, the South and the Environment*, ed. Bhaskar and Glyn, pp.54, 56.
2. OECD, *OECD Employment Outlook: June 1998*, p.165; Bruce Little, "Strikes, Weaker Economy Dampen Productivity Growth," *The Globe and Mail Report on Business*, July 1, 1999; Barrie McKenna, "Canadian Productivity Posts Weak Growth in 1996," *The Globe and Mail*, June 6, 1997, p.B5; Bruce Little, "Productivity Paradox Puzzles Experts," *The Globe and Mail*, April 14, 1997, p.B1.
3. Andrew Jackson, chief economist for the Canadian Labour Congress, argues that less scope exists for the tradeoff of work-time flexibility for WTR in North America because business already enjoys a high degree of flexibility.
4. Four-day-week example at food retailer Ducs de Gascogne from Pierre Larrouturou, *20 Enterprises Déja Passées à la Semaine de 4 Jours* (Paris: 4 Jours-Nouvel Equilibre, 1997).
5. Hinrichs, "Working-Time Development in West Germany," p.52; Jallade, "Working Time Policies in France," p.80.
6. Hinrichs, "Working-Time Development in West Germany," p.50.
7. De Neubourg, "Where Have All the Hours Gone?" p.139.
8. Jallade, "Working Time Policies in France," pp.80, 83.
9. Susan Christopherson "Trading Time for Consumption: The Failure of Working-Hours Reduction in the United States," in *Working Time in Transition*, ed. Hinrichs, Roche, and Sirianni, p.171.
10. National Forum on Health, *Canada Health Action: Building on the Legacy*, vol. I, *Final Report* (Ottawa: National Forum on Health, 1997), p.22.
11. See, for example, Reid, *Work and Leisure in the 21st Century*, p.108.
12. Aznar, "Revenu minimum garanti et deuxième chèque," pp.60-61.
13. Ibid., pp.62-67; Aznar, "Semaine de quatre jours," p.69.
14. Aznar, *Travailler Moins pour Travailler Tous*, p.106.
15. Sirianni, "Self-Management of Time in Postindustrial Society," pp.259-62; Hinrichs, Roche, and Sirianni, "From Standardization to Flexibility," pp.8, 22; Weigelt, "On the Road to a Society of Free Choice," p.227; Roche, Fynes, and Morrissey, "Working Time and Employment," pp.135-36. Rehn's original proposal is outlined in Gösta Rehn, "Towards a Society of Free Choice," in *Comparing Public Policies*, ed. Jerzy J. Wiatr and Richard Rose (1977), pp.121-57.
16. Gorz, *Critique of Economic Reason*, pp.241-42. Rifkin has called for a similar tax, using the funds to create jobs in the non-profit "third sector" rather than to top up incomes. Rifkin, "Civil Society in the Information Age," p.16.
17. Jacques Robin, "Repenser les activités humaines à l'échelle de la vie," *Le*

Monde Diplomatique, March 1997, p.5.

18. Crié, "Taxes Vertes"; Raulin, "Jospin règle le Meccano de la deuxième loi."
19. Aznar, "Semaine de quatre jours," p.69; Aznar, "Revenu minimum garanti et deuxième cheque," p.60.
20. Boulding, quoted in Daly, "Consumption," p.17.
21. Quoted in Pierre Larrouturou and Michel Rocard, "Un nouvel enthousiasme," *Le Monde*, May 21, 1998.
22. Aznar, "Semaine de quatre jours," p.68.
23. Lehndorff, "Redistribution de l'emploi en Allemagne," pp.9, 16.
24. However, if workers accept a less than proportionate reduction in pay, in which they receive hourly pay increases equal to any increase in hourly productivity following the reduction of work hours, there would be no shift in income from labour to capital.
25. Roberts and Brandum, *Get a Life!* p.85. See also Wayne Roberts, Rod MacRae, and Lori Stahlbrand, *Real Food for a Change* (Toronto: Random House of Canada, 1999), pp.69-78.
26. Handy, *Future of Work*, p.9.
27. Interview with Gerhard Scherhorn, Director, Working Group on New Models of Wealth, Wuppertal Institute for Climate, Environment and Energy, Wuppertal, Germany, June 16, 1998.
28. Barbara Brandt, *Whole Life Economics: Revaluing Daily Life* (Gabriola Island, B.C.: New Society Publishers, 1995), pp.190-91; Murray, "History Pushing toward Four-Day Working Week."
29. Roberts and Brandum, *Get a Life!* pp.76-77.
30. Handy, *Future of Work*, p.172.
31. Roberts and Brandum suggest, for example, that union pension funds could offer discounted mortgages to those who volunteer for the four-day week; Roberts and Brandum, *Get a Life!* p.76.
32. Joe Dominguez and Vicki Robin, *Your Money or Your Life?* (New York: Penguin, 1992).
33. Aronowitz and DiFazio, *Jobless Future*, p.349.
34. Heilbroner, "Ghosts of the ATM Machine," p.21.
35. Hutton and Kuttner, "Full Employment in a Free Society." "Incomes policies" and "social pacts" to limit wage pressures under conditions of low unemployment are another option to minimize inflation and the consequent flight of capital.
36. For a discussion of options for far-reaching investment alternatives, see Jim Stanford, *Paper Boom* (Toronto: James Lorimer, 1999), chapter 16.
37. For a discussion of how differences in the progressivity of taxation have affected work hours in Germany and the United States, see "Workaholics Anonymous."
38. Heilbroner, "Ghosts of the ATM Machine," p.21.
39. For example, annual population growth for 2000-2015 is estimated at 0.05 per cent in Denmark, -0.03 per cent in Japan, and -0.30 per cent in Italy; The Economist, *Pocket World in Figures: 1999* (Toronto: John Wiley & Sons, 1999), p.15. Canada, however, is experiencing continued population growth due to significant immigration levels. To maintain the same level of material living standards per capita, GDP growth would have to equal the increase in

population.
40. Nash, *Frugality*, p.9.
41. Victor Lebow, quoted in Durning, *How Much Is Enough?* pp.21-22.
42. Gorz, *Capitalism, Socialism, Ecology*, pp.32-33.
43. Doug Saunders, "Strikers Plan to Chain Theatres Shut," *The Globe and Mail*, Dec. 28, 1996, p.A10.
44. Oliver Bertin, "CN Chops 3,000 More Jobs," *The Globe and Mail*, Oct. 21, 1998, p.A1. Stock option statistics from the Canadian Auto Workers.
45. Michal Kalecki, "Political Aspects of Full Employment," *Political Quarterly* 14,4 (1943), p.331.
46. Gorz, *Capitalism, Socialism, Ecology*, p.12.

Selected Bibliography

Advisory Group on Working Time and the Distribution of Work. *Report of the Advisory Group on Working Time and the Distribution of Work*. Ottawa: Ministry of Supply and Services, 1994.

Aronowitz, Stanley and William DiFazio. *The Jobless Future: Sci-Tech and the Dogma of Work*. Minneapolis: University of Minnesota Press, 1994.

Aznar, Guy. *Travailler Moins pour Travailler Tous*. Paris: Syros, 1993.

Bhaskar, V. and Andrew Glyn, eds. *The North, the South and the Environment: Ecological Constraints and the Global Economy*. London: Earthscan, 1995.

Brandt, Barbara. *Whole Life Economics: Revaluing Daily Life*. Gabriola Island, B.C.: New Society Publishers, 1995.

Canadian Labour Market Productivity Centre. *Case Studies of Alternative Working Arrangements and Changes in Working Time*. Ottawa, April 1997.

Communications, Energy and Paperworkers Union of Canada (CEP). *More Jobs, More Fun: Shorter Hours of Work in the CEP*. Ottawa, 1997.

Cross, Gary. *Time and Money: The Making of Consumer Culture*. London: Routledge, 1993.

Daly, Herman E. and John B. Cobb, Jr. *For the Common Good: Redirecting the Economy toward Community, the Environment, and a Sustainable Future*. Boston: Beacon Press, 1989.

Daly, Herman E. and Kenneth N. Townsend, eds. *Valuing the Earth: Economics, Ecology, Ethics*. Cambridge, Mass.: MIT Press, 1993.

Dobson, Andrew. *Green Political Thought*. London: Routledge, 1995.

Dobson, Andrew, ed. *The Green Reader*. London: André Deutsch, 1991.

Dominguez, Joe and Vicki Robin. *Your Money or Your Life?* New York: Penguin, 1992.

Durning, Alan. *How Much Is Enough? The Consumer Society and the Future of the Earth*. London: Earthscan, 1992.

Goldsmith, Edward et al. *Blueprint for Survival*. Boston: Houghton Mifflin, 1972.

Goodland, Robert, Herman Daly, Salah El Serafy, and Bernd von Droste, eds. *Environmentally Sustainable Development: Building on Brundtland*. Paris: UNESCO, 1991.

Gorz, André. *Capitalism, Socialism, Ecology*. London: Verso, 1994.

_____. *Critique of Economic Reason*. London: Verso, 1989.

_____. *Ecology as Politics*. London: Pluto Press, 1983.

Handy, Charles. *The Future of Work*. London: Basil Blackwell, 1985.

Hinrichs, Karl, William Roche, and Carmen Sirianni, eds. *Working Time in Transition: The Political Economy of Working Hours in Industrial Nations*. Philadelphia: Temple University Press, 1991.

Hunnicutt, Benjamin Kline. *Work without End: Abandoning Shorter Hours for the Right to Work*. Philadelphia: Temple University Press, 1988.

_____. *Kellogg's Six-Hour Day*. Philadelphia: Temple University Press, 1996.

Keynes, John Maynard. "The Economic Possibilities for Our Grandchildren." In *The Collected Writings of John Maynard Keynes: Essays in Persuasion*. Vol IX. London: Macmillan Press, 1972.

Lafargue, Paul. *The Right to Be Lazy*. Chicago: Charles H. Kerr, 1989.

Larrouturou, Pierre. *35 Heures: Le Double Piège*. Paris: Belfond, 1998.

Lipietz, Alain. *Green Hopes*. Cambridge: Polity Press, 1995.

_____. *La société en sablier: Le Partage du travail contre la déchirure sociale*. Paris: Éditions La Découverte, 1996.

_____. *Towards a New Economic Order: Postfordism, Ecology and Democracy*. Cambridge: Polity Press, 1992.

McKibben, Bill. *Hope, Human and Wild: True Stories of Living Lightly on the Earth*. Toronto: Little, Brown and Company, 1995.

Moody, Kim and Simone Sagovac. *Time Out! The Case for a Shorter Work Week*. Detroit: Labor Notes, 1995.

O'Hara, Bruce. *Working Harder Isn't Working*. Vancouver: New Star Books, 1993.

O'Riordan, Timothy, ed. *Ecotaxation*. London: Earthscan, 1997.

Rees, William E. *The Ecological Meaning of Environment-Economy Integration*. Vancouver: University of British Columbia School of Community and Regional Planning, 1989.

Reid, Donald G. *Work and Leisure in the 21st Century*. Toronto: Wall & Emerson, 1995.

Reid, Frank. "Combatting Unemployment through Work Time Reductions." *Canadian Public Policy* XII,2 (1986): 275-85.

Reid, Frank and Morley Gunderson. *Worksharing and Working Time Issues in Canada*. (Forthcoming 1999.)

Renner, Michael. "Saving the Earth, Creating Jobs." *World Watch* 5,1 (1992): 10-17.

Rifkin, Jeremy. *The End of Work*. New York: Tarcher/Putnam, 1995.

Roberts, Wayne and Susan Brandum. *Get A Life!* Toronto: Get A Life Publishing, 1995.

Robertson, James. *Future Work: Jobs, Employment and Leisure after the Industrial Age*. Aldershot, U.K.: Gower, 1985.

Rubin, Marcus and Ray Richardson. *The Microeconomics of the Shorter Working Week*. Aldershot, U.K.: Avebury, 1997.

Russell, Bertrand. *In Praise of Idleness and Other Essays*. London: Unwin, 1976.

Rybczynski, Witold. *Waiting for the Weekend*. Toronto: Penguin, 1991.

Sachs, Wolfgang, ed. *Global Ecology: A New Arena of Conflict*. Halifax: Fernwood Publishing, 1993.

Sachs, Wolfgang, Reinhard Loske, Manfred Linz et al. *Greening the North: A Post-*

Industrial Blueprint for Ecology and Equity. London: Zed Books, 1998.

Schor, Juliet B. *The Overworked American: The Unexpected Decline of Leisure*. New York: Basic Books, 1991.

_____. *The Overspent American: Upscaling, Downshifting, and the New Consumer*. New York: Basic Books, 1998.

Wierink, Marie. "Temps de travail aux Pays-Bas: la voix des femmes." *Futuribles*, November 1998: 39-65.

Von Weizsäcker, Ernst U. *Earth Politics*. London: Zed Books, 1994.

Von Weizsäcker, Ernst U. and Jochen Jesinghaus. *Ecological Tax Reform*. London: Zed Books, 1992.

Von Weizsäcker, Ernst U., Amory B. Lovins, and L. Hunter Lovins. *Factor Four: Doubling Wealth—Halving Resource Use*. London: Earthscan, 1997.

Wackernagel, Matthias and William Rees. *Our Ecological Footprint*. Gabriola Island, B.C.: New Catalyst, 1996.

WEBSITES

32 HOURS: Action for Full Employment, Toronto
www.web.net/32hours

European Industrial Relations Observatory (for updates on work-time issues in Europe)
www.eiro.eurofound.ie

Shorter Work-Time Group/Society for the Reduction of Human Labor, USA
www.swt.org

Time Work Web/Shorter Work Time Network of Canada
www.vcn.bc.ca/timework/worksite.htm

Index